PHILOSOPHY FOR NON-PHILOSOPHERS

ALSO AVAILABLE FROM BLOOMSBURY

PHILOSOPHY FOR NON-PHILOSOPHERS

By Louis Althusser

**Translated and edited by
G. M. Goshgarian**

**With an introduction by
Warren Montag**

Bloomsbury Academic
An imprint of Bloomsbury Publishing Plc

B L O O M S B U R Y
LONDON · OXFORD · NEW YORK · NEW DELHI · SYDNEY

Bloomsbury Academic

An imprint of Bloomsbury Publishing Plc

50 Bedford Square	1385 Broadway
London	New York
WC1B 3DP	NY 10018
UK	USA

www.bloomsbury.com

BLOOMSBURY and the Diana logo are trademarks of Bloomsbury Publishing Plc

First published in French as *Initiation a la philosophie pour les non-philosophes*
© Presses Universitaires de France, 2014

First published in English 2017

© Copyright to the English language edition Bloomsbury Publishing Plc, 2017

G. M. Goshgarian has asserted his right under the Copyright, Designs and Patents Act,
1988, to be identified as Translator of this work.

Translation of the references of this volume was completed by Serene John-Richards.

British Library Cataloguing-in-Publication Data
A catalogue record for this book is available from the British Library.

ISBN:	HB:	9781472592019
	PB:	9781474299275
	ePDF:	9781472592033
	ePub:	9781472592026

Library of Congress Cataloging-in-Publication Data
Names: Althusser, Louis, 1918-1990, author. | Goshgarian, G. M., translator.
Title: Philosophy for non-philosophers / by Louis Althusser ;
translated by G. M. Goshgarian.
Other titles: Initiation áa la philosophie pour les non-philosophes. English
Description: New York : Bloomsbury, 2017. | Includes index.
Identifiers: LCCN 2016016465 (print) | LCCN 2016033536 (ebook) |
ISBN 9781472592019 (hardback) | ISBN 9781474299275 (pbk.) |
ISBN 9781472592033 (epdf) | ISBN 9781472592026 (epub)
Subjects: LCSH: Philosophy—Introductions.
Classification: LCC BD22 .A4813 2017 (print) | LCC BD22 (ebook) | DDC 100—dc23
LC record available at https://lccn.loc.gov/2016016465

Typeset by RefineCatch Limited, Bungay, Suffolk
Printed and bound in Great Britain

CONTENTS

ACKNOWLEDGEMENTS

For their help and support, G. M. Goshgarian thanks Jackie Épain, Sandrine Ferré, Paul Garapon, Christine Gardon, François Matheron, Peter Schöttler, Tzuchien Tho, Jean Touzot, Fabienne Trévisan, Laurie Tuller, Maria Vlădulescu, Yu Shan, the Editorial Board of *Décalages: An Althusser Studies Journal*, and the director, Nathalie Léger, and staff of the Institut Mémoires de l'Édition contemporaine.

INTRODUCTION: PHILOSOPHY FOR NON-PHILOSOPHERS OR NON-PHILOSOPHY FOR PHILOSOPHERS?

Warren Montag

Readers whose knowledge of Althusser derives primarily from the texts published during his lifetime (and perhaps the more well-known posthumous works such as *Machiavelli and Us* and 'The Underground Current of the Materialism of the Encounter') will no doubt find *Philosophy for Non-Philosophers* perplexing. The problem is not its content, that is, the arguments and concepts Althusser advances there: nearly all can be found in previously published work. It is instead the work's form, or perhaps genre, that will surprise readers, the fact that Althusser chose to address an audience consisting of 'non-philosophers', that is, not simply specialists from other academic disciplines, but more importantly a mass audience outside the academic world. The nature (and breadth) of this audience makes it different in kind from a text like *Philosophy and the Spontaneous Philosophy of the Scientists* (published in 1974 but based on the lectures that Althusser delivered at his seminar in 1967) (Althusser 1974) which was addressed to scientists who were non-philosophers, not in the sense that they did not practice philosophy, but because they did so without knowing that they did so, that is, spontaneously. There Althusser seeks to make visible the tendency among scientists irrespective of their field, to accept as simple and obvious what are in fact complex notions imposed on scientists by a (general, not individual) forgetting of the historical determination of philosophical concepts.

In contrast, the genre represented by *Philosophy for Non-Philosophers* requires, above all, the simplification of complex arguments, that is, a reduction of the actual written form of these arguments to what is regarded (but by whom and by what means?) as essential, extracting it from the accidental and contingent that envelopes and perhaps conceals it. Because it is essential, it can be explained and communicated through examples drawn from everyday life and in this way understood by everyone. It is this assumption that will allow Althusser, otherwise known as a 'difficult', even obscure, thinker, to speak (or to think he is speaking) directly to the people in a language that can be understood by those (the vast majority) who have neither the leisure nor the training to read Aristotle or Kant or, for that matter, Althusser's own texts.

This last example should give us pause: is the project of *Philosophy for Non-Philosophers* based on the presupposition, articulated by many of his critics, but never explicitly stated by Althusser himself, that the conceptual density and discursive complexity of his earlier works, even the way Althusser practices philosophy in and through them, is in some sense inessential and unnecessary, constituting a baroque exterior that by calling attention to itself only serves to obscure the otherwise clear and distinct ideas that might be in principle communicated to any rational individual? It is useful to recall at this point that Althusser wrote his *Maîtrise* on the notion of content in the works of Hegel, who insisted that to understand form in its determinate existence is to grasp it as the self-understanding of content and not as something applied to it from the exterior (Althusser 1997). The critiques of Althusser's mode of exposition and even his 'style' assume that in philosophy and in theory more generally a given form may be applied indifferently and indeterminately (that is, determined in the last instance by authorial choice alone) to any content, which would imply, in turn, that the meaning of a text like 'From *Capital* to Marx's Philosophy' (Part I of *Reading Capital*) (Althusser, 1970, 11–69) existed outside of and prior to its textual incarnation and could have been be expressed in different, more common, words. To sustain such a notion, however, would be to reject the very arguments of the text itself and to place Althusser in the paradoxical position of restating (in different, simpler, words and phrases) the argument that arguments always appear in a singular, non-repeatable forms from which they cannot be separated. Has Althusser come to occupy this paradoxical space in order to write a work like *Philosophy for Non-Philosophers*, and, if so, how did he arrive there and what are the consequences of this occupation?

Written (or rather put into final or quasi-final form) in 1978–80, the time of the 'crisis of Marxism' in general and the crisis of Althusser's Marxism in particular, *Philosophy for Non-Philosophers* embodies the contradictory movements of this precise moment. In part, it is a presentation of Althusser's previously stated positions on philosophy (although not all of them, and without any attempt to account for the incompatibilities between the different phases in the development of his thought). But it also exhibits an imitation or mimicry of the affects, and the discourses consubstantial with these affects, of some of Althusser's most hostile critics, as if their critiques had been internalized and the collective rejection of Althusser's corpus incorporated into the fabric of the text. The result was a kind of theoretical stalemate that prevented *Philosophy for Non-Philosophers* from advancing beyond its starting point. Althusser's decision not to publish the manuscript certainly represented in some way an intuition, however dim, that the work was a kind of unstable compromise formation that accumulated within itself contradictions of both form and content. These contradictions, however, cannot be explained by Althusser's worsening psychological state alone; they must also be understood in relation to the conjuncture in which he sought to intervene, as the inescapable effects of an increasingly unfavourable relation of forces. It was this that made the project of speaking directly to the 'popular masses' about philosophy and Marxism appear to Althusser simultaneously urgent and impossible.

Althusser's Marxism separated him from the contemporaries with whom he is often associated. Despite the shared concerns that linked him to Lacan, Derrida and Foucault (among others), Althusser's work differed from theirs in its idiom: when he examined the problem of causality, for example, a problem central to the work of those named above, he invariably situated his investigation in the great debates internal to Marxist theory. Because this theory was itself grounded in the history of the socialist and communist movements, the problems that it posed to itself derived, directly or indirectly, from the practice of these movements: the nature of historical contradiction (and class struggle), the concept of the conjuncture as the site of political intervention, and perhaps most important of all, the notion of base and superstructure (and thus also of ideology, particularly in the light of the Russian, Chinese and Cuban revolutions).

But Althusser was also distinguished from both Marxists and non-Marxists alike by his attention not only to the place and effectivity of philosophy in Marxist theory, but to the question of what philosophy as such actually does and how it acts. Thus, even before he articulated his position in the form of an argument or a thesis to be tested, perhaps even before he knew that he held this position, Althusser had replaced the question of what philosophy is with that of how it operates and produces effects. Further, his insistence on understanding philosophy as a form of practice necessitated a perpetual re-evaluation of the actual effects of his own philosophical utterances, both within the field of philosophy and outside of it. As Pierre Macherey has noted, Althusser could sum up in a single phrase the standard by which he measured the effectivity of his philosophical interventions (Macherey, 2000): did he succeed in *faire bouger les choses*, that is, in getting things moving or shaking things up, was he able to initiate movement within and/or outside of philosophy? He expressed this imperative publicly and semi-publicly in the form of the self-criticism that became an increasingly significant aspect of his philosophical writing after 1968. Most observers were perplexed by this aspect of Althusser's thought and could see it as nothing more than an enactment of a Stalinist (or perhaps Maoist) ritual of self-denunciation which would amount to a barely secularized Communist act of contrition or, in contrast, a cunning attempt to anticipate and pre-emptively neutralize the critiques that his work would provoke and in this way clear a path for his own thought.

The fact remains, however, that Althusser, even before he was able to articulate it in theoretical form, practiced philosophy as if it were an extension of the class struggle, intervening to shift the balance of forces so as to weaken the power of the dominant ideas and thus create the space for ideas (or philosophical theses) adequate to the practice of revolt. In this sense, Althusser's idiom and theoretical/political points of reference were not a matter of choice but were imposed on him by the nature of his project of both laying new foundations for Marxism and participating in the great controversies that traversed the Communist movement in his time: at first, the conflict between the Soviet and Chinese models of revolution and socialism, later, the emerging strategy of guerrilla warfare, above all in Latin America, where Althusser's work was widely read and discussed, and finally the questions of revolutionary strategy in Europe and North America which finally centred on the emergence of Eurocommunism and the problematization of concept of the dictatorship of the proletariat.

But his singular Marxism set him apart from his contemporaries, Marxist and non-Marxist alike, in another way that has often been overlooked or ignored. The great works of 1960–65, that is, the essays collected in *For Marx* and his contributions to *Reading Capital*, were written with an exactitude that determined both his language and his choice of referents and that accordingly allowed few concessions to the reader. It was as if Althusser took the risk that, as he once put it, the words that came to him so rapidly that he often feared he would lose them would, once gathered into a coherent, if extraordinarily dense, discourse, exercise sufficient force to tip the balance of the theoretical conjuncture and upset the prevailing relations of force between concepts and ideas. Further, the 'theoretical prudence' or caution he demanded of himself prevented him from proposing imaginary solutions to the real problems he identified: for many readers, the absence of the conclusion necessary to a proposal of the new theory they expected of him, appeared as a kind of fraud, rendering the reading of his texts, in their eyes, as useless as it was tedious. Similarly, the theoretical line of march that forced him to seek out unfamiliar allies (Machiavelli and Spinoza, as well as Foucault and Lacan) and to mobilize them against the 'poor man's Hegelianism' (Althusser, 2006a, 62) and theoretical humanism that together functioned as a kind of Communist vulgate, produced effects of incomprehension and hostility in many of his readers, not only in the French Communist Party (PCF), but in significant parts of the left internationally. These characteristics led his many critics to charge him with hyper-intellectualism, complaining that Althusser neither spoke effectively to, nor reliably about, real workers and their struggle and that the nature of his writing served only to isolate philosophy and philosophers from the people. Such critiques multiplied after May 1968, when many on the far left (including former students and colleagues) read Althusser's theory, in the light of his failure to break with the PCF, as a left cover for revisionism and a cunning defence of the established order. The charge of hyper-intellectualism was if anything more common in the Anglophone world than in France and was not limited to the far left. In his attack on Althusser in 1972, British Communist John Lewis articulated what was implied but left unstated in most previous critiques: the difficulty of Althusser's work was not objectively determined by the complexity of the problems posed by the movement of history, but arose from what he called 'The Althusser Style', that is, Althusser's 'whole style of life and writing' (Lewis, 25). Lewis charged that Althusser had promised to deliver 'a complete theoretical system' (Lewis, 26), a promise he could not keep, given his vacillation between 'insistent dogmatism' and its opposite, a speculative metaphysics that could only 'tremble on the balancing point of conviction' (Lewis, 26). Althusser's works, according to Lewis, were marked and defined by the absence of 'the kind of healthy immersion in everyday affairs and current issues' (Lewis, 26) necessary to living Marxist theory, in contrast to the dead abstraction of what Lewis calls Althusser's scholasticism. Jacques Rancière saw Althusser's *Reply to John Lewis* (1972) as a little theatre piece in which the master confronts a 'useful idiot' to great comic effect. In fact,

Rancière argued, the previously unknown and not particularly astute John Lewis fit the role so perfectly that he might have been invented by Althusser. Although Rancière takes up Lewis's argument in phrases such as 'Althusser tips his hat in tribute to the workers' movement, only the better to wash his hands of empirical workers' (Rancière, 80), he is careful not to advance a populist critique of Althusser's style of writing or his choice of references. Instead, Rancière argues that Althusser's notion of philosophy as the drawing of lines of demarcation within texts, sometimes even between words, to reveal the stakes of the conflict around which philosophical and political works are constituted, is not only not addressed to the masses, but is designed to exclude their participation. The very line of demarcation between materialist and idealist tendencies in a given form of discourse represents the imposition of a false distinction that denies the fact that the idealist thesis that man makes history may serve just as well to mobilize the people masses as the 'correct' slogan, 'it is the masses who make history'. For Rancière, Althusser's concern with marking distinction and difference served to separate his knowledge from that of the popular masses, and his expertise from their lack of qualification in the matter of theory. And Rancière's critique, even if it is present only in its effects, is central to *Philosophy for Non-Philosophers*.

These criticisms (but only in combination with other factors, both historical and personal) produced some significant shifts in Althusser's philosophical writing, including at the level of style. After 1968, with the exception of a few texts (notably *Machiavelli and Us* and the *Cours sur Rousseau* – the transcription of a tape-recorded lecture course never intended for publication) Althusser's philosophical work was animated by two opposing tendencies: (1) a series of prolonged, typically public, exercises in self-criticism that began with *The Response to John Lewis* and culminated in his *Soutenance d'Amiens*, 'Is it Simple to be a Marxist in Philosophy' (Althusser 1976) (taken from a longer manuscript recently published in French in an edition prepared by G. M. Goshgarian) (Althusser, 2015), (2) a succession of attempts (some nothing more than fragments, others consisting of manuscripts at or near completion) to produce works aimed at a broad left audience which Althusser conceived as situated outside of the academic world. Beginning with *On the Reproduction of Capitalism*, written shortly after the May events, and then throughout the 1970s, Althusser repeatedly (perhaps obsessively) sought to compose introductions to Marxism or to some aspect of Marxist theory, often incorporating parts of earlier unpublished manuscripts. The drafts contained in the Althusser archive reveal that he began and abandoned in fairly rapid succession short books on Communism (*Projet du livre sur le communisme*, 1972 and 1980),

Imperialism (*Qu'est-ce que l'imperialisme*, 1973) and the present text, *Philosophy for Non-Philosophers* (1978–80) which, with *On the Reproduction of Capitalism* (1969), represents the most fully realized version of such a project (which Althusser nevertheless chose not to publish).

These last two texts, written nearly ten years apart and in very different historical conjunctures, reveal in their singular ways the contradictions and ambivalences proper to Althusser's attempts to bypass intellectuals and speak directly to the mass of politicized youth and workers. *Philosophy for Non-Philosophers*, written in part in response to his critics, is profoundly marked by the struggle immanent in the text itself between the omnipotent fantasy, proper to philosophy as such, of 'simply preaching the naked truth, and waiting for its anatomical obviousness to "enlighten minds", as our eighteenth-century ancestors used to say', and an equally powerful defence against such fantasies, based on Machiavelli's notion of '*la verità effetuale*' (effectual truth) and Vico's maxim, '*verum factum*' (truth is made) that if you want to 'force a change in ideas' you must 'recognize the force which is keeping them bent, by applying a counter-force capable of destroying this power and bending the stick in the opposite direction so as to put the ideas right' (Althusser, 1976, 171). The result was a decade of oscillation between producing and then setting aside introductions to Marxist theory (as conceived by Althusser). The ongoing attempt 'to speak plainly and clearly, in a way that can be understood by all our comrades' (Althusser, 1976, 32) as he announced in his *Reply to John Lewis*, that is, to explain Marxism, his Marxism, to them, resulted in a succession of unpublished and perhaps unpublishable fragments and fragments made up of fragments, some fashioned into the shape of a whole. This was, perhaps, the underground current of Althusser's own philosophy.

Nowhere is this contradictory movement more evident than in *Philosophy for Non-Philosophers*. As Goshgarian has noted, Althusser himself labelled the manuscript a 'manual' (*manuel*), a term that has a slightly broader semantic range in French than in English (*Initiation*). It is not simply a 'handbook' (as the term's etymology implies) containing a set of instructions that would allow anyone, irrespective of their class position or level of education, to understand, if not practice, philosophy. '*Manuel*' may also be translated as 'textbook' (*manuel scolaire*). Althusser had, in fact, written a preface for the second edition of Marta Harnecker's *Los conceptos elementales del materialismo histórico* (1972), a book widely read by the Latin American left. Harnecker's text resembled in form, if not content, such works as Stalin's *Fundamentals of Leninism* or *Dialectical and Historical Materialism*, texts designed as vehicles for the communication of a doctrine or vulgate (so called because it is addressed to the *vulgus*, or the masses).

Such endeavours necessarily involve reading for, rather than to, the audience, and reading in precisely the way that Althusser explicitly condemned in *Reading Capital*, that is, by extracting what is defined as essential from the inessential mass in which it lies buried (which can be discarded once the extraction is completed), an operation that he compared to the extraction of a gold nugget, 'from the dross of earth and sand in which it is held and contained' (Althusser, 1970, 36). Thus, even the method that guides what is read for, and then communicated to, the audience contradicts Althusser's insistence that concepts, no matter how basic, can be understood only in the written, textual form in which they appear, a position that demands that texts be read to the letter. How does one summarize not simply the conflicts proper to a text, but even more the 'symptoms' that every text exhibits, the silences, gaps and absences necessarily produced by the work of theoretical practice? Does *Philosophy for Non-Philosophers*, insofar as it respects the conventions of the genre of the manual, then constitute in what it does, if not in what it says, a rejection of the protocol of reading that Althusser establishes in the introduction to *Reading Capital*?

The answer lies in the fact that Althusser proved incapable of writing anything that might serve as a manual or textbook: every manuscript that emerged from this endeavour, whether a fragment or a quasi-finished text, was interrupted or cut short by a deviation or a series of deviations from the straight line that would lead to the production of a manual, as if his own texts were governed by a logic of the clinamen. *On the Reproduction of Capitalism* offers a perfect example of such a logic: the work begins with a simplified account of Marxist economic theory ('What is a Mode of Production?' 'On the Reproduction of the Conditions of Production', 'Infrastructure and Superstructure'), followed by a description of the extra-economic conditions of reproduction ('The State, Law, and the Repressive State Apparatus/ Ideological State Apparatuses'), most (but not all) of which corresponds to what would be expected of a textbook. The section 'On Ideology', however, marks a caesura and a point of divergence in the exposition: Althusser's theses on ideology and the ideological state apparatuses have little to do with what until then had been associated with the term 'ideology' and, because they are unprecedented, cannot be understood as summaries. Further, they culminate in a highly elliptical and allusive presentation of the thesis that posed and continues to pose great difficulties for Althusser's readers, namely the thesis that ideology, which has a material existence, interpellates individuals as subjects. Indeed, it appears as if Althusser's repeated attempts to compose a manual or guide for militants forced him to confront the impossibility of summarizing or simplifying concepts that, while necessary to Marxist theory, were absent from it. It is not easy to summarize an absence, and all the more when this absence takes the form of a text's 'own words' (Althusser, 1970, 22). In the case of ideology, Althusser simply supplied what was lacking without noting that he did so, thereby imputing to Marxism the theory that it both required and for which it provided a basis, but lacked. Significantly, from the entire manuscript of *Reproduction*, Althusser published only a part of the section on ideology, precisely the section that had no place in a textbook because it marked a break with all previous theories, a fact that conferred upon it an exploratory, tentative and sometimes contradictory character that is inscribed in the letter of the text itself.

The case of *Philosophy for Non-Philosophers* is in certain ways even more complex. The original French title, *Initiation à la philosophie pour les non-philosophes*, captures something of the work's strangeness. First, 'initiation': the title could be translated as 'An Introduction to Philosophy for Non-Philosophers', and in fact there exist in the French language introductory texts whose object is philosophy in general or the work of specific philosophers, but whose titles offer an initiation into, rather than an introduction to, philosophy. A review of the titles of twentieth-century French philosophical texts of this genre, however, reveals that 'introduction' is far more common than 'initiation' by a ratio of nearly ten to one. Gilbert-Sibertin Blanc is thus right to call attention to the term in his preface to the French edition of *Philosophy for Non-Philosophers* and to note that 'initiation' suggests an introduction into a secret and secretive realm set apart, its movement presupposing a secularized version of the separation of the sacred and the profane (Althusser, 2013, 11). The very idea of an initiation into philosophy is at odds with the notion of a manual, which assumes that anyone can learn to philosophize, or perhaps learn that they are already engaged in the work of philosophy, and that what is lacking is only the consciousness of this work. Is philosophy then situated in a space separated from everyday life, as the sacred is demarcated from the profane? 'Initiation', however, also serves to remind us of the ritual by which one is admitted to a cult (and always by someone else, someone endowed with authority, given that one cannot initiate oneself) and made acquainted with its secrets and mysteries. The term thus calls attention to the material disposition of philosophy as it currently exists: set apart, assigned the task of understanding the world without participating in it, as if the vocation of contemplating the world as totality demands a removal from it. But if it is removed from the world, where does it go? The speculative activity whose object is the whole, that is, 'the way the sciences, the arts, literature, economics and politics are related to each other, interconnected and articulated into a whole' (Althusser, 1974, 80–1) paradoxically can exist, despite its denials, only in the form of a practice embedded in an apparatus with walls and barriers both to confine and protect it: the university.

It would thus appear that the project of a philosophy manual is even more questionable than a manual of Marxism: Marxist theory is incarnate in the practical forms of class struggle, including the organizations that emerge out of this struggle. It is from the vantage point of this struggle (Althusser was fond of quoting Machiavelli's adage that 'one must be the people to know the Prince') that its theoretical expressions become intelligible even in their literal form. The case of philosophy is quite different: its institutional forms are designed to maintain a separation whose function is to protect it from the contagion of these struggles. In fact, philosophy, that is, what philosophy says (and Anglophone philosophy is closest to the ideal type) is marked by its struggle to protect itself from the effects of struggle, social struggle, immunizing itself by means of a language that renders struggle unthinkable and by a phobic avoidance of all but a few of the texts produced in the course of the history of philosophy. Althusser devotes surprisingly little attention here to the question of the material and institutional existence of philosophy: the single word, 'initiation', neither explained nor repeated, and finally eliminated altogether from the English version of the text, serves to remind us that the very possibility of a manual would require the shattering of real obstacles and the profanation of sacred spaces to release philosophy from its captivity.

If Althusser fails to acknowledge this problem, he nevertheless proposes a kind of solution by declaring that philosophy is not the property of philosophy teachers (a synecdoche for philosophy's institutional existence) but, as Lautréament said of poetry, *philosophie doit être faite par tous*, in other words, 'everyone is a philosopher' and only the consciousness of it is lacking. It thus appears that the initiation into philosophy instructs the initiate in the secret that there are no secrets and therefore nothing to be initiated into because philosophy, reputed to dwell behind walls, is not there but in the mutual immanence of bodily action and thought, the element in which we live, move and have our being. Religion furnishes the proof of his thesis: even if we cannot say that there has always been philosophy, we can say that religion has always existed in some form or another and religion, insofar as it recognizes the existence of necessity (in the form of fate or destiny), represents philosophy in an alienated form. But this thesis poses another problem: what is the cause of philosophy's self-alienation?

The answer lies in the fact that philosophy is not a realm of homogeneity or harmony, even a harmony based on the reign of reason. On the one side, a materialist tendency arises from the daily practical activity of the people who are instructed by experience to regard even philosophy as a practice and to elevate practice above theory. Their struggle for existence appears as a generalized resistance against the forces, human and natural, that threaten this existence, as if the acts of subjecting and exploiting the people are responses to an original and ever-present resistance. On the other side are those who must devalue the world of bodies and practices and invent another ideal or immaterial world that justifies their place in this one. Philosophy, according to Althusser, emerged from religion at the moment that Plato invoked not the Gods but the ideal forms of geometry in order to exploit mathematics in the service of the transcendence that explains the necessity of submission and servitude. This is the idealist tendency in philosophy: 'idealism talks about Truth; but behind Truth, it is power that appears on the horizon, and with power, Order' (Althusser, 2017, 43). It might appear at this point that the divisions in philosophy are homologous with those in society as a whole, above all, the division between those who work and those who live off the labour of others, making it possible to distinguish between a natural and spontaneous materialism of the exploited and an equally natural and spontaneous idealism of the exploiters. Indeed, such notions inevitably informed the anti-intellectual tendencies on the French left for whom Althusser's enterprise constituted a denial of the intelligence of the masses.

In contrast, Althusser argues that Plato's idealism is neither consistent nor coherent but 'carries materialism inside itself, present, albeit refuted. It does so not to give it the floor, but to ward it off, to get the jump on it; it does so to occupy in advance positions that materialism might capture, and to bend the materialist arguments themselves, roundly refuted or turned against themselves, to idealism's service' (Althusser, 2017, 43–4). If both idealist and materialist philosophies contain their adversaries, keeping them in custody so to speak, with the objective of neutralizing them, both run the risk of being captured from within by a revolt of their prisoners whose mere existence poses a threat to their captors.

If the contradiction between idealism and materialism is in this way compromised, Althusser nevertheless preserves it in the transmuted from of the contradiction between philosophy and non-philosophy. A philosophy, if it is able to subject itself to a critique capable of accounting for its historical conditions of possibility, must begin by abandoning 'the philosophy of the philosophers in order to analyse concrete human practices', a phrase that clearly places the philosophy of the philosophers (and what other philosophy is there?) outside the realm of concrete human practices, as if it is neither concrete nor a practice. Only if philosophy abandons 'the philosophy of the philosophers', that is, itself (which raises the question of what is abandoned and what or who performs the act of abandoning), can it undertake 'the perilous venture of making *the Big*

Detour through non-philosophy' (Althusser, 2017, 47), philosophy's other, in order return to itself laden with the knowledge both of what philosophy is and what it might become. Non-philosophy must not be understood as the totality of what is not philosophy (that is, the philosophy of the philosophers), but rather as 'everything that the dominant idealist philosophy ... has *neglected, rejected, censored, or abandoned* as the refuse of existence and history, as objects unworthy of its attention' (Althusser, 2017, 47). Both the idealist tendency in philosophy (and the materialist tendency insofar as it is compelled by an idealism able to borrow force from the existing order to take idealist questions as its own) have refused to examine such objects as matter, labour and even the body. The implicit identification of the philosophy of the philosophers with the dominant idealist philosophy allows Althusser to replace the notion of the conflict internal to philosophy with the image of a struggle between philosophy and non-philosophy, between an inside and an outside, with the result that philosophy is deprived of its contradictory character. The theoretical costs of such a manoeuvre are clear: Althusser charges that Spinoza, even Spinoza, 'talks about the body and says that its powers are unknown, but he says nothing about sex'. From this, Althusser deduces that Spinoza (whose philosophy he had described only a few years earlier as 'the greatest lesson in heresy the world has ever seen') (Althusser, 1976, 132) had, despite appearances, made nothing more than 'an insignificant detour', and, worse, a detour that would allow him the better 'to fall back into line' (Althusser, 2017, 48). Because Spinoza never left the philosophy of the philosophers his words were emptied of their heretical or materialist sense and allowed to produce only apologetic effects.

It is precisely the elimination of philosophy's internal contradictions that explains the necessity of what he calls the Big Detour. To understand it, Althusser asks us to recall the navigators of the fifteenth and sixteenth centuries who sailed far beyond the frontiers of the known world and brought back with them a sense of other worlds whose unimaginable difference allowed them to know their own. Their journeys, as he imagines them, are always circular, always a return to the point of origin, no matter how great the distance travelled and how difficult the conditions: 'One can never venture too far afield in quest of the adventure of coming home.' Philosophy has to go 'as far as possible from itself, so that it can come home laden with comparisons and know a little better what it is' (Althusser, 2017, 47). Here, somewhat surprisingly, Althusser offers a very Hegelian description of the activity of the explorers. He might have imagined a journey outward in search of the absolutely other, an unknown land from which they may not return, whether because of the perils of journey or because they have chosen an irreversible movement to an alterity from which there is no return. Similarly, he might have spoken not of explorers, but of the mutineers of the Bounty and the island they found in their flight from the savage justice of British maritime courts. Thousands of miles from the nearest land, they agreed to burn their ship, thereby cutting off any possibility of a return home. Instead, Althusser suggests that philosophy can have no other destination than home, its activity necessarily a return to itself, not to abolish its existence so that something new may be born, but on the contrary to fortify the original foundation. From this perspective, philosophy's identity is never in question no matter how far from itself it travels; as in the case of the colonial regimes the explorers served, the encounters with what is other only enrich the metropole.

But this was not the first or the last time that Althusser would compare philosophy to the act of exploration. In 1963, when he was perhaps at the height of his powers, he wrote to Franca Madonia that he felt like one of those 'explorers who come upon an immense river without knowing where it leads. They hollow out a log and entrust their craft to the current for months simply to discover the sea' (Althusser, 1998, 386). Similarly, near the end of his life, Althusser composed the parable of the Materialist Philosopher who always catches a moving train without knowing 'where he comes from (origin) or where he's going (goal)' (Althusser, 2006b, 290). These are not circular journeys, but movements of no return, as if Althusser sought to capture in an image the simultaneity of philosophy's abandonment of the origin and the origin's disappearance into the mists that envelope the river at dawn.

Finally, to read *Philosophy for Non-Philosophers* to the letter is to discover the contradictions in Althusser's attempt to eliminate contradiction from the philosophy of the philosophers in favour of the opposition of philosophy and non-philosophy, which he in turn links to the opposition of the abstract and the concrete. He shows us that philosophy never returns to itself, because the 'it' to which philosophy would return is precisely a historically specific conjunction of philosophy and non-philosophy, the latter an outside always present in philosophy as a foreign body that it contains but cannot assimilate. If there is an initiation here, it is that of the philosopher who will be permitted to know the secret that philosophy is inhabited or possessed by the non-philosophy that it had sought in vain outside of itself. But it is difficult not to see in *Philosophy for Non-Philosophers* an image of the explorer's last hope: without a compass to guide him, he entrusts his craft to the current and is carried off by the immense river, dreaming of the sea he will never find.

Works cited

Althusser, Louis, 1970, *Reading Capital*, London: New Left Books.

Althusser, Louis, 1976, *Essays in Self-Criticism*, London: New Left Books.

Althusser, Louis, 1990, *Philosophy and the Spontaneous Philosophy of the Scientists and Other Essays*, London: Verso.

Althusser, Louis, 1997, *The Spectre of Hegel*, London: Verso.

Althusser, Louis, 1998, *Lettres à Franca*. Paris: Stock/Imec.

Althusser, Louis, 1999, *Machiavelli and Us*. London: Verso.

Althusser, Louis, 2006a, *Lenin and Philosophy and Other Essays*, New York: Monthly Review Press.

Althusser, Louis, 2006b, *Philosophy of the Encounter: Later Writings 1978–87*, London: Verso.

Althusser, Louis, 2012, *Cours sur Rousseau*, Paris: Le Temps des Cerises.

Althusser, Louis, 2014, *Initiation à la philosophie pour les non-philosophes*, Paris: Presses Universitaires de France.

Althusser, Louis, 2015, *Être marxiste en philosophie*, London: Presses Universitaires de France.

Althusser, Louis, 2017. *Philosophy for Non-Philosophers*, London: Bloomsbury.

Lewis, John, 1972, 'The Althusser Case', *The Australian Left Review*, 1(37), 16–26.

Rancière, Jacques, 2011, *Althusser's Lesson*, London: Continuum.

NOTE ON THE TEXT

by G. M. Goshgarian

'My ambition, you know, is to write manuals', Althusser declared in a 28 February 1966 letter to Franca Madonia. It took him a long time to realize it. Of the two 'manuals' he failed to finish in the 1960s, only a few fragments ever saw the light: an extract from the introduction to a sprawling manuscript on the union of theory and practice that appeared in the *Cahiers marxistes-léninistes* in April 1966 under the title 'Matérialisme historique et matérialisme dialectique', and a nine-page 'provisional definition of philosophy' that became the first chapter of 'Sur la reproduction des relations de production' ('On the reproduction of the relations of production'), the book-length 1969 manuscript from which Althusser extracted, in 1970, his well-known paper on ideology and ideological state apparatuses.

That provisional first chapter of the 1969 manuscript was supposed to find its sequel in a second volume, which, after the 'big detour' constituted by Volume 1, was to elaborate, according to a prefatory note, 'a scientific definition of philosophy'. But the first volume of 'Sur la reproduction' did not see the light in French until 1995, five years after its author's death (it first appeared in English in 2014 as the main text in a collection titled *On the Reproduction of Capitalism: Ideology and Ideological State Apparatuses*). As for the second volume, it was never written. In the mid-1970s, however, Althusser *re*-wrote, as it were, this unwritten philosophy manual: first in 1976, in the form of a 140-page manuscript, which was followed, one or two years later, by a heavily revised version released only in 2014, under the title *Initiation à la philosophie pour les non-philosophes. Initiation* is here translated into English for the first time.

Althusser initially called his book *Introduction à la philosophie*, a title he later changed to *Être marxiste en philosophie*, echoing the title of the lecture that he had given at his June 1975 habilitation and published in French and

English shortly thereafter as 'Est-il simple d'être marxiste en philosophie? (Soutenance d'Amiens)' ('Is it Simple to Be a Marxist in Philosophy?'). He finished the first draft of *Introduction* in July or August 1976, as is indicated by a letter accompanying a photocopy of the manuscript that he sent Pierre Macherey late that summer. Worried, as he confessed in this letter, that the text would be too demanding for the 'non-philosophers' who were its intended readers, he proceeded to rewrite it in 1977 and (?) 1978. The new avatar of the 'manual', which Althusser eventually recast from one end to the other, revising and reorganizing it several times, ultimately only vaguely resembled its predecessor. Comprising 154 typed pages in a version he showed his friend Sandra Salomon, presumably in early 1977, it included a little more than half of the 'Note on the ISAs' in a state anterior to the one on which he put the final touches in February 1977, as is revealed by his correspondence with Peter Schöttler, who published a German translation of the 'Note' late that year. Althusser subsequently incorporated more material into this already well advanced text, notably, some twenty pages on the relationship between the practice of production and the Aristotelian notions of *poiesis* and *praxis*. Preserved in his archives at the Institut Mémoires de l'édition contemporaine (Imec) in Caen, the resulting manuscript of some 175 typed pages (Manuscript 2) is covered with several hundred undateable handwritten corrections and addenda. Althusser also wrote a new version of the first section of this manuscript (everything that now precedes Chapter 6), with the result that the fifteen-page introductory section of Manuscript 2 grew into the seventy-four typed pages of a manuscript physically quite distinct from its companion (Manuscript 1, also held by the Imec). Manuscript 1, in its turn, bears more than 200 handwritten corrections and addenda.

A page of instructions that Althusser drew up for a typist suggests that he wanted to work further on a retyped version of both manuscripts, if only to eliminate redundancies due to the augmentation and reorganization of the first part of his text. His archives do not, however, seem to contain a version of the text in a state posterior to that represented by the hand-corrected Manuscript 1 and Manuscript 2, with their two different introductory sections. These two manuscripts served as the basis for the 2014 French edition, the one translated here, which contains only the more recent version of the introductory section.

Those familiar with Althusser's work will note that his 'manual', while initiating 'non-philosophers' into philosophy, initiates them more particularly into its author's philosophy, above all as elaborated after his 'anti-theoreticist' turn of 1966–67. Thus elements of several posthumously published (and one or two still unpublished) texts written during or after that turn are either summed up or clearly anticipated in *Philosophy for Non-Philosophers*. These include, besides 'Note on the ISAs' and 'On the Reproduction of the Relations of Production', the fifth and final lecture (still unavailable in English) of *Philosophy and the Spontaneous Philosophy of the Scientists* (1967); 'On Feuerbach' (1967); the fragmentary 'Livre sur l'impérialisme' (1973, unpublished); 'Is it Simple to be a Marxist in Philosophy?'; 'The Transformation of Philosophy' (a lecture first delivered in Granada in March 1976); *Les vaches noires: Interview imaginaire* (1976, Presses universitaires de France, 2016, English translation forthcoming from Bloomsbury); 'Marx in his Limits' (1977–80); and the 1982 manuscript partially published in French in 1994 and English in 2006 under the title 'The Underground Current of the Materialism of the Encounter'.

We do not know why Althusser decided not to publish *Philosophy for Non-Philosophers*, despite the fact that the text is, stylistically unpolished passages aside, in virtually finished form.

1 WHAT NON-PHILOSOPHERS SAY

This short book is addressed to readers who, rightly or wrongly, consider themselves to be 'non-philosophers', yet would like to have some idea of what philosophy is.[1] What do these 'non-philosophers' say?

The blue-collar worker, the farmer, the office-worker: 'We don't know the first thing about philosophy. It's not for us, it's for intellectuals and specialists. It's too hard. And no one ever told us anything about it: we left school before we got that far.'

The manager, the civil servant, the doctor: 'Yes, we had our philosophy class.[2] But it was too abstract. The teacher knew his stuff, but he was obscure. We don't remember anything about that class. Besides, what's philosophy good for?'

Someone else: 'Sorry, but I found philosophy very interesting. I must add that we had a spellbinding professor. With him, one understood philosophy. But, since then, I've had to earn a living. And, well, what can I say: there are only twenty-four hours in a day. I've lost touch. It's really too bad.'

If you ask them: 'But then why don't you consider yourselves philosophers? Who, in your opinion, deserves to be called a philosopher?', they will all answer, in unison: '*Philosophy teachers*, of course!' And they are absolutely right. Except for people who, for personal reasons – that is to say, for pleasure or their own benefit – continue to read philosophers and 'do philosophy', the only people who deserve to be called philosophers are in fact the ones who teach philosophy.

Naturally, this *fact* throws up a first question or, rather, two.

1. Is it really by chance that *philosophy* is so closely bound up with *teaching* and those who teach it? All indications are that it isn't; for, after all,

the marriage of philosophy and teaching doesn't just go back to our philosophy classes, it doesn't date from yesterday. At the very beginnings of philosophy, Plato taught philosophy, Aristotle taught philosophy . . . If this marriage between philosophy and teaching isn't due to chance, it must express a secret necessity. We shall try to find out what that necessity is.

2. Let us take another step. Since, *or so it seems*, philosophy isn't much use in everyday life, as it doesn't produce knowledge and has no concrete applications, we may well wonder: what earthly purpose does it serve? We can even ask ourselves the following strange question: might it be that *the one purpose philosophy serves is the teaching of philosophy*, and nothing else? And if the only purpose it serves is the teaching of philosophy, what might that mean? We shall try to answer this difficult question.

You see how things go in philosophy. One need only consider the *least of its aspects* (here, the fact that all philosophers are philosophy teachers) for interesting, surprising questions to surge up before we can blink. And those questions are such that we have to ask them, although we lack the means to answer them. To answer them, we have to make *a very long detour*, and this detour is nothing other than philosophy itself. The reader will therefore have to practise patience. Patience is a philosophical 'virtue'. Unless one is patient, one cannot gather the least notion of what philosophy is.

To take another step, let us cast a discreet glance at the people known as philosophy teachers. Like you and me, they have husbands or wives, and also children, if they wanted to have children. They eat and sleep, suffer and die, in the most ordinary way imaginable. They may love music or sports, and be involved in politics or not. Granted: these things aren't what makes them philosophers.

What makes them philosophers is that they live in a world apart, in a *closed world*, constituted by the great works in the history of philosophy. That world has no outside, or so it seems. They live with Plato, Descartes, Kant, Hegel, Husserl, Heidegger and others. What do they do? (I mean the best of them, of course.) They read the works of the great philosophers, and reread them, indefinitely, comparing and contrasting them from one end of the history of philosophy to the other in order to understand them better. This *endless rereading* is astonishing, after all! One never sees math or physics teachers endlessly reading and rereading a treatise on mathematics or physics, or 'ruminating' on it that way. They transmit knowledge, and they explain or demonstrate that knowledge, full stop, *without going back over it.* Yet to practise philosophy is to go back over one's texts interminably. Philosophers know this very well, and tell you why to boot! It's because a philosophical work does not yield up its meaning, its message, on a single reading. It is overloaded with meaning: it is by nature inexhaustible and, so to speak, infinite, and it always has something new to say to someone who knows how to *interpret* it. The practice of philosophy is not just reading, or even demonstration. It is *interpretation, interrogation, meditation*. It aims to make the great works say what they *mean* or *might mean*, in the unfathomable Truth that they contain or, rather, indicate – indicate mutely, by 'gesturing' at it.

The consequence is that this world with no outside is *a world without history*. Although it comprises all the great works consecrated by history, it has no history. The proof is that, to interpret a passage in Kant, a philosopher will invoke Plato as well as Husserl, as if there weren't twenty-three centuries between the latter two, or a century and a half between the first and the last; as if before and after hardly mattered. For a philosopher, all philosophies are, so to speak, *contemporaneous*. They answer each other and echo each other, because, ultimately, they only ever answer the same questions, which make philosophy what it is. This explains the famous thesis that 'philosophy is eternal'. One can readily see that, to make perpetual rereading and the uninterrupted labour of meditation possible, philosophy has to be both infinite (what it 'says' is inexhaustible) and eternal (all philosophy is contained in embryo in each philosophy).

Such is the basis for the practice of philosophers – I mean philosophy teachers. Under these conditions, if you tell them that they *teach* philosophy, watch out! For it leaps to the eye that they don't teach in the same way as other teachers, who present their students with knowledge that they have to learn – knowledge, or in other words, (provisionally) *definitive* scientific results. For the philosophy teacher who has understood Plato and Kant well, *philosophy cannot be taught*.[3] But then what does the philosophy teacher do? He teaches his students *to philosophize* by interpreting the great texts or great philosophers in their presence, helping them, by his example, to philosophize in their turn. In short, he inspires them with a *desire-to-philosophize* (the Greek word *philo-sophia* can be freely translated that way). The philosophy teacher who feels himself equal to the task can go a step further and engage in *personal reflection*; he can, that is, sketch an original philosophy. This is living proof that philosophy produces – what, exactly? Philosophy and nothing else, and that all this happens in a closed world. There is nothing surprising about the fact that this world of the philosophers is closed. Since they make no effort to leave it – since, quite the contrary, they plunge ever more deeply into the works' *interiority* – they put a wide gulf between their world and that of ordinary people, who observe them from afar, as if they were some species of strange animal.

Well and good. But, the reader will object, we've just described a limit situation, an extreme tendency: to be sure, that tendency exists, but things don't always happen like that. And the reader is right: what we've just described is, in relatively pure form, *the idealist tendency, the idealist practice* of philosophy.

One can, however, philosophize very differently. The proof is that, in history, certain philosophers – let us say the 'materialists' – *have* philosophized very differently, and that some philosophy teachers try to follow their example. These philosophers do not wish to belong to a separate world, a closed world turned *in on itself*. They leave that world behind for the *external* world: they want to encourage productive exchanges between the philosophical world (which exists) and the real world. In principle, that is philosophy's very function, as they see it: whereas idealists consider philosophy to be above all *theoretical*, materialists consider it to be above all *practical*, to have its source in the real world and to produce, unbeknownst to itself, concrete effects there.

Note that, despite their fundamental opposition to the idealists, materialist philosophers can, let us say, 'agree' with their adversaries on a number of points: for example, the thesis that 'philosophy can't be taught'. But they don't assign this thesis the same meaning. The idealist tradition defends it by elevating philosophy above concrete knowledge [*connaissances*] and calling on everyone to activate the philosophical inspiration *in his inner self*. The materialist tradition doesn't elevate philosophy above concrete knowledge, and it calls on people to look *outside* themselves, to the practices, knowledge and social struggle – without, however, neglecting works of philosophy – for that with which they can learn to philosophize. A small difference, but one with far-reaching consequences.

Take another example, which idealism cherishes like the apple of its eye: the inexhaustible nature of philosophical works, something that obviously distinguishes philosophy from the sciences. Materialism 'agrees' to acknowledge *the fact* that a work of philosophy cannot be reduced to its letter or, let us say, its surface, because it is *overloaded with meaning*. Materialism goes still further: it acknowledges, as idealism also does, that this superabundant meaning has to do with the very 'nature' of philosophy! However, since its conception of philosophy is utterly different from idealism's, the philosophical work's *superabundance of meaning* doesn't reflect the *infinite* nature of interpretation, in materialism's view, but, rather, the extreme *complexity* of the philosophical function. If, for materialism, a philosophical work is overloaded with meaning, it is because philosophy must unify a large number of significations in order to exist as philosophy. A small difference, but one with far-reaching consequences.

Take one last example: the well-known idealist thesis that all philosophies are, as it were, contemporaneous, that philosophy is 'eternal' or has no history. However paradoxical it may seem, materialism can 'agree' with this – but with a reservation, for materialism holds that *something historical* is produced in philosophy [*qu'il se produit* de l'histoire *dans la philosophie*], that there occur in it real events, conflicts and revolutions which alter the philosophical 'lay of the land'. With that one reservation, however, materialism too affirms in its fashion that 'philosophy has no history', inasmuch as the history of philosophy is *repetition of the same basic conflict*, the one that opposes the materialist to the idealist tendency in every philosophy. A small difference, but one with far-reaching consequences.

From the examples thus briefly reviewed, we shall draw the lesson that, although philosophy is *one*, there are, at the limit, *two* contrary ways of philosophizing, *two contradictory practices of philosophy*: the *idealist* and the *materialist* practice of philosophy. But we shall also draw the lesson that, paradoxically, idealist positions *encroach on* materialist positions, and the other way around. How can philosophy be one, yet subject to two contradictory tendencies, the idealist and the materialist tendency? How can philosophical adversaries have something in common (as is shown by the fact that they encroach on one another)?

We are once again asking questions we can't answer right away. We have to make the Big Detour first. Patience!

Patience – but also, straight away, a surprise. For if there exists 'a way of philosophizing' different from that of idealist philosophy teachers, a practice of philosophy which, far from removing philosophers from the world, puts them in the world and makes them everyone's brothers – if there exists a practice of philosophy which, far from handing down a Truth to people from on high in a language workers can't understand, *knows how to shut up* and *learn from* people, from their practices, suffering and struggles – then this philosophy can turn our initial hypothesis upside down.

For we have put our question to people who do different kinds of work and have different social positions. All of them told us about *philosophy teachers*. That was only to be expected: philosophy is taught in secondary schools and universities. In their modesty or indifference, they identified philosophy with the teaching of philosophy. What did they do if not repeat, in their own fashion, what the institutions of our society declare, namely that *philosophy belongs to philosophy teachers*? Intimidated by this fait accompli of the social order, awed by the difficulty of the philosophy of the philosophers, they didn't dare to challenge a *philosophical prejudice*. The division between mental and manual labour and its practical consequences, the domination of idealist philosophy and a terminology reserved for insiders, intimidated them or discouraged them. They didn't dare to say: no, philosophy doesn't just belong to philosophy teachers. They didn't dare to say, with the materialists (such as Diderot, Lenin or Gramsci): *'Everyone is a philosopher.'*

Idealist philosophers speak on everyone's behalf and in everyone's stead. They think, and no mistake, that they possess the Truth about everything. Materialist philosophers are much less talkative: they know how to shut up and listen to people. They do not consider themselves privy to the Truth about everything. They know that they can become philosophers only gradually, modestly, and that their philosophy will come to them *from outside*. So they shut up and listen.

We need not go very far to discover what they hear – to observe that there exists among the people, among workers who haven't received any philosophical education and never had a 'master' whom they could follow in the art of philosophizing, a certain *idea of philosophy* precise enough for us to be able to refer to it and discuss it. This plainly means that, as the materialists claim, 'everyone is a philosopher', even if the philosophy he carries around in his head is, as one can well imagine, not exactly the philosophy of the great philosophers or the professors.

What might this philosophy that is 'natural' to everyone be? If you ask people you know, 'ordinary' men and women, they may well, out of modesty, let you insist a bit before coming out with it, but they will eventually admit that they do in fact have a kind of philosophy all their own. What is it, exactly? A way of 'looking at things'. And if you pursue your questioning, they will say: 'There are things in life I know well, from first-hand experience. For example, my work, the people I associate with, the parts of the world I've travelled through, or what I learned at school or have learned from books. We can call these things *knowledge*. There are, however, lots of things in the world I've never seen and don't know. That doesn't prevent me from having some *idea* of them. In that case, I have *ideas that go beyond what I know*: about, for example, the origins of the world, death, suffering, politics, art or religion. But there is something more: these ideas came to me pell-mell, from all sides, and separately: they didn't hang together at first. Yet, bit by bit, I don't know why, they were unified, and something strange even happened: I collected all or almost all my knowledge *under* these general ideas, *under their unity*. That was when I put together a sort of philosophy for myself, a general view of things, the things I know first-hand and the things I don't. My philosophy is my knowledge unified under my ideas.' And if you ask: 'But what use is this philosophy to you?', your interlocutor will answer: 'That's simple: *I use it to orient myself in life*. It's like a compass: it helps me to get my bearings. But, you know, everyone comes up with his own personal philosophy.'

That is what an ordinary person would say. An observer, however, would add the following comments. He would say that everyone does indeed come up with 'his own personal philosophy', but that *experience shows* that most of these philosophies are similar, that they are just personal variations on a common philosophical stock. Setting out from this common stock, people go their different ways in their 'ideas'.

He would say that we can form an approximate idea of the common stock of this philosophy that is 'natural' to everyone: when we say about someone, for example, depending on how he bears up under suffering or trials which deeply distress him, that, despite all, he takes life's setbacks 'philosophically'; or, if life is good to him, that he knows how not to abuse its blessings. In that case, the relations he maintains with things good or bad are tempered, carefully considered, well controlled and wise, and we say that he is a 'philosopher'.

What do we find, at bottom, in this 'philosophy'? Gramsci explained the matter very well when he said: a certain idea of the necessity of things (the things one has to endure); and, therefore, a certain *knowledge* [*savoir*] on the one hand and, on the other, a certain way of using this knowledge in negotiating life's ups and downs; and, therefore, a certain *wisdom*. Hence a certain theoretical *attitude*, combined with a certain *practical* attitude: a certain wisdom. In this 'spontaneous' philosophy of the common man, we thus find two great themes that run through the whole history of the philosophy of the philosophers: a certain conception of the *necessity* of things, the order of the world, and a certain conception of human *wisdom* in the face of the course of the world. Would anyone dare to say that these ideas aren't already philosophical?

Yet the contradictory, paradoxical nature of this conception is quite striking. For it is, basically, a very '*active*' conception. It assumes that people *can do* something about natural and social necessity; it presupposes deep reflection and close attention to self, as well as great self-control in situations of intense grief, or others in which good fortune hands us everything on a platter. Yet the fact is that when this apparently active attitude isn't 'educated' and transformed – by political struggle, for example – it usually expresses a withdrawal into *passivity*. It is clearly, if one likes, human *activity*, yet it is activity of the kind that can be profoundly *passive* and *conformist*. For it isn't a question, in this 'spontaneous' philosophical conception, of acting positively in the world, as even certain idealist philosophers would like, or of 'changing' it, as Marx would like, but of accepting it and avoiding all its extremes. This is one meaning of the remark by an 'ordinary person' that we cited a moment ago: '*everyone comes up with his own personal philosophy*' in solitude ('every man for himself'). Why? So that he can bear a world that is crushing or could crush him. And while it is clearly a matter of bringing the course of things under control, it is less by trying to transform it than by submitting to it 'philosophically' in order to make the best of a bad deal. In short, it is a matter of coming to terms with a necessity that exceeds an individual's powers, one he had best find a way to accept, since he can do nothing to change it. Activity, then, but passive activity; activity, but *resigned* activity.

Here I am simply summarizing the thought of the Italian Marxist philosopher Gramsci on this point. You can see, from this example, how a materialist philosopher reasons. He doesn't 'tell himself stories'; he doesn't make lofty speeches; he doesn't say that 'everyone is a revolutionary'. He lets people talk and he tells things the way they are. There is no denying the fact: in the broad masses of people *who have not yet been awakened to the struggle*, or even in the case of those who have fought, but were defeated, there is an underlying resignation. It goes all the way back to the earliest periods of history, which has always been the history of class societies, hence of exploitation and oppression. Men of the people, shaped by this history, may have revolted; but, since their revolts were always put down, they had no choice but to resign themselves to the *necessity* to which they were subjected and to accept it 'philosophically'.

This is where religion comes in.

2 PHILOSOPHY AND RELIGION

This necessity that one has no choice but to accept is, to begin with, that of nature, whose laws 'we can master only by obeying her' (Hegel). But it is also and above all that of the social order, which individuals, taken separately, cannot change and must therefore accept in its turn. Hence the generally resigned cast of this 'philosophy': 'injustice has always reigned on earth, rich and poor have always been with us', and the like. This resignation may spare those who cultivate it (or so they suppose) evils that they would only have made worse by revolting. Nevertheless, when it spreads to broad masses of people, it reinforces the established order and the havoc it wreaks – the established order of the dominant class, which exploits workers and has a powerful interest in their taking things *with a 'philosophy' of resignation*.

We find in this conception of a life that must be taken 'philosophically' not just recognition of the *necessity* of 'things', but also an indication of the *uncontrollable* nature of this necessity that rules people's lives. An accident, a crisis, a catastrophe or a brutal intervention of the powers-that-be can occur at any time and turn life upside down. People are helpless in the face of these 'strokes of fate', which reflect their inability to anticipate events or the caprices of power. This power (nature's, the state's) accordingly appears to *be beyond* human capacities, to be endowed with almost supernatural force and to be unpredictable in its 'decisions'.

It is clear that *the model or epitome of this power is God*. That is why, at this level, non-philosophers' conception of things is above all *religious*. However far back we go in human history, we find the presence of this omnipotent force that exceeds individuals' or human groups' ability to anticipate and react. Individuals accordingly submit to their existence as if to a fate decided by forces beyond them; and, since they see no one taking the decision, they believe that the author and organizer of the whole of this order to which one can only submit is *God*.

That is why *resignation* generally dominates 'ordinary' people's spontaneous philosophy when they aren't mobilized in struggle. That is why the personal philosophies that everyone works out for himself are all so similar. For every personal philosophy has *religious underpinnings* that have nothing personal about them, but are social: the still living heritage of humanity's long history. And it is a well-established fact that, except for certain moments in history in which religion served the *revolt* of the humble (the early Christians, the Peasant Wars, or various sects, such as the Cathars and others), and except for certain contemporary Christians' attempts to take part in the working class's battles, religion has historically been massively associated with *resignation* in the face of earthly trials, in exchange for the 'promise' of a reward in another world.

If *philosophy has not always existed*, it is a well-established fact that religion has always existed in one form or another, even in the first, communal, so-called 'primitive' societies. Religion preceded philosophy, and the advent of philosophy did not bring on its demise. Quite the contrary: it has been rightly said that the idealist philosophy which inaugurated the history of philosophy with Plato was a 'daughter of religion', like who can say how many other philosophies since Plato. There remains, in the common consciousness, something of this long domination of religion, which has given ground, but hasn't disappeared from our world. Similarly, there remains something of the long domination of philosophical idealism, which was so closely linked to religion that philosophy was able to detach itself from religion only on the absolute condition that it maintain religious dogmas and itself take up the big religious questions as if they were so many philosophical questions. The sole difference was that philosophy treated these old questions in a *new way*. It accepted them, however, as 'obvious'.

For instance, religion asked the question of questions, the question of the *Origin of the World*.[1] Why is there something rather than nothing? Why is there Being rather than Nothingness? Why does the world exist, why do people exist? Religion answered: the world was created by God out of Nothingness, and if God created it, it was so that plants and animals could provide people with nourishment, and people, God's children, could be saved at the End of Time.

Philosophy inherited this question of questions, the question of the Origin of the World, which is the question of the World, humanity and God. It had no choice but to maintain it (to criticize it was a heresy punishable by burning at the stake). But philosophy did not maintain it in its religious simplicity, that of a narrative or sequence of grand mythical images. It filled it with *conceptual* content, that of abstract, rational thought. Thus it was that the personal God of the Gospels, who sends his son into the world and has him born in a manger, became, to the indignation and despair of Pascal, who was a true 'believer', *'the God of the philosophers and scientists'*:[2] he became a very abstract concept playing a theoretical role in a system of concepts. Plato had already conceived of God as the *Idea of the Good*,[3] capable of organizing a hierarchical social world. Aristotle conceived of him as the *Prime Mover*[4] who could introduce motion into the world. Descartes conceived of him as the infinitely perfect *First Cause* of a world reduced to a mechanism.[5] For Spinoza, he was *Infinite Substance*, or omnipotent Nature's power to produce its effects[6] (that this Spinozist God was identical to Nature earned the philosopher an accusation, which was well-founded, of atheism). Leibniz conceived of him as *Infinite Calculator* of the best of all possible worlds[7] and so on.

By thus changing God's name, rigorously defining him and drawing the theoretical consequences of this modification, philosophy in fact altered God's 'nature' *in order to subject the God imposed on it by religion to its own philosophical ends*: in order to make this God take *responsibility for*, and *guarantee*, a world profoundly altered by scientific discoveries and social upheavals. It harnessed God to its service, but it simultaneously served him. To this end, idealist philosophy (with a few exceptions) treated the question of 'the radical Origin of things' (Leibniz)[8] as its own for a very long time, striving to pierce the 'mystery' of this question, to think it in rigorous conceptual terms ... as if it were a meaningful question.

It is, however, one of materialism's achievements *to have realized that there exist meaningless questions*. In this question of the radical origin of things, the materialists, and even Kant,[9] were to see a mere theoretical imposture inspired by religion, an imposture that philosophy had purely and simply to eliminate. To give some idea of it, I shall say that the question *'Why is there something rather than nothing?'* is as absurd as the question with which one amuses children: *'Why doesn't the ocean overflow, although countless rivers pour into it?'* When we ask: 'Why is there something rather than nothing?', we forget that, if there were not 'something' (being), no one would be there to ask the question about nothing, and thus that the question of nothingness is a feint that pretends to believe that being *might not be* – when we have no choice in the matter!

Since we are taking our time, I would like to cite an illuminating example in connection with this famous question of the Origin of the World (which continues to inspire the philosophy of modern philosophers such as Heidegger), in order to show how idealism and materialism go about things.

Idealist philosophy says: God created the World out of Chaos – in other words, out of *Nothingness*. Before God decreed the creation of the world, therefore, there was nothing (other than God). Note that the little word 'before' poses formidable problems, for it designates temporal anteriority. But did time exist before the world was created? Or did time appear only with the creation of the world – was it created as well? If time too was created, then there was no time before time, just the eternity of God plus the Nothingness from which he drew the world by pure creation (*starting out from nothing*). This strikingly underscores God's omnipotence (for, in the human world, nothing can ever be 'created' from nothing: there has to be some pre-existent matter). The more powerful God becomes, however, the less comprehensible he becomes. Idealist philosophy is self-consistent: it goes so far as to say that God is 'incomprehensible', is beyond all our human ideas and that, if we talk about him, it is 'by analogy' (due allowance made, for he is incommensurable with us). But try to see whether you can understand how God can exist alone in the company of Nothingness and can draw the existence of the world out of nothing! This does indeed make him the absolute Origin of the World, but it also makes him incomprehensible.

Now take a materialist philosophy such as that of Epicurus. This philosophy talks about not the Origin of the world (a meaningless question), but the *beginning* of the world. It doesn't bring the omnipotence of God into play to draw the world out of Nothingness. Before the beginning, there is neither God nor Nothingness. What is there, then? *There is* – a materialist thesis par excellence – *always already something, always already matter*, which is not Chaos: it is matter, subject to certain laws. What is this matter? It is an infinite number of atoms, indivisible particles all falling in the infinite void as a result [*sous l'effet*] of gravity (a law), falling side by side without ever encountering one another. The Roman philosopher-poet Lucretius expounded the philosophy of Epicurus, whose own manuscripts have been destroyed: in a poem titled *On the Nature of Things*, Lucretius says that, before the beginning of the world, the atoms were '*falling like rain*'. This would have gone on indefinitely, had the atoms not been endowed with an astonishing property, '*declination*', the capacity to deviate from the straight line of their fall, imperceptibly. The *slightest* [*un rien de*] *deviation, the slightest 'deviance'*, is enough for the atoms to *encounter each other* and agglomerate: there we have the beginning of the world, and the world. Neither God nor Nothingness at the Origin: no Origin, but the beginning and, to account for the beginning, pre-existent matter, which becomes a world thanks to the (contingent, arbitrary) *encounter* of its elements. And this encounter which commands everything is the figure of contingency and chance, yet it produces the necessity of the World. Thus chance produces necessity by itself, with no intervention by God.[10] This is tantamount to saying that the World produces itself, and that by substituting the materialist question of the beginning (or the event, the advent) for the idealist question of the Origin, *we eliminate meaningless questions*: not just the question of the Origin of the World, but also everything connected with it – the question of God, of his omnipotence, of his incomprehensibility, of time and eternity, and so on.

Similarly, religion raised the question of the *End of the world* (in both senses of the word 'end': death and its beyond; the destination of the world). Why, after all, is man on earth? What is his destination, what is the meaning of his existence and his history, what is that history's ultimate purpose [*finalité*]? The Christian religion answered with the dogmas of original sin, God's incarnation in Christ, and the redemption of humanity at the end of time thanks to Christ's passion. For a long time, philosophy continued to ask this question, and had to ask it (it still does when it is idealist or spiritualist). But, naturally, it didn't maintain the form of the question – these grand images of the Christian narrative. It thought the question in philosophical concepts, abstract notions linked one to the other as rigorously as possible. It developed the theme of the state of nature and the inevitable fall into the state of society (to preserve people from the evils brought on by the state of war, the result of the anarchy of the state of nature), and it thought the conditions for the ultimate triumph of freedom in history. Here too, it transformed the terms of both question and answer *as a function of the historical variation of the stakes of political and ideological struggle*, and also as a function of each philosopher's own position. But it retained the questions of the Meaning of human existence and the Meaning of history, before Marx's materialist philosophy squarely denounced the theoretical imposture involved, taking its inspiration from a long tradition in which Epicurus, Machiavelli, Diderot and others all figure.

Yet another meaningless question. We can form some idea of it by noting that this question of the Meaning of human existence and human history (as if some all-powerful personage had assigned them a final goal in advance) is as absurd as Malebranche's naïve question: 'But why does it rain upon sands, upon highways and seas?'[11] The implication of the question is that this makes no Sense, since there is no lack of water in the sea, while the dunes and highways, where nothing grows, need no water, *so that this is no use at all*. This surprise makes sense only for a conception of the world that is religious, even if it presents itself as philosophical – for a conception which has it that *an all-powerful Being has assigned every being in the world a purpose and function.* To which materialism responds: but why not admit that the world is full of things that 'are of no use at all'? Let us go further: why not admit that neither the world nor human existence nor human history have a Meaning (an end, a goal established in advance)? Is it because that would be *disheartening*? But wait a moment: why not frankly admit that the surest condition for acting in the world, modifying its course and thus investing it with *meaning* through work, discovery and struggle, is to admit that *the World has no Meaning* (no pre-established meaning determined by an all-powerful Being, who is a pure fiction)?

Philosophy, then, descended of religion, took up religion's questions again. It must not be supposed that it did so just to be prudent – because, for centuries, there was a *prohibition* on thinking outside of religion. It must not be supposed that philosophers were all (for there are exceptions) men who advanced 'masked' (Descartes)[12] and that their thought was, therefore, duplicitous – that they all had a 'double doctrine'. In the eighteenth century, this thesis was a widespread way of explaining the conflictual relations between philosophy and religion. The presupposition was that philosophers, by virtue of the specific nature of philosophy, which was, it seems, 'pure Reason', had always thought and possessed the Truth, but that, because it was forbidden to proclaim it publicly on pain of inquisition and death, they had fabricated another doctrine *for public consumption*, advancing 'masked' so as to hide what they really thought and protect it from the religious or political authorities' sanctions, while simultaneously communicating something of the Truth.

This idealist conception does not correspond to the historical truth. In reality, we have every reason to believe that, certain exceptions aside (Spinoza), the philosophers who spoke of God were not just bowing to the ideological requirements of their day. They too believed in this God whose name they changed; they too believed in the religious questions of the Origin of the World and the Meaning of the existence of things; they thought within this 'problematic' (a system of questions) of absolute Truth, inherited from religion. For they needed God to 'ground' their philosophical systems, to 'think the whole', not as 'pure' philosophers who had to dissimulate their thought, but *as the convinced idealists* they were.

The proof that one could *think differently*, in a very different 'problematic', in the same hard times for philosophy, is provided by the existence of a tradition different from the idealist tradition. This was the *materialist* tradition, which thought not only outside religion, but also outside religious questions transformed into philosophical ones, and thus on a very different 'basis', within a very different 'problematic', by denouncing and rejecting *questions devoid of meaning*.

These few remarks have just one purpose: to show that philosophy's relationship to religion is neither a simple nor a 'pure' relationship, with philosophy always being pure Reason and religion being only unreason and social imposture. This is not only because religion can, under certain conditions of social struggle (which, it is true, have been rather rare so far), be something other than simple *resignation*; it is also because philosophy is not determined *exclusively* by its relationship to religion, by religious questions, but, behind this relationship, by its adoption of properly philosophical *positions*, idealist or materialist, which have other stakes as well, and incline it to accept or reject religious questions about the Origin of the World and the Meaning of human existence and history. The positions adopted do not depend on the existence of religion alone: they are attributable to opposed ideas and orientations that cannot be explained without reference to the major social, ideological and political conflicts at work in the history of the world.

All this will be explained in what follows.

Yet if most of philosophy's questions initially came to it from religion, we obviously must ask: *just what is religion*? This is a hard question.

For most people in the long course of human history, religion posed no question and had nothing mysterious about it. For religion itself answered the question by dint of the services it rendered and, quite simply, because it was part of the very order of things, as a 'self-evident truth' not open to debate. *It was there*, represented by its priests and churches, its myths and dogmas, its sacraments and practices. It was there as the Truth of things, there to utter this truth, teach it, and see to it that it reigned over the world. It was established, recognized, supported by the state. Since the order of things always operates to the dominant class's advantage when it is extolled, the conclusion long ran that religion was simply the 'opium of the people', in the early Marx's phrase, a drug intended to avert the revolts of the exploited, hence to reinforce the domination of the exploiters.[13] And, in fact, religion quite clearly plays this ideological class role in all class societies, even when the class struggle brings some believers over to the revolutionaries' side.[14]

Something resembling religion, however, existed long before class society, in 'primitive' communal societies, where it performed other functions. With its myths, it served to *unify* the social group in its struggle against nature, from which the group laboriously wrested its subsistence. It also served to *regulate the group's practices of production*, enabling its magicians or priests to announce auspicious dates for sowing, harvesting, or fishing and hunting, so as to bring people together and organize them in a form of work in *common*. Thus the priests possessed, and even kept to themselves, certain knowledge of a theoretical kind that grounded their authority over others.

But that is not all. What then stood in for religion also presided over all the events in an individual's life: *birth, pubescence, sexual and social initiation, the formation of couples, childbearing and death*. Life, sex, society, death and perhaps language as well: an endless cycle. Not by accident were these events sanctioned in this way by special ceremonies, for they ensured the social group's biological *reproduction*, while also ensuring, thanks to the law of exogamy (marriage outside the group), the community's relationship to other communities, its renewal and its alliances.

If religions no longer play the role, dominant in this period, that they once played in unifying society, along with their role in organizing production, most of the religions we know in our own societies have abandoned nothing of their role of initiation into existence, sexual life, and death. They continue to sanction birth, marriage and death with their ceremonies and sacraments, and they still control, by way of the confession of 'sins', individuals' evolution towards sexuality and sexual 'normalcy'. *Thanks to some obscure connection, religions are thus bound up with birth, sexuality and death*, with death usually acting as a mask for birth and sexuality.

Death in fact haunts the whole history of human civilization. It has been observed that human beings are the only animals who bury their dead; better, who erect gravestones for them; better yet, who have even buried them with all the implements they used in daily life, and even with their servants and spouse, sacrificed on this occasion as if to guarantee them a visible, manifest *afterlife*. From time immemorial, death has gone hand-in-hand with the theme of the afterlife in the religions, even in cultures that do not recognize it and apparently do not fear it (Madagascar): for to fail to recognize death and hold feasts on the graves of the deceased is still to pretend to believe that *life goes on*.

Religion was there to answer the troubling question of death, with all its mythology about the creation of the world and of humankind, their fall, their misery in the world here below, and the salvation that guaranteed them eternal life in another world, peaceful and happy at last. Transformed, that religion could one day become the instrument of the powerful, serving their cause by preaching to the exploited a *resignation* in this life that would be *rewarded* in the life to come, and it could practically be reduced to this function of ideological subjugation [*asservissement*]. Religion was nevertheless also a source of comfort that assuaged people's anxieties and afflictions, conferring a semblance of meaning on the lives of those crushed by servitude and exploitation, allowing them to experience, or look forward to, some vision of brotherhood, and giving them the hope – an illusory hope, yet a hope nevertheless – of another life. The troubling question of a death that might surprise them at any moment did not, for these unfortunates, arise only at the end of their lives. For death is also the nothingness of life, this life which is, as the phrase from the Gospels has it, 'but ashes and dust'. Why must one suffer this way, in an 'existence that is not life'? Religion responded to this *living death* with the promise of an afterlife, *another life*. It is easy to see that it thereby served the exploiters' interests, since it preached resignation, making what was unbearable in this life bearable with the promise of recompense in a life to come. But, like it or not, all this revolved around death, the fear of death, the question of death, the 'mystery' of death and suffering, which accompanies the whole history of humanity, like the tombs of its dead. *Why death and suffering? Why must people suffer and die?*

Doubtless the most difficult thing for people to accept is the idea, defended by the materialists, of death's 'existence' in the world and dominion over the world. It is not just a matter of saying that human beings are mortal or that life is finite and has a limited span. It is a matter of affirming that there are a great many things in the world that make no sense and serve no purpose; in particular, that *suffering and evil can exist with nothing to make up for them, with no compensation in this world or anywhere else*. It is a matter of recognizing that there are *losses* that are absolute (that will never be made good), *failures* without appeal, events without meaning or sequel, undertakings and even entire civilizations that come to naught and vanish without a trace in the nothingness of history, like those big rivers that disappear in the desert sands. And inasmuch as this idea is based on the materialist thesis that the world itself has no (pre-established) Meaning, but exists only as a miraculous accident that has surged up among an infinite number of other worlds which, for their part, have perished in the nothingness of the cold stars, it can readily be seen that the risk of death and nothingness besets people on all sides, and that they may well be frightened by it when the life they lead, far from making them forget death, makes its presence all the more real.

If we do not forget that, lurking behind the question of death, are *both* the question of birth *and* the question of sex, and that religion proposes to answer these three questions (birth, sex, death) which concern the biological reproduction of every human 'society', we will understand that religion is not reducible to its role of 'opium of the people' in the class struggle. To be sure, it is constantly enlisted in the class struggle, almost always on the side of the powerful. But if it can be enlisted, it is because it exists, and it exists because there subsists in it this core of functions, of questions and answers which, behind the grand affirmations of the Origin of the World and End of the World, *relate it to death, sex and birth.* These questions, which concern the biological reproduction of human societies, as I just noted, are 'experienced' by people unconsciously, amidst anguish or unconscious anguish. The anxiety the questions cause has not disappeared with the advent of class societies – quite the contrary, but we cannot say that that anxiety is confined to class societies, for it is older than they are. It is this anxiety which seizes the child and makes him seek the protection of his parents; it is this anxiety which makes someone who has escaped an accident tremble afterwards, makes soldiers engaged in battle pale before the assault, and overcomes old people at the approach of an inevitable end rendered still more harrowing by illness.

The capacity to confront the naked reality of death, fearlessly and with utter lucidity, whether amidst the dangers of work, war, illness or even love ('one is alone before love as one is alone before death', Malraux), is a grand tragic theme of popular wisdom and materialist philosophy. Freud, suffering from a serious case of cancer of the jaw, knew that he was doomed, yet he kept working down to the last minute, wracked by pain of the worst kind, knowing that he was going to die, and *knowing when.* He treated death for what it is: *nothing.* But what suffering for this nothing!

I mention Freud: this is an example and, because of Freud's fame, a well-known example. But how many hundreds of millions of nameless men and women have attained the terrible calm of death, what is called 'the peace of death', only after unspeakable, interminable suffering? When we recall that sexuality too can cause excruciating anguish, and that existence (birth) is a mystery (why me and not 'someone else'?), we can see that the religious acts that objectively sanction the biological reproduction of individuals and make social men and women of them are underwritten by a human anguish that cannot be laid to rest by Reason alone.

Materialist philosophy long contended that religion owes its existence to the fear of death ('fear creates the gods'). To combat religion, materialist philosophers undertook to rob it of death by doing away with the fear of death and demonstrating that death is *nothing.* As early as the fourth century BC, Epicurus reasoned as follows: for someone still alive, death is nothing, since he is alive; for one who is dead, death is nothing, since he no longer knows anything about it.[15] In the eighteenth century, other materialists showed that a human being is simply matter in organized form, which, when it disintegrates (in death), returns to its former state. These arguments could be accepted by minds that were already strong, but they were too feeble to convince most people, who sought refuge in religion. It is certainly true that death in the proper sense is no longer anything at all for a corpse, and is, for someone still alive, only an infinitesimally brief moment that he must get through. This is, however, false as far as *the suffering* that precedes so many deaths is concerned, and false for the survivors, who are taught the eternal lesson of human finitude by the dying and see in advance, in death, the inexorable destiny awaiting them too: the lesson of fear.

Yet it is here, notwithstanding the fact that philosophical demonstrations are not enough to deliver people of the fear of death, that we can sense a certain divorce, or a radical divorce, between the religious and philosophical conceptions of the world.

When Plato declares that 'to philosophize is to learn to die',[16] he is plainly echoing the themes of religious resignation, but by way of reflection and reasoning: to die is to be separated from the sensory and the body so as to be able to contemplate the Truth. When Spinoza declares, in a materialist sentence, that '*to philosophize is to learn not to die, but to live*', he goes further than Epicurus's demonstration: rather than showing that death is nothing – that is, rather than calling attention to death – he treats it as if it were nothing – that is, treats it by passing it over in silence, and talks about life alone.[17] These two *opposed* attitudes (opposed because one of them reinforces religion, while the other treats it very critically), the former idealist and the latter materialist, have at least one thing in common: they proceed by reasoning, and painstakingly *seek out* rational proofs and demonstrations.

How persuasive they are is another question. When Plato explains that the body is, for man, a 'tomb' that prevents him from seeing the Truth, and that 'to die' is to free oneself of the body (= to turn away from sense impressions) and behold the Truth, it takes considerable goodwill to follow him.[18] When Epicurus produces his demonstration about death, it hardly convinces us, irrefutable though it may be. Yet the fact remains that the reasons cited by philosophers are *reasons*, even if they are sometimes artificial or arbitrary, especially in the idealist tradition, and they are reasons *sought* by a painstaking effort of Reason, which undertakes to produce a *consistent* rational discourse in which everything coheres. What a contrast with religion! Religion has always had its reasons, *without going to the least trouble to look for them*, without expending the least effort to find them, without establishing a coherent rational order among them. It has received its reasons from God himself in the Revelation, and since it has also received the absolute guarantee of their Truth, it runs no risk of ever being deceived. It is forever sure of what it says, and when it talks about death or someone in his death agony, it does so in order to transfigure this ordeal by frightening people (sinners will go to Hell) or consoling them – but, always, by exploiting it to reproduce its own power.

It is quite striking that this divorce between materialism and religion manifests itself in the most concrete, the most pedestrian everyday practice of the ordinary people who consider themselves 'non-philosophers'.

I said earlier that the *passive, resigned* aspect of the philosophy of non-philosophers had something *religious* about it. One need only recall the onerous heritage weighing them down to confirm this: their long centuries of servitude and all their abortive revolts, drowned in blood. It is understandable that they should be instinctively suspicious and wary of the omnipotent power – Nature and the dominant class – that bears down on and crushes them. It is understandable that, instructed by an age-old prudence, they should resort to cunning to counter the effects of this power, and strive simply to survive by avoiding these effects.

At the same time, however, we find the germs of an altogether different, counterposed conception in the same people's spontaneous philosophy, one which *inverts the order of the arguments*. This conception returns fearlessly to the idea that to be human is to be subject to finite conditions of life and finite capacities and, ultimately, to be mortal. Rather than appealing to God and lapsing into *resignation*, however, it draws its conclusions from people's real practice, judging that *it is precisely this finite condition of destitution and need that makes people work, transform nature and search painstakingly* – a task religion spares them – *for a little truth about the world*.

There is, in Plato, a story about the beginnings of humanity. It is told by the materialist philosopher Protagoras, for Plato has given him the floor. Protagoras explains that, unlike animals, whom nature protects from the cold with fur, people are born into a hostile world *completely naked*. Animals reproduce themselves without making a fuss [*sans histoire*]: for, precisely, *animals have no history* [*n'ont pas d'histoire*]. Human beings, however, have had to gather in groups, shivering, and go to work to survive. They have *transformed their destitution into productive activity*: they have invented society and the arts and sciences, endowing themselves with a history thanks to this effort and producing all the marvels of the arts and crafts.[19] This opens up infinite perspectives. But, to add a word to Protagoras's tale, it is surprisingly true that people are born *completely naked*. In other words, a human baby is 'premature' (unlike animals' young, which can walk and do without their mother's care as soon as they are born) and wouldn't survive if their mother didn't provide them with the indispensable nourishment, care and love they need simply to survive. Born naked in the beginning, human beings discover the same nakedness again in each of their children: to conduct a child towards humanity is to invest it with all that humankind has achieved in its history, to introduce it into this history, a product of the effort and struggle that constitutes what is specifically human. 'Man is an animal who works' (Kant).[20] 'Man is a tool-making animal' (Franklin,[21] Marx[22]). Man is a historical animal.

This may be observed even in everyday life. For people do not just passively endure the events of natural and social life. *They transform* something in nature and society insofar as *they work*, insofar as *they act*. Every worker knows that he has only to apply his labour-power properly to the tools he uses to work on a given material in order to produce a *new* result: a product that didn't previously exist in nature. He can see that he has only to act on other people, directly or indirectly, in order to produce, under favourable circumstances, certain effects which, if enough individuals unite in the same action, can likewise culminate in a *new* result that didn't previously exist in society.

This experience strengthens people's conviction that there are reasons for things, comprehensible and controllable reasons, since one succeeds in producing defined results by respecting the laws of their production, which are laws of nature and society. Production and action are thus proof of the truth of these laws. And, since those who act are human beings, they know the laws that govern what they do, for they have to respect them. An eighteenth-century Italian philosopher, Giambattista Vico, said '*verum factum*', which means that 'what is true is what has been made' or 'truth is revealed by activity'.[23] In the same mode, religion can declare that if God knows the world, it is because he 'made' or created it. The worker can reply that the first to have this experience wasn't God – for go see if he exists! – but the worker himself, in his practice of production. The scientist can say the same thing, for he will not obtain scientific results unless he puts an elaborate experimental array in place and has such exact knowledge of its laws that he can trust his results.

A vast experiment [*expérience*] is performed in this way by all who work (from labourers, craftsmen and farmers to scientists). It accumulates in the course of human history, producing and reinforcing a *materialist* conception of the world based on determinism and the laws governing things, laws discovered in the practice of transforming nature and society. *In principle, this philosophy no longer has anything religious, passive or resigned about it. On the contrary, it is a philosophy of work and struggle, an active philosophy* that seconds people's practical efforts. Unlike idealism, which is a philosophy of *theory*, materialism is a philosophy of *practice*. By this we mean not that this philosophy neglects theory, but that it puts practice 'above' theory, or affirms the 'primacy of practice over theory'.

If this is indeed the case (we shall explain what all these expressions mean), we cannot avoid asking the following question. If it is true that people spend *the better part of their lives* at work, where they are confronted by the necessity of the things of nature, and in struggle or submission, where they are confronted by the necessity of the things of society, then how are we to explain the fact that the first of the great philosophies of the philosophers (Plato's) was *idealist, and that idealism has represented, throughout the history of philosophy, the dominant tendency* – with materialism represented by only a handful of philosophers courageous enough to go against the current? It will doubtless be said that religion already existed and dominated philosophy to the point of making it its 'handmaiden', imposing the idealist standpoint on it. We saw a moment ago, however, that this explanation falls short of the mark, and that the philosophy of the philosophers had *reasons of its own*, more complicated reasons, to surge up in history in the form of idealism.

It is time to say a few words on the subject and, therefore, to discuss the *beginnings* of the philosophy of the philosophers. Why did this philosophy surge up in the world of the fifth century BC in Greece?[24]

Historians have proposed several different answers to this question. Some have said that philosophy sprang up in Greece on the basis provided by the existence of a market and *currency*, since currency provided an example of 'abstraction' that inspired philosophical abstraction. Others have said that philosophy sprang up in Greece on the basis provided by *democracy*, since democratic rules provided an abstract model for philosophical abstraction and imposed a confrontation between differing viewpoints. We shall adopt one feature of these explanations: their insistence on the *abstract* nature of philosophical notions and reasoning. But must we look for the origin of philosophical abstraction in money or in democracy? It seems not.

We should look for it, rather, in the first true *science* to have irrupted in the history of human culture, precisely in sixth-century and fifth-century Greece: geometry. Involved here was a veritable *revolution* in knowledge, the apparition of a way of thinking and reasoning *that had never before existed* and that no one had foreseen. Previously, *empirical* mathematics had been highly developed by the peoples of the eastern Mediterranean basin, but it had been unable to attain *theoretical* form. What does that mean? It means that people were familiar with a great many properties of numbers (arithmetic) and figures (geometry). These properties had been derived from the observation of combinations of real numbers and comparisons of concrete figures. At the time, people reasoned about *concrete objects*: the number of oxen, the distances and surface areas bounded by fields, and so on. They knew how to perform various operations on numbers and geometrical figures: the proof is that architects and shipbuilders or the builders of temples could, in practice, solve very difficult problems using technical rules and formulas. Their solutions compel our admiration even today. Mathematics of this kind produced *correct* results. It had, however, nothing to do with the mathematics we know, which arose in Greece around a more or less mythical figure named Thales towards the sixth century BC. Why? Because these *correct* mathematical results were simply the result of empirical observations and practices: *they had been neither explained nor demonstrated.*

With Thales, everything changed. People began to reason in a completely different way about a different kind of object. They stopped *observing* combinations of concrete numbers and transformations of concrete figures in order to reason about *abstract* objects considered as such: pure numbers and pure figures, abstracted from their content or from concrete representations of them. And those who reasoned about these abstract objects began to use different methods of reasoning, abstract in their turn, which proved to be enormously productive: no longer empirical comparison, but 'pure' demonstration and deduction. Thus, when they studied the properties of the angles '*of the*' triangle, they did not reason, even if they drew a triangle in the sand, about that concrete triangle drawn in the sand, but *about the 'pure' triangle*, representing all possible triangles. And once they had *demonstrated* a property, they were absolutely certain that it was *incontestable* and valid for all possible triangles. That, however, was not the sole interest of this stunning discovery, because the 'pure' mathematician's practice was not confined to *demonstrating* the validity of already discovered properties; it also multiplied the properties of its object by revealing in it new properties that empirical mathematicians had not only not known, but could not even have suspected. 'Demonstrations', a philosopher was to say, 'are the eyes of the soul'; they see infinitely further than the eyes of the body.[25] What, until then, had seen infinitely further than the eyes of the body, the limited human body that is destined to die? *Religion.* There can be no doubt that this 'qualitative leap' in human knowledge, the prestige and fecundity of the new mathematics and, above all, its total autonomy and its capacity to produce demonstrations beyond the reach of time and death, through the effort of the human 'mind', had, in some fashion, undermined religion.

It was in this way that the philosophy of the philosophers, which had been stagnating in *cosmologies* (theories of the universe: the nature of the basic elements composing it – water, fire, cold, warmth and so on), reached a decisive turning point, conquering, with Plato's grand undertaking, an *irreversible historical existence*. Although the beginnings of philosophy can be considered to predate Plato, they were just its first stammers. The philosophy of the philosophers came into being only with Plato, and these philosophers referred to Plato as the Founder, the Foremost of their contemporaries, the first to establish the existence and form of philosophy and impose it in history. What the philosophers still do not know is *why this form was invented* and *why it is still a viable form.*

We may indeed suppose that religion, which 'cemented' Greek society and unified its ideas and was, therefore, its dominant ideology, was put to a severe test by the sudden emergence of mathematical science, and that its pretensions to possessing *every Truth* were dealt a serious blow. For the first time, religion saw its field of operations restricted by the achievements of a secular science that stated incontestable truths and spoke a language completely different from the one religion spoke: the language of pure demonstration. A threat now hung over the dominant ideas and their religious unification.

What did Plato do? He came up with *the 'unheard-of' project* of restoring the unity of the dominant ideas undermined by the advent of mathematics – not by combating mathematics in the name of religion, nor by contesting its methods or results, but, quite the contrary, by acknowledging their existence and validity, and *borrowing* from them the novelty they had introduced: *the idea of pure objects to which pure reasoning can be applied.* That is why he had this famous sentence engraved on the lintel of his school of philosophy: 'Let none who is not a geometer enter here.'[26] Yet the same Plato, who had apparently gone to school to mathematics, conducted this whole operation for the sole purpose of making mathematics go to school to his philosophy. He put mathematics not in first place, but in second in his philosophy … after philosophy itself. He thereby managed, by subordinating mathematics to his philosophy, to gain control over it, or, in other words, *to put it back in its place* in the established order – the order, that is, of the moral and political values that mathematics had momentarily threatened or might threaten. Thus he beat back the threat that the discovery of mathematics represented for the dominant ideas of his day.

Of course, this gigantic political-ideological operation, which restored the jeopardized unity of the dominant ideas, was not a pure and simple retreat. For something quite different from a cosmology or myth was needed to dispel the menace: a new discourse operating on pure objects, *the 'Ideas'*, using a new method, *rational* and *dialectical demonstration*. It is easy to understand why: to gain control over the existence of mathematical ideas and put them back in their place, subordinate to philosophy's, what was required was a discourse *on a par with* them. This new discourse was, quite simply, that of the philosophy of the philosophers.

The consequence, however, was that philosophy, which was born of this counter-attack, simultaneously took its place in the other camp: that of religion, or, rather, of the ideas and the dominant ideology unified by religion. For it was quite as if the advent of the new science had put a tear in the relatively unified fabric of the dominant ideas; this tear had to be 'patched up'. Do you know the kind of people who, when they feel they've been 'cornered' in a debate, shift ground to get out of a tight spot or repair the damage done? Allowance duly made, things happened much the same way here. Plato's invention of philosophy represented the 'change of terrain' that was indispensable to overcoming the difficulties encountered on the old terrain, indispensable to repairing the damage caused by the apparition of science in a world unified by religion. That is what allows us to say that Platonic philosophy merely *shifted the problems and role of religion onto the terrain of 'pure' rationality.* If philosophy makes its appearance, it is to ward off the threat of science so as to restore order: religion's order. But it does so with one difference: philosophy's God was to be, as we have already seen, a God different from the God of simple believers – he was to be 'the God of the philosophers and scientists'.

Order was restored, to be sure, but the result of this spectacular thrust and parry, this dazzling philosophical riposte, was that there were now *two new characters* on the stage of existing culture, *characters whose existence no one had foreseen.* One was an authentic *science,* 'pure' mathematics; it supplanted empirical mathematics and was to undergo phenomenal developments, which began in Antiquity with the work of Euclid and Archimedes, before making the birth of Galilean physics possible in the sixteenth and seventeenth centuries. The other character was *philosophy.* The philosophy that emerged at this time, in a victorious operation, did not in any sense break with religion, *pace* the eighteenth-century rationalists. It emerged as a replique and a rejoinder to the emergence of mathematics, as a defensive manoeuvre, the purpose of which was to restore the jeopardized unity of the dominant ideas and, consequently, of religion.

This philosophy openly announced itself as *the philosophy of the philosophers* (and philosophy teachers), for, to practise it, one had to 'be a geometer' – that is, versed in the new science and its methods, and capable of reinterpreting religion in a rational discourse.[27] That wasn't given to everyone. On Plato's own witness, this philosophy was idealist: it rang in the long, the interminable domination of materialism by idealism in the history of philosophy, a domination that coincides with the existence of class societies and persists in our own time. For only an idealist could successfully hold mathematical truths and all the material practices making up human existence at bay, subordinating them to *Ideas* superior to *concrete knowledge* [*connaissances*]. For only an idealist could successfully enlist a discourse of a rational cast in the service of religious values and questions. It is to be an idealist thus to affirm philosophy's and the philosopher's absolute *power* over all things and all truth, a position that makes the Truth a (religious and political) power and makes philosophers a small group of initiated intellectuals in sole possession of the Truth, which they consent to hand down from on high to the common herd and also to kings, should they be inclined to lend an ear to it. For the kings and priests, and all those holding any sort of power whatsoever, *have a stake in this philosophy*; it is the only one capable of putting things in order and reinforcing the order of things so that everyone stays in his place and performs his social function: so that the slave remains a slave, the craftsman, a craftsman, the merchant, a merchant, the freemen, freemen, the priests, priests, the warriors, warriors and the king, a king. Idealism talks about Truth, but, behind Truth, it is power that appears on the horizon, and, with power, Order. Philosophers seem to withdraw from the world: they do so to set themselves apart from the ignorant, from common men and materialists. But they withdraw from the world only to intervene in it and dictate the Truth to it: the Truth of power and Order.

It will be objected that it is strange that a handful of men should *presume to* exercise a power of this kind. For what forces can they call on, their discourse aside? The only possible answer is that *their discourse has power because it serves the powers-that-be, borrowing its force from the forces philosophers serve*: quid pro quo. But what can the discourse of idealist philosophers really *give*? What does it *add* to the social forces it serves (the religious powers-that-be, the political powers-that-be and so on)? Might it be that the political authorities and religion need a *supplement of force* which takes, precisely, the form of idealist philosophy? But to what end? We shall leave this new question in abeyance. Patience!

To conclude our discussion of Plato's philosophy, which inaugurates the whole history of philosophy, here is one last surprising trait: *this idealist philosophy carries its adversary, materialism, inside it*! Plato, who ranges himself with the 'Friends of the Ideas', combats the materialism of the 'Friends of the Earth';[28] yet, in several passages, their materialism figures in his own thought. This is a strange property that we never observe in the sciences: carrying one's adversary inside oneself! Plato's idealist philosophy, however, carries materialism inside itself, present, albeit refuted. It does so not to give it the floor, but to ward it off, to get the jump on it; it does so to occupy in advance positions that materialism might capture, and to bend the materialist arguments themselves, roundly refuted or turned against themselves, to idealism's service.

Let us generalize: *every philosophy, idealist or materialist, carries its adversary inside itself,* with the aim of preventively refuting it. Well and good. But why must it refute it? Why must it carry its adversary's arguments inside itself, even if these arguments are turned against him? Why can a philosophy not be quite simply and serenely idealist, or quite serenely materialist, without troubling itself about its foe? Is there not place in the sun for one and all? Is there so little available space that one has to squabble over it? *Why are there necessarily adversaries in philosophy and why does this combat necessarily revolve around idealism and materialism?*

Strange.

THE BIG DETOUR

The Big Detour starts here. At the end of it, we will be able to answer the questions that we have already encountered and posed. That the philosophy we wish to explain has to make this Big Detour reminds us that the explorers of the fourteenth to the sixteenth centuries had to venture into the unknown and past the tips of the continents, sailing round the Cape of Good Hope and negotiating the Straits of Magellan, to conquer other seas and other worlds for human knowledge, to take the measure of the earth and confirm that it was round. By the time they returned to port, their caravels battered, with sails in shreds, they had a completely different idea of the little world in which they lived. One has to leave one's own world behind and make the Big Detour of the world to know one's own world. One can never venture too far afield in quest of the adventure of coming home.

The same holds for philosophy. If a philosophy truly, honestly wants to *know itself*, to discover the place it occupies in the philosophical world and that which properly distinguishes it from all other philosophies, it has to make the Grand Detour through the history of philosophy and engage other works near and far, indeed, as far as possible from itself, so that it can come home laden with comparisons and know a little better what it is. All great philosophies make this Big Detour. Kant went looking for ways of knowing himself in distant Plato and in Descartes, who was close at hand. Marx went to the ends of the earth to look for ways of defining himself, in Aristotle and in what was nearest, but also farthest, in Hegel. We too, therefore, shall make this Big Detour. To do so, we shall call on the philosophers farthest from us and closest to us. *Simultaneously, however, we shall make another Big Detour*, taking our distance from the philosophy of the philosophers in order to analyse concrete human practices. We shall engage in the perilous venture of making *the Big Detour through non-philosophy* in order to discover, once we have 'come home', what philosophy might be.

There exist countless Histories of Philosophy, and some of them are good. But who has ever seen fit to write a *History of Non-Philosophy*? Who, I mean, has ever seen fit to write a History of everything that the dominant idealist philosophy (and even the dominated materialist philosophy, which has all too often been forced, under pressure from the other, to think exclusively in terms of the other's questions) has *neglected, rejected, censored or abandoned* as the refuse of existence and history, as objects unworthy of its attention?

Above all, *matter*, its ponderousness and power; above all, *labour* and its conditions, exploitation, slaves, serfs, proletarians, women and children in the hell of the factory, and slums and disease, and the attrition due to usury and also physical attrition; above all, the *body* and the desire that comes to it from its sex, that suspect part of man and woman which countless authorities have surveyed and still do; above all, *woman*, long man's property, and *children*, monitored from earliest infancy and in the stranglehold of an elaborate system of controls; above all, *madness*, condemned to the 'humanitarian' prison of the asylums; above all, *prisoners*, hunted down by law and Right, and all the exiles, the condemned and the tortured; above all, *the Barbarians* for the Greeks and the 'wogs' or 'foreigners' or 'natives' for us; above all, *state power* and all its apparatuses of coercion and 'persuasion', concealed in seemingly neutral institutions, the family, the School System, the Health Care System, the Administration, the Constitution; above all, class struggle; above all, war. *No more than that.*

Aristotle does of course talk about slaves, but only to say that they are animals.[1] Hegel does of course talk about war, but only to say that it regenerates the nations as a blast of wind from the heavens stirs up still waters to keep them from stagnating.[2] Spinoza does of course talk about the body and says that its powers are unknown, but he says nothing about sex.[3] An insignificant detour, only to fall back into line.

And to whom did it ever occur, for centuries, at any rate,[4] to write a History of these non-philosophical 'objects' in order to show that if the dominant philosophy has so thoroughly *scorned* them, it is because it has an interest in hushing up its own relationship with the official censorship of them, its own complicity with the dominant class's religion, morality and politics? What if this complicity went a good way towards defining philosophy itself? Before the war, the French philosopher Nizan defined philosophers as 'watchdogs'. On all these burning questions, philosophers did not even have to bark. All they had to do was *keep their mouths shut.*

In this short book, we cannot, for material reasons, touch on all these questions. On the Big Detour that we are about to make, we shall discuss only some of the human practices in the domain of *non-philosophy*, the most important for understanding what philosophy is. But everyone should keep the existence of the others in mind – for they silently accompany everything that will be said here.

3 ABSTRACTION

Let us go back to the double advent of the world's first science and the philosophy that took shape *in response* to it.

The reader will no doubt find that we have got ahead of ourselves. We have been invited to witness this double event, and we have understood that philosophy is in some sense charged with the task of 'patching up' the tear that science puts in the fabric of the dominant ideology. Well and good. But we have been told that the characteristic feature of this first science was to break with the empirical practice of the mathematics of an earlier day and reason on the basis of demonstrations about 'abstract' objects. We have also been told that philosophy had to follow suit in order to carry out its task of ideological restoration. Yet no one has explained to us what this science really was, or what the bases on which it could come about were, or, above all, what the much-vaunted 'purity' and 'abstraction' distinguishing its objects and reasoning were. What might this 'abstraction' be, and what proves that it was born, miraculously, with this science – that it was not preceded by other forms of abstraction?

To answer, we have to begin again at the beginning: with the practical experience of the broad masses of people who work, suffer, struggle and make history, even when they simply endure it. We have to try to see whether we can find something in this practical experience that resembles *abstraction* and the *abstract*.

The spontaneous, common-sense reaction, based on experience of real practices, is to say: 'But that's impossible! Everything that exists is concrete! What could be more concrete than a man and a woman? What could be more concrete or more material than a field, horses, a tractor, a factory, a commodity, money? Everything is what it is: it exists, it's defined, it consists of all its parts, it coexists with an infinite number of other things that are just as concrete. What are you after with your abstraction? You're well aware that if someone starts telling you stories that make no sense, you say: "All that's just abstractions" – in other words, just a string of statements that take no account of the real, the concrete. And you show him the door'.

'We're quite sure that we're living in the concrete world: from cradle to grave, we live in the concrete and under the domination of the concrete. It's tough enough as it is, without us having to make things up to boot and believe in things that don't exist! Leave us alone with your abstractions!'

In this reaction, there is a profound protest against what we shall call 'bad abstractions', which the whole materialist tradition (Spinoza)[1] and certain idealists (Hegel)[2] have condemned. The fact is that when one 'abstracts from' reality, it is usually in order to lose oneself in daydreams, which are sometimes motivated by personal interests; and, in that case, it is because someone wants to divert people's attention from reality, to mislead them about it.

Abstraction, however, does not always bear on 'all of reality'; one can abstract from *part* of reality in order to focus on the rest. The farmer ploughing his field and the worker on his assembly line 'abstract from' quite a few things while working, so that they can think about nothing but their work. Similarly, in order to consider this or that aspect of the reality they are studying, scientists 'abstract from' the rest. It is not that the rest doesn't exist: they simply set it aside temporarily, as the farmer at his plough temporarily sets his wife and children aside. Let us generalize: *every specific practice* (labour, scientific research, medicine, political struggle) *abstracts from the rest of reality in order to concentrate on transforming one part of it*. To abstract is 'to detach' a part of reality from the rest. Abstraction is, to begin with, this operation and its result. The abstract is opposed to the concrete as *the part detached* from the whole is opposed to the whole.

But a long way that's got us! For when you detach (when you abstract) one part of the real, that part too is real. In what sense can you call it 'abstract' not in a negative, but in a *positive* way? If the part abstracted is made of the same 'stuff' as the concrete whole from which it has been abstracted, what remains of the abstraction? The act of carving things up. The butcher who carves a piece of lamb 'following the articulations' (Plato) cuts away first one part, then another.[3] Is a leg of lamb an abstraction? The butcher will laugh in your face: it's mutton like all the rest.

We need to broach things differently, then: the way they are broached in an example adduced by Descartes, who reflects on the imagination of painters.[4] However far the imagination goes, it cannot go beyond existing nature, existing beings. But the painter can combine parts of reality, taken here and there from beings that don't possess all of them at once. Thus if you take a woman's body, a lion's claws and an eagle's head, and paint all that end to end, you come up with a creature no one has ever laid eyes on, a completely new, unprecedented creature, a creature that doesn't exist: a chimera. The chimera is the product of a series of abstractions, because the woman's body is 'abstracted' from this or that woman, the eagle's head from this or that eagle and the lion's claws from this or that lion – or pictures of them. *All this comes from nature; yet the result isn't found in nature.* Quite the contrary: the result of this series of combined abstractions *adds* something to nature that wasn't in nature. This time, the definition of abstraction is *positive*. It is, however, also quite paradoxical, since it adds something to nature without leaving nature behind. It is the product of the imagination of the painter, who doesn't confine himself to carving something up, like the butcher, but *composes* something.

'But that's a matter for painters,' it will be objected. 'What in the world does it have to do with life? The overwhelming majority of people aren't painters. They don't live in the land of chimeras and the imagination; they live in the concrete.'

Quite. But what if we said that the first 'abstraction' that people have to do with, in all their everyday acts, day and night (yes, 'and night': in their dreams), was *language*?

What, after all, is a word, if not a sound, an articulated sound, and thus something that exists in nature that has been 'extracted', hence 'abstracted', from the whole set of sounds existing in nature? Yet this abstract [*abstrait*, which also means 'abstracted'] thing known as a word possesses the existence of abstraction only because, as a sound, it is combined or associated with the thing it designates. Thus when we say: 'I call a cat a cat',[5] we mean that the sound 'cat', produced by a certain configuration of the muscles of the mouth and tongue, is associated with a natural reality: the animal that goes chasing after mice and miaows when it's hungry, the one called 'cat'. 'Cat' is thus a sound become a word because it has been associated with the living thing that is a cat.

It is also plain that, as with the chimera, this composition consisting of two elements 'extracted' from nature (the sound 'cat' and the animal, the cat) is totally *arbitrary*. Plato long ago pointed out the arbitrary nature of the choice of the words used to designate things, although he was inclined to think that there was a natural correspondence between word and thing, sound and thing. He cited many different examples in Greek;[6] we can cite others in French. For example, when we talk about a *murmure* [murmur], we see, as it were, the lips open partway and close again, twice, in order to produce the sound; it is as if we were seeing the sound that they make in enunciating the word. Similarly, when we pronounce the word *brouhaha* [brouhaha], it is clear that the sound of the word imitates the noise a crowd makes. Even when we pronounce the word *tremble* [he trembles], whether it is a question of the tree known by the name *tremble* [trembling poplar] or a naked man gripped by the cold, it is as if we were seeing the movement of a slender trunk battered by the wind or a shivering body like the one we can admire in a famous painting by the fifteenth-century Italian painter Masaccio, a picture of John the Baptist on the banks of a stream: a man is pouring the baptismal water over his nude body, and he is shivering.[7] To paint a shiver . . .

However, apart from a handful of words which, as it were, reproduce the thing, but are nevertheless not the thing because they are words or signifiers, the immense majority of words reproduce absolutely nothing of the thing they designate. The words 'man' and 'woman' bear no resemblance at all, whether of sound, smell, taste, form or anything else, to the real beings known as a man and a woman. And 'God', for those who believe in him, bears no resemblance, *as a word*, to the 'reality' that God is supposed to be, so much so that an entire school of theologians (the word designating people who are supposed to know and say what God is) defended the idea that there is no relation between God and any name in language; they held that we should give God no name at all and that the only way to name him was to use names *while simultaneously negating them*. Thus one could only name God by saying that he was the not-existent, the not-powerful, the not-perfect, even the not-God. This is a way not of doing away with him, but of saying that he is beyond 'all possible names', for he is beyond all possible realities.

The overwhelming majority of words are thus perfectly arbitrary with respect to the things they designate. This means that there is no natural, material relationship between the sound and the meaning of words. It was this fact that the linguist Saussure noted in developing the theory of the '*arbitrary nature of the sign*'.[8] He showed that there is no natural, necessary relation between the sounds or written signs known as words and the things they designate, but that, in contrast, a necessary, if arbitrary relationship (arbitrary: with no natural basis, whether of correspondence or resemblance) had been established between signs and things.

How was this relationship established? It was obviously not established by God, although believers of all religions claim that he or his messenger bestowed language on humanity. If it was not established by God, then it must have been established by human beings. Here, however, insuperable problems crop up (which eighteenth-century philosophers tried in vain to resolve): for in order for human beings to agree to assign definite words, and the same words, to things, they had to live in society; to live in society, however, they had first to have concluded a social pact or convention among themselves, and to conclude that convention, they obviously needed language. Thus we find ourselves in a theoretical vicious circle, which we can get out of only by supposing, as Rousseau does, that language has an unknown origin, and yet a beginning, because it has not always existed, since human beings were animals to begin with, and animals do not talk.[9]

While there is no relation between names and things that is not arbitrary and conventional, Saussure showed that there exist, in contrast, necessary relations between the sounds of a language, and that it is the regulated difference of the phonological system that distinguishes the different words. This means that no phonological element exists in isolation; it exists only by virtue of the difference distinguishing it from, and relating it to, the other phonological elements. (Thus p does not exist in itself, but in its difference from b; d does not exist in itself, but in its difference from t, and so on.) Hence language is, as far as its sounds are concerned, simply a 'system of differences'. It is this rule of similarity and difference that results in the constitution of units of sound enabling us to identify words, hence to tell words apart and, thanks to words, to distinguish things by naming them.

Similarly, Saussure showed that there exist relationships of proximity and opposition between words (often called 'signifiers' from this new standpoint), and that language has available to it a whole series of words and constructions whose sole function is to bring out this affinity or difference. For instance, the French word *son* means both 'sound' and 'bran'. Special words or phrasal constructions allow us to distinguish two meanings of the same word: 'the sound of the trumpet' [*le son du clairon*]; 'he's playing the ass to get bran' [*il fait l'âne pour avoir du son*].[10] Language, albeit arbitrary, constitutes a double system that is at once phonological (its different sounds) and grammatical (the arrangement of its words in sentences), and those sentences are regulated by laws that are necessary and necessarily respected. If they weren't, everyone would be completely at sea.

It is this strange reality, language, which makes the operation known as abstraction possible. *All those who speak, therefore, make 'natural' use of abstraction*, of this new abstraction.

They would be quite surprised to be told that, just as Monsieur Jourdain was surprised to hear that he 'had been speaking prose'. Yet it is true. The proof is that we may take any word at all, with just one exception – we shall see which one (the proper name, and even then, only with reservations) – to bring out the fact that *all people make use of this abstraction*. In other words, even while they live in the concrete, they live in abstraction as well, whatever their acts, even their most concrete acts.

Take a farmer who says: '*the* cow died'. For him, it is a question of *his* cow, not just any cow: Gracieuse, who died last night while calving because the veterinarian had had an accident. Thus it is a question, when the farmer talks about 'the cow', of 'his cow' and, among his cows, of a single cow, precisely *the one* that died last night. Thus it is a question of an animal that can be confused with no other, the most concrete, and the most singular thing imaginable.

Yet any farmer at all could say, of *his* cow, or any cow, provided that he designates it either in language or with a gesture, '*the* cow' [*vache*]; and if the conditions of concrete designation are fulfilled, no one will misunderstand him. In other words, in each case, that is, in every case, that is, in any case at all, *the most abstract, the most general of forms, namely the two words 'the cow', unfailingly designates the most concrete of objects,* this cow and no other; and no one misunderstands. Exactly the same thing would happen with a worker who said, 'The boss is a bastard [*vache*]',[11] or 'The boss is a nice guy, but he's still a boss.' In every case, *the abstraction of language serves to designate the most concrete of concrete things.*

This is what the German philosopher Hegel showed in a famous passage of *The Phenomenology of Spirit.*[12] Suppose anyone at all, said Hegel, in any situation at all. Suppose that this person wants to designate something he is pointing to, or something he means, with the shortest and most concrete of words, a word that is hardly even a word, but a gesture designating the most singular thing in the world. The effect of this word or gesture is simply to show the concrete thing; it comes down to saying '*this*', and nothing more. The thing that is the 'this' will be shown, and no one can mistake the thing shown: it's plainly this one, not that one. To make quite sure that this thing is indeed itself and will not disappear (for, a second later, it can be replaced by some other thing), the person will spell out: '*this* this, here, now'. But, Hegel says, the person in question need only turn around; if he looks for the concrete, singular object, the 'this' that was 'here, now', he is quite likely to discover (like someone in a train watching the scenery slip by) that the 'this' that was 'here, now' has completely changed. Another 'this' has taken its place, 'here and now'. Hegel quite rightly concludes not that concrete immediacy does not exist, but that the language whose function it is to designate it as concrete is itself *abstract, general.*

Of course, we can ask whether there do not exist means other than the abstraction of language for 'grasping' the concrete. When a man eats a pudding, he makes no mistake about what he's eating: he knows it's *this* pudding and no other. When a man embraces a woman and penetrates her, he makes no mistake about which woman is involved, except in Marivaux's comedies: it's clearly *this* woman, not another. But, and this is precisely the point, he doesn't speak: it is his arms and sex which 'have the floor' [*ont la parole*, literally, 'have the word'].

The same thing applies when a worker works on 'his' part: he designates the concrete object by holding it and working on it with the tools he has in his hand. We may conclude from this that there is an *appropriation of the concrete that proceeds by way of not language, but the human body*, whether a person works on raw material, is united with another person in the sexual act, consumes bread and wine to nourish himself or takes state power. In every case, impostures aside, there is no mistaking the concrete object involved, and the person appropriates the concrete without a word.

What is missing from this act of appropriation, however, is social communication, the ability to say to others: this is my woman, this is my bread, this object is my horse or my tool. What is missing, consequently, is *social, public recognition of the act of appropriation of the concrete*. But everything goes to show that, to live in society – and people do live in society – an individual not only feels the need to appropriate concrete things physically; he also feels the need for social recognition of this act of appropriation, in the form of others' tacit consent or of *property law*. Otherwise, anyone at all could happen along and borrow or steal his horse and tools. Thus the act of physical, bodily appropriation has, in some way, to be redoubled by a sanction that makes the detour through a particular language, the *language of law* [*droit*], which publicly affirms, before all men, that this woman is well and truly his (not some other man's), that this horse is well and truly his, and so on.

Even the most 'concrete' kind of appropriation thus has to have the social sanction of the *language of law*, that is, of an abstract system of relations, if it is to be accomplished without risk – and not just without risk, but with all possible guarantees. When the concrete appropriation of the concrete does not submit to this abstraction and this sanction, it runs the risk, at the limit, of not being socially recognized, hence of violating the law, hence of being qualified as theft or crime: as such, it comes under yet another abstract rule, the law that prohibits taking other's property. This rule produces the public offence and the punishment for it, which, for its part, is always concrete: the penalty inflicted on the delinquent or criminal.

There we have the 'dialectical' circle of the concrete and the abstract. There is no abstraction without the existence of the concrete. People can only maintain a social relation to the concrete, however, thanks to the abstract rules of language and law. If they break them, they pay 'concretely' for their infraction. For abusive language, insults or lies almost always have consequences for their authors *in person*, as do thefts, violent crimes and other 'affronts' to the Law.

'Granted,' the objection will run, 'we live under language and Law. But we don't spend our whole lives doing that. Existence isn't made up of words alone and the Civil Code doesn't govern everything we do. Law states general rules that apply to everyone; that's why they're called abstract. We have only to respect them to be left in peace. The rest of our time is our own: for instance, work, our personal lives, our desires and pleasures. That's the *truly concrete aspect of our life: what we do on our own.'*

Yes and no. Yes, because it is true that the individual who works is a concrete human being who applies his efforts to concrete matter using concrete tools, investing all his competence and patience in his task, even when he works for someone else, and all the more when he works for himself. Yes, because – to go from one extreme to the other – it is true that a man making love is a concrete man united with a concrete woman (with her and no other), who devotes all his attention and passion to the act. No, because we need take just a short step back from things to see that each of these concrete men succeeds in working or loving only by repeating gestures he has learned, which are subject to relations no less abstract than the relations of language and Law.

A worker, however skilful he may be, would not make such-and-such a gesture unless *the form of his work*, and thus the form of his practical gestures, were not *imposed* on him by the existing raw material and the existing tools or machines, which he has not made himself (they are products of a long history of social relations that have established this form independently of him), and unless the existing relations of production had assigned him his place in the organization and division of labour. His movements are of course his own, yet he merely repeats the same movements that millions of workers the world over are repeating at the same moment: movements established in advance, 'abstractly', for him and his peers, by the relations of production dominating the societies in which all of them live.

No, because we have to take just a short step back from things to see that every concrete man who makes love to a concrete woman (to her and not another) and tries to tell her of his love and affection merely repeats, as a rule, give or take a few variations, and even when he tries to find other words and gestures all his own, the same few poor words and gestures which the tradition established and attempted to exalt long before he was born, and which the press and novels, as well as the radio – and songs! – diffuse the livelong day. And if we take a little more distance from things, we shall see that there exist, in every culture, determinate, specific words and gestures, *different* words and gestures, for declaring one's love, or, sometimes, silence, when relations between the sexes are established in advance by the family or religion and are beyond appeal. Where do these words and gestures come from? *From a certain standing idea* of what is at stake in the relations between a man and a woman, or, rather, from a certain set of ideas about *what it is appropriate to do as a function of what is at stake* in the relations between a man and a woman. This set of ideas (love, always; the couple, happiness, the children; the idea that the initiative belongs to men, who are superior to women; abandonment, remorse, return, death) makes up what may be called a *practical 'ideology'*. These 'ideas' exist only by virtue of their *relations*, which are obligatory for the vast majority of men and women, and it is these relations which inspire and govern the ordinary words and gestures of even the most concrete romantic ceremonial.

We have taken these two examples, simple examples, so as not to complicate our exposition of an elementary truth. This truth is that it is not only language which is abstract (it is linked to concrete things, but is arbitrary and exists independently of them, and this makes it possible for it to have *general* value, the characteristic feature of all abstraction), and not only Law which is abstract (since it 'abstracts from' all particulars, is general and applies to everyone); there also exists an infinite number of *abstract gestures* that are linked to concrete practices, yet exist independently of them, and this makes it possible for them to have general value and *serve these concrete practices*.

Let us sum up what we have established so far. Abstraction is not detachment of a part belonging to the concrete whole. Abstraction is bound to the concrete and derives from the concrete in ways that can vary (language is not 'abstracted' from the concrete the way law is, or the way the abstract gestures of every practice are). Yet the peculiarity of abstraction is to be something other than part of the concrete, since abstraction *adds* something to the concrete. What does it add? *The generality of a relation* (linguistic, legal, social, ideological) that concerns the concrete. Better: *this relation dominates the concrete without the latter's knowledge, and it is this relation that constitutes the concrete as concrete.*

Thus we have something on the order of a cycle. The concrete is there at the beginning; then comes the abstract; then comes the concrete again. That is what we explained above: social appropriation of the concrete proceeds by way of the domination of abstract relations. There are, accordingly, two concretes: the concrete that is not appropriated socially, which at the limit *is nothing*; and the concrete that is not just socially appropriated by individuals, but *produced as concrete by this appropriation*. This means that, without language and law, without the relations of production and ideological relations, nothing in the world is concrete for man. For I can neither name it, nor attribute it, nor produce it, nor make my intentions known to it.

Oscar Wilde has a story in which he recounts, in his fashion, the creation of the world and the Garden and, in the Garden, Adam and Eve. God was distracted back then and forgot to give Adam and Eve language. Wilde explains that Adam and Eve never encountered each other and, because they never encountered each other, nothing happened the way it was supposed to: neither the serpent, nor the fruit of the tree of good and evil, nor, consequently, sin, nor, consequently, the whole string of catastrophes, nor, consequently, the Incarnation, nor, consequently, the Redemption of the World. And why did Adam and Eve (who did in fact cross paths) never encounter each other? *'Since they didn't know how to talk, they couldn't see each other.'*

4 TECHNICAL ABSTRACTION AND SCIENTIFIC ABSTRACTION

But, it will be objected, if we are always in abstraction, or, rather, if we always live under the domination of abstraction, of abstract relations, if we must always proceed by way of abstraction to attain and transform the concrete, what difference is there between this abstraction that reigns everywhere and the abstraction of science that we discussed a moment ago? Is it simply a difference of degree?

One might well think so. For every practice seems to have its own abstract relations, which make it what it is; and if we make our way up the 'hierarchy' of practices, it seems reasonable to assume that we will observe a difference of degree in moving from the most common practices (language, production, human relations) to the practice regarded as 'the highest' practice: scientific practice. We should, however, beware of this notion of a 'hierarchy' of practices (hence of a difference in value or dignity). It is very likely to stem from something other than observation of the practices' respective places – namely from a social value judgement reflecting the organization of society. This appears very clearly, for example, in the 'hierarchy of practices' in Plato,[1] a 'hierarchy' that merely serves to maintain and legitimate a social Order, or, rather, legitimate its restoration.

We shall therefore say, provisionally, and in order to avoid this risk, that each practice has a nature of its own, and thus its specificity. We shall add that the passage from one practice to another, as observed in the real world, must in its turn be analysed with an eye to its specificity and specific difference.

Everyone will grant this difference if he compares, for instance, the *productive practice* of a farmer who owns a little land, has a herd of animals and still uses traditional farming methods with that of a big capitalist farmer who owns hundreds of acres in the Beauce region, has a machinery park and uses industrial methods: they do not have the same productive practice. A fortiori, the big landowner who does not work, but lives off ground rent (tenant farmers' rent) and speculation on his income (invested in the stock market or industry), does not have the same practice, because he does not produce anything; he lives off direct exploitation (of his tenant farmers) and indirect exploitation (of workers, through his 'investments' in industry and shares). The wage-worker who works on the assembly line in a factory that does not belong to him, on machines that do not belong to him, has yet another practice, and the same goes for his boss, who does not work, but exploits his workers and speculates on his revenues by 'investing' in his firm or by 'working' with the banks and other branches of industry in which he invests his profits.

However, if we now consider not these workers' or non-workers' *immediate* practice (what one *sees* them doing), but *the practice which is realized* in their tools, machines and methods (including the capitalists' financial methods), commands their immediate practice and furnishes them with the *means* of *doing what they do*, we find ourselves dealing with a completely different practice. It presupposes not only habits, 'tricks of the trade', familiarity with the 'methods' (of work and 'business'), but also material realities such as machines, plant and institutions. In short, it presupposes the considerable *technical know-how* that is invested in these realities and therefore in the corresponding practices as well.

Here the nature of the abstraction changes once again. If we can agree that the ensemble constituted by such realizations (factories, machines, methods of financial speculation, the organization of the labour-process) represents the *realization of a* highly elaborated *technique*, then the abstraction present in this technique is that of knowledge: not just of know-how [*savoir-faire*], but also of an abstract, relatively coherent body of knowledge [*savoir*], recorded in treatises (on agricultural production, tool-making, the organization of the labour-process, capital investment and so on) – know-how and knowledge that can be taught and transmitted. And this knowledge is verified by practice, because one can apply it to produce results.

In our societies, in which the sciences play a very big role in production, this technical knowledge is, *to some extent*, 'fallout' from scientific knowledge, insofar as one whole part of its realizations depends on the application of scientific results. I say 'to some extent', because there are idealist philosophers, such as Kant, who uphold the idea that *technique* is merely the '*consequence*' of scientific theory and is, therefore, pure theory, not a practice in its own right.[2] That, however, is to neglect the *materiality* of technical know-how and technical knowledge, the opacity and resistance of their object (which is irreducible to the transparency of 'pure' theory), in order to promote the notion of a 'pure theory' contained in a 'pure' abstraction. It is also to neglect the fact that know-how and technical or practical knowledge existed long before the sciences made their appearance.

Well before the advent of 'pure' mathematics, as we have seen, people *knew how to carry out* mathematical operations to obtain results not just in calculation and measurement, but also in architecture, hydraulics, navigation and weaponry. They *knew how to carry out* operations in physics, in statics and dynamics, in order to transport enormous masses over great distances or launch projectiles using 'machines'. They *knew how to carry out* operations in optics and chemistry, and could also, of course, perform all the agricultural operations required for cattle-rearing or the cultivation of crops. To be sure, all this knowledge was 'empirical'; it had not been obtained by demonstrations bearing on 'pure' objects. Yet it was immense; and, without it, the discovery of 'pure' mathematics – which initially provided demonstrations of results that had already been obtained (by the Babylonians, Egyptians and others) before going beyond them – would have been unthinkable.

Where do this technical know-how and technical knowledge come from? They come from the *technical discoveries* that punctuate all of human history from the prehistoric period on, and have not disappeared from the history of our present. Without going all the way back to the Old Stone Age and the discovery of fire and stone-knapping, we may note that humanity had discovered metals, the wheel, water-power and wind-power, and wheat when it made the transition from grazing to cultivation of the soil. No one knows how these 'discoveries' were made. But they can only have emerged from elements already present, from an encounter between various earlier techniques and, doubtless, a 'chance event' (an event or element that might not have been present) which precipitated a discovery in an unforeseen encounter of completely disparate elements. These discoveries can only have occurred on the basis of previous know-how and, in addition, on the basis of a representation of the world in which people lived.

For let us not forget that these people, even if they were very primitive, lived in society. We have seen that the *reproduction* of such societies presupposed an entire system of ideas and rituals sanctioning both the community's biological reproduction and its relation to nature. It is hard to imagine that this 'religious representation of the world', which made it possible to identify each object and each practice and assign it its social significance, did not play a role in the simple perception of things, and in the 'discovery' of new properties or the invention of tools and the earliest machines.

That is why, if we can speak of know-how and technical or practical knowledge, we have to beware of imagining that they were acquired through simple *direct contact* with things, which revealed their properties to people in a purely *empirical* mode. As empiricism sees it, truth is in things, and knowing it is a matter of simply seeing it or extracting it: I 'separate out' from the thing everything that is not its 'truth', and I have its truth. That is too simple to be true, for I always stand in *practical* relations to things: I work on them, and have to work on them to know them. When I work on them, I always have ideas in mind in which knowledge [*savoir*] and ideology are inextricably intertwined; this ideological relation is an integral part of my work, research and discovery, since it has always 'framed' my concrete knowledge [*connaissance*]. *Thus there is no pure 'empirical' knowledge*: we can talk about 'empirical' knowledge only *by contrast*, in order to bring out what is peculiar to scientific knowledge in its difference from practical-technical knowledge.

This thesis is important, for the notion of pure empirical knowledge on which all empiricist philosophies are based is an idealist myth that serves idealism as a justification or foil when it asserts the omnipotence of Ideas or Pure Forms of knowledge.

I have dwelt on technical-practical knowledge because it constitutes one of idealist philosophy's blind spots. Idealist philosophy *does not wish to see* that this practical knowledge, a product of people's labour over the centuries and their trial-and-error discoveries, has a specificity all its own. It is determined to reduce it at all costs either to the myth of an 'empirical knowledge' that does not exist in its supposed purity, or to science pure and simple, in its 'applied' form. Idealist philosophy does not wish to see that technical-practical knowledge preceded science and that, without it, science could not have emerged in history. This philosophy does not wish to see that, in our times, which are dominated by the sciences, discoveries are still made, as they were in Archimedes' or Leonardo da Vinci's times, *which do not come by way of science*, but are appropriated by science after the fact. It does not wish to see that simple human practice, which works on or experiments with its object, can succeed in grasping what science, with pretensions sustained by the reigning ideology, has neglected, rejected or scorned.

I spoke earlier of the History of non-philosophy: the history of all the mute human practices which have been relegated to the shadows, yet sustain or accompany all the visible practices and produce discoveries that sometimes irrupt in the world of 'culture' as a surprise and a scandal intolerable for the dominant ideas. Would you like examples of discoveries resulting from practices scorned by the dominant philosophy? Machiavelli, who served Princes and knew what he was talking about when he said that 'one must be people to know the Prince' – and who knew about the endless war that the 'fat' wage on the 'lean'.[3] Marx, who played an active part in the Workers' Movement and knew what he was talking about: 'history is the history of class struggle'.[4] Freud, who squarely confronted hysteria and knew what he was talking about: we have unconscious thoughts and desires, and they are sexual.[5]

I have dwelt on technical-practical knowledge, which we may simply call practical knowledge, for another reason as well: because it is not 'pure'. Not only does it not produce demonstrations or experimental proofs, as the sciences do; it is also always conspicuously entangled in the silent relations of the 'representation of the world' or the ideology of the society or social group that produces it. *To put the accent on practical knowledge is also to highlight the condition for all knowledge that we call ideology.* Many philosophers have recognized the existence of pre-scientific notions and erroneous ways of picturing things among men: the different errors inventoried by Bacon, among them the 'idols of the tribe', the social errors linked to the existence of authority and religion.[6] Very few philosophers, however, have ever maintained that these preconceived or erroneous ideas should be thought not singly, but with an eye to the *system* they form, and in a way that is not negative (simple errors), but *positive*. We find this intuition in Spinoza, who puts what he calls the first kind of knowledge, or 'imagination', before scientific knowledge (the second kind of knowledge).[7] All perception is given in this first kind of knowledge, all things are named by it, and each perceived and named thing is situated by it in the system of the imagination, the order of things as they are imagined in this *necessary illusion*.[8] It is the illusion not of a psychological 'faculty' (Spinoza rejects the notion of faculties),[9] but of a world, which is always a social world. Not until Marx was further progress made in the theory of this reality, ideology: the discovery that ideology too is constituted by abstract relations.

Why this long discussion?

Because we had first to situate *both practical knowledge* and the *ideological relations* in which, and under the domination of which, practical knowledge is produced in order to go on to present *scientific knowledge*.

It was on the basis of practical knowledge and a particular ideological conjuncture that the first science, mathematics, irrupted in history. Similar irruptions occurred again, always on the basis of a pre-existent body of practical knowledge and a particular ideological, philosophical (for philosophy existed once mathematics had emerged) and scientific conjuncture, in the case of all other sciences: physics, chemistry, biology and so on. In each case, however, we can speak of either a 'break' or a 'shift in terrain' to mark the difference between earlier practical knowledge and the nature of scientific knowledge in the strong sense of the word. This mutation always takes the form of a paradox from the standpoint of earlier answers: where new answers might be expected, science begins by changing the questions (Marx). Where Scheele saw a solution (phlogistic), Lavoisier saw a problem (the discovery of oxygen, inaugurating chemistry) and so on.[10] Thus the advent of a science coincides with a mutation in *the system of questions* that science puts to nature, in the system of problems that science confronts: a mutation in the *problematic*. Naturally, this mutation affects the concepts in which science thinks its problems: mutation of the problematic inherited from practical knowledge goes hand-in-hand with transformation of old notions into new concepts and, correlatively, of old 'objects' into new 'objects'. The triangle about which Thales reasoned was not the triangle drawn in the sand. The motion about which Galileo reasoned was not motion as conceived of by Aristotle. The chemists' bodies are not the alchemists' bodies.

What is the essential difference between scientific and practical knowledge? We know that practical knowledge bears on concrete, empirical objects and the operations that make it possible to obtain concrete results. Since, however, what is in question here is knowledge, this knowledge *adds* something to the concrete objects about which it talks. What does it add? An abstraction which takes the form of *generality*, which, in other words, bears on, and *bears only on*, the finite set of concrete, enumerable objects, or the set of properties observed. Simply, it has been established by practice that such-and-such a formula applies *generally* to *all observed cases*, but only to them.

In contrast, scientific knowledge bears on directly abstract objects, which are, consequently, endowed with an abstraction *that is no longer generality, but universality*. A scientific concept, theorem, or law holds for all the objects defined by that concept, theorem or law, without exception – although the scientific demonstration was carried out *with respect to a single case*: with respect, precisely, to an abstract object that has the property of representing the infinite set of objects of its kind.

The leap from generality to universality, where the result demonstrated with respect to a single abstract object holds for all objects in the same category, brings about a radical transformation of the scope of knowledge. Knowledge is no longer limited to observed cases, since it now applies to all possible instances of the same type. The properties established for a 'pure' triangle hold for all possible or real triangles.

The most striking feature of this new knowledge is that, by putting the new universal concepts to work on new universal objects, one can produce new abstract objects and know them. This opens up a new field for scientific investigation. Science is no longer limited *by the limitation of the observed cases* about which practical knowledge reasons. Science cannot dispense with observation of the concrete, but this concrete is not the immediate existence of pure facts. Science's concrete is the *experimental* concrete, the 'purified' concrete, defined and produced as a function of the problem to be posed, and inserted into an array of instruments that are merely, as Bachelard puts it, 'realized theories'.[11] It is because this experimental concrete is subject to the conditions of its insertion *into the experimental set-up* that it becomes a 'representative of its own species', that is to say, a representative of all the concrete instances identical to it. It thus makes it possible to know them by knowing only it, since it is produced in theoretically defined conditions guaranteeing its universal validity.

It should not be supposed that the irruption of science, even when it occurs on the basis of practical knowledge, releases science once and for all from its relation to the 'concrete'. Even in ideology, a relation to the 'concrete' subsists – we shall see how. In practical knowledge, the relation to the real concrete is clearly a relation of knowledge, but only of *general* knowledge bearing on the set of observed cases, extended by a few limited 'inductions'. In the case of scientific knowledge, the relation to the real concrete is objective, but *universal*. In science, accordingly, the relation to the concrete subsists: not only the concrete from which science sets out (the experimental concrete), but also the concrete at which it arrives: knowledge or the 'concrete-in-thought' (Marx).[12] Moreover, as knowledge is always commanded by social practice, it returns, once produced, to social practice in the form of technical procedures or 'principles' of action. Such is the cycle *concrete-abstract-concrete*.

We have so far maintained these terms (concrete, abstract), for they seemed to go without saying. But now that we have learned, in the course of our discussion, that there is no concrete except for a practice and no abstract except for a theory, we can replace our initial formulation with another and talk about the cycle *practice-theory-practice*. We shall therefore say that every theory leaves practice only in order to return to it, in an endless cycle embracing the whole history of human culture.

The thesis of the 'primacy of practice over theory' refers to this cycle. Everyone knows this expression, which belongs to the Marxist materialist tradition. Yet it also belongs to idealism! For a philosopher such as Kant also affirms the primacy of practice over theory.[13] One must, however, be careful with words. In Kant, 'practice' designates *moral* practice, the fulfilment of duty, whereas, in the Marxist tradition, it designates the activity of production and social struggle. Thus the same expression has two completely different meanings. The Marxist thesis of the 'primacy of practice over theory' is nevertheless liable to misinterpretation, because of the little word 'primacy' and the sharp distinction between practice and theory. It is idealism which radically separates practice from theory and, in general, puts theory in power over practice. In fact, there is theory (knowledge) in all practice, as there is practice in all theory (all knowledge results from labour). The pair theory-practice designates not two distinct objects, but a variable relationship between two inseparable terms: the unity of practice and theory. As for 'primacy', we should not regard it as the index of a hierarchy between two objects, one of which is 'higher' or 'more dignified' than the other, for this implies a value judgement. The primacy of practice over theory should, in my opinion, be understood as a connection in which practice plays something like the role of the balance weight on the wheel of a moving locomotive: *the role of the ballast that conserves and prolongs the movement.*

It is not, consequently, a matter of saying that practical knowledge is superior to theoretical (scientific) knowledge because it preceded scientific knowledge chronologically, because science emerged on the basis of the achievements of practical knowledge. Of course, scientific knowledge eventually went a long way beyond practical knowledge, yet practical knowledge continues to exist; it stimulates and extends the power of theory and, in addition, realizes the concrete knowledge [*connaissances*] produced by theory, since it possesses the knowledge [*savoir*] of the technical applications of theory. And behind practical knowledge is practice *tout court*, the social practices of production and of the economic, political and ideological class struggle, which precipitate the movement (or non-movement: consider the stagnation or even forgetting of the sciences in the Middle Ages) of theory, including the return (or non-return: consider the crisis of Marxist theory today) of theory to practice, not just the practice of production, but also that of class struggle.

The fact that the primacy of practice over theory can be thus formulated in terms of movement, precipitation, stimulation and prolongation is crucial to breaking with the idealist opposition between theory and practice, which merely serves to isolate scientists and philosophers from ordinary people in order to entrust the former (and them alone: the theorists) with the possession, maintenance and dissemination of a Truth beyond the ken of simple 'practitioners', who are just barely good enough to come under the authority of this Truth.

5 PHILOSOPHICAL ABSTRACTION

Can we, setting out from these remarks, shed a little more light on philosophy by comparing it to practical knowledge and scientific knowledge? That is not impossible. We must, however, bear firmly in mind that our conclusions will be limited, since, in making the comparison, we have to confine our reflections to just one point: the specific nature of philosophical abstraction.

We have seen that people, by virtue of their language and practices, the knowledge that emerges from those practices and, later, the scientific practice that emerges from that knowledge, never leave abstraction behind. The reason is not that they live outside the 'concrete'. They are, however, condemned to using abstraction to target, name, know, attain and appropriate it.

We have also seen that abstraction does not always have the same 'quality' or 'look', depending on whether it is the 'abstraction' of language, ideological (religious) abstraction, practical knowledge or scientific knowledge. Philosophy confronts us with a kind of abstraction altogether different from those we find in practical knowledge and scientific knowledge. Paradoxically, philosophical abstraction is rather similar to ideological abstraction.

Philosophical abstraction manifestly does not resemble practical abstraction. It does not bear on a limited number of actually observed cases, because it claims to hold good for every being in the world, for *the 'totality' of beings*, whether real or simply possible, that is, non-existent. Idealism, in any case, clearly makes this claim. Thus Plato declares that the philosopher who is a dialectician (hence a true philosopher!) 'sees the whole'.[1] Kant grants himself the whole, not as a totality of beings, but as the idea of the infinite totalization of knowledge.[2] Hegel proclaims that 'the true is the whole', and says that philosophy's specific task is to 'think the whole' as the result of its logical and historical development.[3] To take a contemporary example, Sartre talks not about the whole, but about totalization as humanity's most profound philosophical project.[4]

Whether or not this 'whole' comprises actually existing beings, it is inordinately pretentious of idealist philosophy to claim to 'see' the whole, 'think' the whole, or aspire to 'totalization'. What gives philosophy this superhuman power?

And idealist philosophy does not leave it at that. It can go so far as to consider this real 'whole' as the realization of one *possible* world among an infinity of others, which thus exist only as possibilities – in other words, do not exist. That is Leibniz's position. He adopts God's standpoint to show us his infinite intelligence combining simple principles in an infinite number of combinations. There results, in God's mind, an infinite number of possible worlds. Out of goodness, he chooses to create the best of them; rather, 'the best of all possible worlds' automatically chooses itself in his intellect, which works somewhat like a computer. Obviously, the philosopher, who 'adopts God's point of view' in order to explain this divine calculation to us, does not know *the other* possible worlds, for he is just a human being living in the only created world there is. He knows, however, that God proceeds this way; hence he knows that, in principle, the possible precedes the real, and that a philosopher possessed of God's infinite intelligence would understand not only the real world, but also this 'calculus' of the divine combinatory, and thus 'the radical origin of things': the infinity of possible worlds in its entirety, a point of departure for the choice of 'the best of all possible worlds'. Leibniz, however, allows us to go even further than that. For only one possible world exists: the other possible worlds *might have existed*, but do not. They enter into God's calculus, and thus also into the philosopher's thinking, as the *non-existent* that must be thought in order to think the actually existing 'whole'.[5]

All this is a way of saying that idealist philosophy has something like an abiding tendency to up the ante. It wants to think the 'whole', and it is obviously a matter of the 'whole' made up of all the things and beings that *exist*, since idealist philosophy wants to account for 'all things'. To account for the 'whole' of real beings, however, it has to attain a supplementary degree of abstraction, conceiving of them as a function of the whole of all *possible* beings (or as a function of the system of their conditions of *possibility*). Yet as soon as it grants itself the whole of all *possible beings* (as in Leibniz), it thinks possibilities that have not come into existence and thus do not exist. This shows just how far this philosophy's pretension goes! The whole of all existing beings plus the whole of all possible beings, and among them, let us say, *'things' that do not exist*, yet play a decisive part in the existence of the things that do, and/or in the knowledge of them.

However surprising it may seem, the fact is that when philosophy wants to think 'the whole', it is irresistibly led to add a 'supplement' to the things that exist. The paradox is that it needs this supplement in order to 'think the whole', but *this supplement does not exist!* This supplement is a 'thing' which does not exist; better, which is sometimes explicitly conceived of as not existing. For example, the void in Democritus and Epicurus as the condition of possibility for the encounter of atoms, hence for the constitution of the 'whole' of the world (this void is posited as existing, but the thought of it is negative: we can say that it is not thought). For example, nothingness in Plato, Hegel, Sartre and others. For example, the thing-in-itself in Kant (it cannot be said to 'exist', because it is not accessible to the senses) and so on.

Hence, paradoxically, it is as if the philosophy that wishes to 'think the whole' were practically obliged, in order to make good its pretensions, to think not just the 'whole' of all real things, but to go on to think the whole represented by all 'possible' things and, finally, *to think 'things' that do not exist* – that is, to think well beyond 'everything' that exists, hence well beyond not only everything that has been observed, but also everything that is observable. Idealist philosophy does not hesitate to take the plunge. Its propositions accordingly display a degree of 'abstraction' that has nothing to do with the abstraction of practical knowledge, because they are 'totalizing' propositions, and because their 'totalization' goes far beyond the real.

For that very reason, however, philosophical abstraction [which does not resemble practical abstraction] does not resemble scientific abstraction, either. We shall say that the abstraction of idealist philosophy is 'totalizing', whereas scientific abstraction is 'universal', which is something quite different. The abstraction of a given science is not 'totalizing', for it does not claim to explain the 'whole'. It is universal, but in its kind: it bears on all the objects in conformity with the same concept, but not the others. Thus a proposition demonstrated with regard to the 'pure' triangle of mathematical practice holds for all triangular objects, but not for all the things in the world. We can put the same thing differently: every particular science (mathematics in each of its branches, physics, chemistry and so on) is *finite*: it has to do with a *limited* object. The fact that scientific investigation of this limited object is infinite, or, rather, indefinite [*indéfini*], that is, endless, is one thing. The 'finite' [*fini*] nature of the object of any science is quite another. Even when two sciences 'converge' (as chemistry and molecular biology are doing today), that does not make an infinite science of them – in other words, a 'totalizing' science that could claim to account for the 'whole' of existing things.

We doubtless do regularly observe, in history, the phenomenon of a finite science being presented by scientists or philosophers as the infinite, 'totalizing' science capable of explaining the ensemble of existing things. Galileo himself, after discovering the first laws of physics, concluded that the 'Great Book of the World was written in mathematical language' and could be understood in its entirety by means of geometrical figures.[6] Descartes took up this claim, presenting analytical geometry, which he had discovered, as capable of explaining everything in a *mathesis universalis* (universal mathematics).[7] Leibniz followed suit: but, for him, the 'universal science' was the infinitesimal calculus.[8] Thus the temptation of the infinite periodically haunts scientists when they are also philosophers: the temptation to charge their finite science (limited to its object) with the 'infinite' function of an infinite, 'totalizing' philosophy (valid for all real and possible entities). This temptation is, however, always overcome by practice and history. In the end, science is always left to confront its finite object again, while philosophy is left confronting its infinite project.

Thus we can understand why philosophy should need God (as can be seen in Plato, Descartes, Leibniz and Hegel): it has to justify its pretension to being infinite. Self-consistently, it thinks the originary 'principle' of this infiniteness in the form of an imaginary being (denounced as abstract by true believers, for example, Pascal, who wants no part of the 'God of the philosophers and scientists'). This imaginary being is God. Philosophy conceives of this God, whom it 'finds' in existing religion and must, for ideological reasons, take charge of, as *infinite* in his turn, endowed with infinite attributes (understanding, will, goodness and so on), and it assigns him the infinite power to create the world, hence to encompass the ensemble of all real and possible beings.

We are so used to regarding this God as part of these philosophies that we risk losing sight of what characterizes him. He has, doubtless, been taken over from religion. But what is he for the philosophy that calls on his theoretical services, if not a *supplementary* and therefore *non-existent* being? Yet, like the void, nothingness, or the thing-in-itself that we mentioned a moment ago, he is indispensable to founding the infinite, 'totalizing' character of philosophy. It is because God exists for the philosopher, and is infinite, that philosophical propositions know no limits, are not bound by the finitude of all science and all concrete knowledge, and can present themselves as infinite: as capable of accounting for *everything* that exists in the world.

As a result, the abstraction of philosophy is similar to that of the dominant ideology, whether the latter takes the form of religion or some other form (legal or political, for instance). In ideological 'knowledge', as will appear in due course, one abstracts from the *finite* character of every science and all concrete knowledge, for ideology too is 'totalizing': it claims to account for everything that exists in the world, to convey its Truth and Meaning, and to establish its precise place, function and destination (think of religion). Ideology too can exist and function only on condition that it endow itself with imaginary beings not subject to any of the conditions of finite existence: for instance, God himself (in religion); for example, the 'human person' (in legal-moral ideology); for example, the subject of knowledge, desire and action (in philosophical ideology).

This strange kinship between ideology and idealist philosophy, both of which are 'totalizing', calls for explanation.[9]

All these remarks on abstraction lead us to an important conclusion. If, as soon as they begin to lead a social existence, people always live in abstraction and can never escape it, not even when they try physically to appropriate a concrete being, because the conditions of that appropriation are themselves abstract, the implication is that we should give up a certain number of illusions about both the concrete and the abstract that are sustained by the ideologies as well as the idealist philosophies.

The implication is, in sum, that we should give up what philosophers have called the state of nature.

6 THE MYTH OF THE STATE OF NATURE

The state of nature is a mythic state in which idealist philosophers imagine that people lived before entering the state of society: Robinson Crusoe's solitude, for example, or a community without the 'drawbacks' of society as we know it. In many religions, this state of nature is called paradise. To take the example of Christianity, paradise was the condition of a human couple whom God created without sin and entrusted to the bounty of nature. Nature was generous then: it provided people with nourishment and, what is more – this is important – was *transparent* for them. Not only was it enough to stretch out one's hand to pick fruit that was always ripe in order to satisfy one's hunger and thirst; it was also enough for Adam to see something with his eyes or take it in his hand in order to know it completely. Contrary to what is all too often supposed, human beings had the right to know all things: this knowledge was provided by the senses, was identical to the understanding in man, was identical to the words designating it, and was perfectly *immediate and transparent*. Adam did not have to work, produce or seek in order to know. He knew, as the 'Christian philosopher' Malebranche puts it, 'by simple sight'.[1] The truth of things was in things, in their empirical existence, and, in order to possess it, it was enough to *extract* it from them by simply looking at them. The abstract was identical to the concrete. This image typifies, better than any other, the theory of knowledge known as *empiricism*. It has not disappeared with the religious myth of paradise, as we shall see.

There was, however, something else in this myth: the idea that nature was generous and that it was enough to reach out and pick fruit that was always in easy reach. In a word, *people did not have to work to survive any more than they had to work to know.* There is a clear connection between the empiricist notion of knowledge and the fact that people did not have to work to produce their means of subsistence. In one case as in the other, Nature, that is, objects, that is, the object, suffices for everything. There is no need to transform it to satisfy human needs; the answer is inscribed in the object in advance. It is enough to extract it; this extraction is, in its simplicity and immediacy, the empiricist form of abstraction. We see, then, that idealist philosophy can depict such abstractions, in which everybody lives, as a simple effect of the contact between people and nature, in other words, between people and objects. At the same time, we see that this distorted conception of abstraction concerns both the practice of knowledge, reduced to 'simple sight', and the practice of production, reduced to the mere picking of fruit that is always ripe and always to hand ('*handgreiflich*', Hegel).[2]

There was something else again in this myth, of course: the idea that human relations were as transparent as the relations between people and natural objects. And it is understandable that relations between people should display this transparency, given that all the problems of the relations between people and nature have been resolved in advance by nature's generosity. Believers or philosophers accordingly attribute to man in this state of paradise or nature a body that is, in its turn, transparent for his soul or understanding. Hence the body is no longer Plato's 'tomb' or 'shroud':[3] a barrier to knowledge of nature or the self that comes between the human understanding or soul and the nature of things or the body – this opaque thing that desires, is hungry, and feels pleasure and pain. The body is just a tool that obeys without resistance, has neither passions, nor desires, nor an unconscious and, since it is merely practical transparency, is, for that very reason, also theoretical transparency.

In these conditions, in which human relations are simple, clear and without remainder, since everyone obeys the 'movement of nature', which is good, it is plain that there are also no legal or political problems, none of the problems that give rise to the horrors of war and peace, of good and evil, and so on. God guides people in paradise towards what is good for them: they need only obey right reason and the 'movement of nature'. Hence all the social abstractions we have mentioned, notably law and the state, which guarantee physical appropriation of the concrete, are absent from paradise, or the state of nature. Since relations between people are transparent and without any opaque remainder, since there is never any conflict or crime, there is no need for law, courts, or the state. Nor is there any need for morality, because its place is taken by the 'movement of nature', or the 'heart', as Rousseau will later put it.

Yet everybody knows that this story is too beautiful to last and always finishes badly: paradise ends in sin and the state of nature ends in the catastrophes of the state of war. In both cases, what precipitates the tragedy is, by a coincidence that will surprise no one, something involving morality, law and politics – precisely the social abstractions which people cannot do without and which the myths of paradise and the state of nature leave aside, from which they 'abstract'.

The myth of original sin is well known: the human couple in paradise knew everything by simple sight, everything *except 'good and evil'*, symbolized by a tree that bore fruit, like all the other trees. There was nothing unusual about the fact that the knowledge of good and evil was thus in easy reach, for all knowledge was available to people the same way: it was in easy reach, so that people had only to reach out and take it. What *was* unusual was that God forbade people to pick, precisely, the fruit – that is, the knowledge – of the tree of good and evil.

The Christian myth provides no reason for this prohibition, except that God knew in advance that, if people attained to knowledge of the difference between good and evil, all manner of conflicts and catastrophes would ensue; that is why he forbade them to acquire it. This argument may seem odd, since God was omnipotent. We can only assume that his omnipotence reached its limits at the frontiers of the knowledge of good and evil, and that he could do nothing to halt the inexorable course of events precipitated by disregard for his prohibition. That is yet another way, an inverted way, this time, *of acknowledging the omnipotence of certain abstractions*, since God himself, although he created all things, is helpless in the face of some of them. And the fact is that, once human beings (Eve) had reached out and picked the fruit of the tree of good and evil 'by distraction' (this is how Malebranche explains original sin,[4] which is otherwise inexplicable, inasmuch as this distraction is itself a form of abstraction, albeit a form that is concrete, punctual and thus sui generis), all the bliss of paradise was wholly lost, human beings were expelled from it, and they saw that they were naked and had to work to eat – and to know as well.

The theorists of the state of nature, from Locke to Rousseau and Kant, tell the same story using other arguments. This time, however, it is not morality (good and evil) which is at the origin of the loss of the state of nature, but the 'origin' of good and evil, *private property*, the physical appropriation of the earth, fruit, animals and money, which, as it is generalized, spawns conflicts over boundaries and a war that tends to be general: the state of war. Only with great effort did people succeed in establishing among themselves the *social abstractions*, the *social relations* represented in the social contract by law, morality, the state and politics, so that there might reign among them the benefits of civil peace, which bears but a remote resemblance to the peace of the origins, the lost peace of the state of nature.

There is a very profound materialist truth in all these myths, the idealist form of their thought notwithstanding. For we find in them the idea that, in creating the world, *God himself is incapable of abstracting from the universal law of abstraction*, and thus that he is himself subject to it. This is a way of indirectly acknowledging the omnipotence of this law. We find in these myths the idea that if we try radically to expel all abstraction from human life, *abstraction takes refuge somewhere and becomes, precisely, the object of a prohibition*.[5] It is this prohibition that forms the absolute condition of possibility for the immediate relation – that is, the relation without abstraction – between people and the world, and also between people and other people, including the relation between men and women, who discover (what a surprise!) that they have a *sex*, that 'abstraction' essential to their human existence, at the same time as they discover the difference between knowledge of good and knowledge of evil – in other words, genuine knowledge.

We discover in these myths that people, once they have lapsed into 'sin' – that is, their true condition, the one no longer misrepresented by an imaginary state of nature – are obliged, under the domination of social relations, to have sexual relations, to work in order to eat, and to perform the labour of seeking knowledge, which now comes to them not by 'simple sight', but from real practice, the practice that transforms nature. We discover in them, in short, that people have left behind the *imaginary 'abstraction'* (forged for reasons that, obviously, reflect the interests of established religion) in which they have an immediate, direct relation with things that immediately deliver up their truth, in order to enter the world of real life, in which one must work to produce and know. In this world, the meaning of abstraction changes. It is no longer this simple 'reading' or 'picking', this simple, immediate '*extraction*' of the truth of things from things. It becomes, rather, a veritable *labour* in which one needs, in order to know, not just raw material, but also labour-power (human beings) as well as know-how and instruments of labour (tools, words).

This brings us to a conclusion about philosophy (and even religion) that is not without interest. For what have we seen in our analysis? We have seen that this religious and this philosophical conception of the world, that of paradise and the state of nature, however religious or idealist both may have been, nevertheless contained, in a way that might be called *inverted* or, rather, *displaced*, recognition of the material reality of the conditions of existence of human (sexual) reproduction, production and knowledge. Of course, to arrive at that conclusion, we have to be able to 'interpret' these myths and philosophies. But our interpretation is not arbitrary. On the contrary, it is based on elements that well and truly figure *in these myths* and philosophies, and doubtless do so not by accident, but by a profound necessity.

For now, we can pinpoint this necessity by saying that these myths and philosophies were produced not by isolated human individuals thinking and writing for themselves alone, but, rather, by historical individuals who wrote with an eye to being understood and obeyed by the popular masses. It has been said that the word 'religion' is derived from a Latin word meaning 'bond'. A religion is, accordingly, a doctrine intended to bind all the members of a people together. Religious myths thus have the function of allowing the men and women to whom they are addressed to establish mutual bonds based on shared beliefs, and to 'form a single people'.

The same holds for the philosophical myths of the state of nature. It is no accident that they sprang up in the formative period of the rising bourgeoisie, expressed its aspirations, reflected its problems and held out its solutions – that they were intended, accordingly, to *cement its unity*, rallying round it all those who had a stake in its social and political triumph. But when addressing masses of human beings in a religious or philosophical myth, if one wishes to be understood, one plainly has *to take account, in the discourse of the myth itself, of the existence of these masses, their practical experience and the reality of their condition.*

In religious or philosophical myth, consequently, the reality of these masses' living conditions, of their experience and needs, has to figure *somewhere*. When I say that *the masses must be won over*, the word should be taken in a very strong sense: their resistance has to be broken in advance and their opposition has to be anticipated and forestalled. Their opposition to what? To, precisely, the conception of the world presented to them, which serves not their interests, but those of very different human groups: a priestly caste, the Church, the social class in power and so on.

Thus we have begun to form a somewhat richer idea of what philosophy is, even when it still shelters behind religion. It does not just content itself with stating propositions (or 'Theses') about all existing beings, or all merely possible and therefore non-existent beings; it states these propositions in a way *that has to do less with knowledge of these beings than with the conflicts of which they may be the stakes.* That is why every philosophy (let us not hesitate to go that far) is haunted by its opposite. That is why idealism is haunted by materialism, just as materialism is haunted by idealism; for every philosophy reproduces within itself, in some sort, the conflict in which it finds itself engaged outside itself.

Thus the meaning of the very special kind of *abstraction* that we have observed in philosophy is beginning to emerge. It is a very strange abstraction indeed, for it aims not to produce knowledge of things that exist in the world, as science does, but, rather, to speak about all that exists (and even all that does not) in a mode that implies *a previous conflict*, still present, involving the place, meaning and function of these beings, a conflict which commands philosophy *from without* and which philosophy has to bring *within itself* in order to exist as philosophy. It is, then, an *active* and, as it were, *polemical abstraction*, divided against itself, which concerns not just its ostensible 'objects', inasmuch as these can exist or not, but also its own positions, its own 'theses'. For these theses can be affirmed only on the paradoxical condition that they are simultaneously negated by contradictory theses which, to be sure, are relegated to the margins of the philosophy in question, yet are present in it nonetheless. It is, obviously, this very surprising characteristic of philosophical abstraction which distinguishes it from the abstraction of both technical-practical and scientific knowledge. At the same time, this feature of philosophical abstraction is what makes it, as we have already noted, strangely similar to ideological abstraction.

7 WHAT IS PRACTICE?

But can we leave it at that? We cannot, because the preceding remarks are superficial, and do not provide us with what we need to make our entry into philosophy. To enter philosophy, we have to make a double detour, by way of scientific practice on the one hand and ideological practice on the other – and we have to bring up other practices that either command these scientific and ideological practices (the most frequent case), as the practice of production does; or that accompany them, as aesthetic practice does; or that can shed light on them, as psychoanalytic practice can.

First, however, it may be worth our while to examine the little word 'practice', which we have been making constant use of. *What is practice*, which, we have said, has primacy over theory? Can we propose a 'theory' of practice without lapsing into contradiction, if every theory is secondary with respect to practice, or to a practice?

We can begin by noting a well-known distinction drawn by the Greek philosopher Aristotle. Aristotle distinguished two senses of the word 'practice'.[1] In the first sense, practice is *poiesis*, that is to say, production or fabrication. It designates the action or process by means of which an individual's (or a team's) labour-power and intelligence, using instruments of labour (tools, machines), transform raw material (already processed or not) into an object that is produced industrially or hand-crafted.

In the second sense, practice is *praxis*. Here it is no longer the object that is transformed by an external agent and external means, but the subject himself who is transformed through his own action, his own practice. In this sense, Aristotle speaks of the *praxis* of the physician who heals himself or the sage who transforms himself. We find these two senses in Marx: transformation of raw material in the 'labour-process' and self-transformation in the 'revolutionary process' ('Theses on Feuerbach').

It is clear that what distinguishes these two senses is not the presence or absence of raw material, instruments of labour, or labour-power, for all three are present in both processes. It is the *exteriority* or *interiority* of 'the object', which is an external object in the first case and, in the second, is the subject himself, who is at once his own raw material, his own labour-power and his own instruments of production. Formally, therefore, the schema is identical as far as its contents and components are concerned, but different when it comes to the nature of the object to be transformed. This distinction will prove eminently useful later in our analysis.

The word 'practice' points, then, to *an active relationship to the real*. Thus we say that a tool is *très pratique* when it is especially well suited to a particular type of work on a particular kind of material, and produces the desired results. Thus we say that someone has a *bonne pratique* of English, meaning that his contact with that language is direct enough to allow him to 'put it into practice', in other words, to use it effectively. In the same sense, we say that someone has no *pratique* of farm machines when he knows them only from books, from theory, but has never actually used them hands-on and does not know how to run them.

The idea of practice thus implies the notion of active contact with the real, while the idea of activity inherent in it implies the notion of a *human agent* (or subject). Since a human subject or agent is, unlike an animal, a being capable of 'forming a plan of action in his mind', at least in theory, we shall agree to use the word 'practice' to designate only the kind of *active contact with the real that is peculiarly human*. Thus we shall not speak of 'bees' practice', despite the marvels that bees can accomplish, but of the practice of the carpenter, mechanic, architect, engineer, physician, jurist, politician and so on.

We can see straight away, however, that since this idea of *practice* is associated with human beings, and since human beings are animals endowed with 'consciousness' – in other words, the capacity to distinguish and detach a representation of external things from the things themselves, work on this representation and form a plan of action in their minds – we can see straight away that the idea of *practice* answers to the idea of *theory* as if it were its inverted echo.

It must not be supposed that theory is specific to 'theorists'. Their theory (that of scientists and philosophers) is simply the most abstract, refined and elaborate form of a capacity that all human beings possess. The word 'theory' comes from a Greek word meaning 'to see', 'to contemplate'. It implies that one *does not handle what one sees* and, consequently, leaves things as they were. Thus the hand [*main*], which 'handles' [*manie*] or 'manipulates' [*manipule*], which works, is contrasted to the eye, which sees at a distance, without touching or transforming its object. Implied by the word 'theory', accordingly, is the notion of a distance taken from immediate reality and maintained; the word expresses, by its nature, what is commonly called *consciousness*, that is, the capacity to gather and store perceptions of the real, and also, thanks to this step back from reality and the 'play' it allows, the capacity to make connections between these perceptions and even to anticipate them. *In this sense, everyone is a theorist.* The farmer who sets out on his tractor in the morning has planned out his day in his mind, and sees far beyond that one day. He could hardly run his farm if he didn't.

We have employed the term 'consciousness' to designate people's capacity to receive and store perceptions of the real, and anticipate them as well. We have done so for the sake of convenience, imposed by long usage. For 'consciousness' is another of idealist philosophy's favourite terms. We express the same idea when we say that human beings possess *language*, for it is language which puts this distance, in advance, between immediate reality and the representation of it: in advance, inasmuch as language contains this distance simply by virtue of its abstractness. In this sense, we can say that *all human beings are theorists*, less because they see *than because they speak*. And we know why: because language is made up of abstractions (sounds that we abstract in order to treat them as words designating concrete realities that we abstract).

That is why the opposition between theory and practice has to be treated with great caution.

In the concrete reality of people's relations to the world, we never find ourselves dealing with, on the one hand, practice alone (blind, purely animal labour) and, on the other, theory alone (pure contemplation in the absence of all activity). In the most elementary practice (the ditch-digger's), there are *ideas* about how to go about things, the plan to follow and the tools to use, and all these 'ideas' exist only in language – even if the people using this language are unaware that it is already theory. And, in the loftiest theory, that of the most abstract of mathematicians, there is always practice: not just the work the mathematician does on his problems, but the *inscription* of those problems in mathematical *symbols* in chalk on the blackboard – even if the mathematician is unaware that such symbolization is a practice.

The philosophical question of the primacy of practice over theory (which defines the materialist position) or theory over practice (which defines the idealist position) is posed in the context of this complex interdependency. In affirming the primacy of theory, idealism affirms that, in the last instance, contemplation or the activity of reason determines all practice. In affirming the primacy of practice, materialism affirms that, in the last instance, practice determines all knowledge.

The very generality of these positions, however, affords us a glimpse of something important: the general and, therefore, 'abstract' character of human practices. We said that practice designates people's active contact with the real. Of course, there exist practices that are apparently utterly singular (such as the practices of madness, said to be 'abnormal'). One can even defend the idea that there exists no practice that is not individual in some respect, since every practice calls for an individual human agent. We are all familiar, for example, with the high praise bestowed on the medieval artisan, who singlehandedly produced an object in a single exemplar intended for a single client. Yet even this artisan reproduced *a general social practice*: he applied certain socially recognized procedures inherited from a collective past to a socially defined demand. He was, certainly, alone before his 'work', but, alongside him, silently, thousands of other artisans were making the same gestures using the same tools in order to furnish the same market with the same products. And if he added a 'personal touch' to his work, he did so within the social limits laid down by both the utility of the object produced and the fashion reigning in his society.

This is a crucial point, for the practices we shall be discussing can be individual only to the extent that they are first of all *social*. What holds for the artisan producing in apparent solitude holds a fortiori for workers subject to the collective organization of work, producing in order to satisfy existing society's 'creditworthy' social needs and, at the same time, so that the capitalist class can accumulate wealth.

Thus every practice is social. As such, it brings into play a set of elements so complex (in the case of production, these elements are the raw material, the agents of production and the instruments of production, under the domination of the social relations of production) that it is impossible to conceive of it as a simple *act* or even a simple *activity*. (For both act and activity lead us to imagine that they have a cause or an author – namely a subject or an agent – and that it would be enough to trace things back to this cause or origin in order to understand everything that goes on in a practice.) We are thus naturally led to conceive of social practices not as acts or simple activities, but as *processes*: that is, *as a set of material, ideological, theoretical, and human (the agents) elements sufficiently well adapted to each other for their reciprocal action to produce a result that modifies the initial givens.*

We shall therefore use the word 'practice' to designate *a social process that puts agents into active contact with the real and produces results of social utility*. It is no doubt possible to speak of 'social practice' as a whole, when this expression is justified – that is, whenever we want to think the interdependency of the different practices. But we must beware of this expression, which, when it is not justified, has the disadvantage of making distinct practices 'melt' into the all-devouring night of 'social practice' – the disadvantage of not marking each practice's *specificity*, and thus of subordinating, say, scientific or philosophical practice to political practice as its 'handmaiden' (consider the example of Lysenko under Stalin). To grasp what practice is, we have first to recognize *the existence of distinct, relatively autonomous social practices*. Technical practice is not scientific practice, philosophical practice is not assimilable to scientific practice, and so on.

This methodological precaution once taken, however, we can provide some idea of what a legitimate use of the notion of '*social practice*' as a whole would be. When we invoke this notion, it can only be with a view to assigning a meaning to the primacy of practice over theory in a social formation in general.

In every social formation, we observe a certain number of practices at work: the practice of production, the practice of technical and, later, scientific knowledge, political practice, ideological practice, aesthetic practice and so on. The question that then arises is less to identify and classify all the existing practices than to establish *the determinant practice in the totality of practices*.

This question is not purely speculative, as might be supposed: it has practical effects, insofar as the way we visualize the determination of the practices,which can originate in either an ideology or a science, is itself part of the practices. Of course, such practical effects are relative, for ideology's impact on a society's evolution is itself relative, depending as it does on the balance of power between the classes. And it is because this question is not purely speculative that it is one of the major philosophical questions.

For idealist philosophy, which affirms, sometimes in very subtle forms, the primacy of theory over practice, the practice that determines the other practices in the last instance is to be sought among *the most 'theoretical'* practices, in the realm of ideology, science or philosophy. Thus Hegel was able to show, in an imposing system that encompassed the whole of human history – all the practices, from political production to science, religion and philosophy – that the philosophical Idea governed the world. All the practices inferior to philosophical practice were in themselves philosophical, without being aware of it; they simply paved the way, through labour, class struggles, wars, religious crises and scientific discoveries, for the advent of the 'self-consciousness' of their own philosophical nature in Hegel's philosophy itself. This mammoth enterprise was not innocent, for it provided the bourgeois ideology of history ('ideas rule the world') with its own guarantee in the form of a philosophical 'demonstration'.

In contrast, Marxist materialist philosophy, defending the primacy of practice over theory, upholds the thesis that the practice which, in the last instance, determines all others is the *practice of production* – that is, the unity of the relations of production and the productive forces (means of production plus labour-power) under the domination of the relations of production. Materialist Marxist philosophy does not merely defend the idea, which idealists do not contest, that to have a history and to live in politics, ideology, science, philosophy and religion, people must first of all simply live, must subsist physically and must therefore materially produce their means of subsistence and instruments of production. For that would be a 'two-term abstraction' (human beings plus their sustenance).

Marxist materialist philosophy defends the idea that this relation that people have to their means of subsistence is governed by the relation of production and is thus a social relation (a 'three-term abstraction'). It is because the practice of production includes this basic relation *as its condition* that the relations governing the other practices can be *put into relation with* this first relation. Marxism does not say: depending on whether you produce this or that object, you have this or that society. It says, rather: depending on *the social relation of production* under which you produce your subsistence, you have such-and-such political, ideological (and other) relations. And since this social relation is, in class societies, a conflictual, antagonistic relation, determination by production (the base) is not mechanical, but includes a 'play' that comes under the dialectic. That is why this determination is said to be 'in the last instance': in order clearly to bring out the fact that there exist 'instances' other than production, and that these instances, which are relatively autonomous, enjoy a certain latitude and can 'exercise reciprocal action' on the base, on production.

To underscore this determination 'in the last instance', Marx presented his general hypothesis on the nature of social formations and history in the form of a *topography*. A topography is a space in which one arranges certain realities in order clearly to bring out their respective positions and relative importance. Marx expounds this topography in the 1859 Preface to the *Contribution*. He shows there that every social formation (society) can be likened to a house with one or two upper floors. On the ground floor, 'base', or 'infrastructure' is production (the unity of the relation of production and the productive forces under the domination of the relation of production). On the first floor is the 'superstructure', which comprises law and the state on the one hand and the ideologies on the other. The base is 'determinant in the last instance'; the 'superstructure', albeit determined by the base, exercises reciprocal action on it. This topography is a simple way of indicating or spatially arranging the 'nodes' of determination, the ensemble of 'instances' and their social efficacity. All the real work remains to be done. It cannot be done on 'society' or 'the social formation' in general, but only on social formations that exist in the present or have existed historically.

This indication, firm, yet quite cautious, of 'determination in the last instance' is invaluable for the study of the superstructure and the ideologies, and of science as well. For the paradox in Marx is that *scientific practice figures nowhere in his topography*. Does this mean that we must at all costs fill in this gap, and range science either with the ideologies (and thus lapse back into the idea of bourgeois science and proletarian science dear to Stalinist ideologues) or with the productive forces, or even make it 'a productive force' in the full sense of the word? The fact is that Marxist theory does not make such demands. It does not claim to provide an exhaustive account of all the practices as a function of its topography. It has a *limited object*. Marx aspired to lay the foundations of a science of class struggle, *and that is all*. That scientific practice can be influenced by ideology, and thus by class struggle, is all too clear. That the results of science and a certain philosophical idea of science can be enlisted in the ideological class struggle is all too obvious. That science is to a large and ever-increasing extent driven by the 'demands' of production is certain. That it therefore stands in close relation with production and, equally, with ideology, philosophy and, consequently, the class struggle is beyond doubt. These relations, however, vary with the conjuncture and, in any case, scientific practice is irreducible to the other practices, since it is the only practice to provide objective knowledge of the real. Hence we must study it in its specificity in order to discover, in each instance, the relations to which it is subordinated, without letting ourselves be intimidated by the demand, which Marx never made, to range all the practices with either the base, which is well defined, or the superstructure, which contains only the state and the ideologies.[2]

That is why we are taking the liberty, in the present initiation into philosophy, of discussing the principal existing practices (considered in detail, there is an unlimited number of practices): not only those that figure in Marx's materialist topography, but also those that do not, such as scientific practice, psychoanalytic practice and aesthetic practice. We shall, however, discuss these practices without losing sight of the programmatic philosophical indications of the Marxist topography, the basic aim of which is to illustrate the primacy of practice over theory.

8 THE PRACTICE OF PRODUCTION

The practice of production seems to show that the first of the two concepts distinguished by Aristotle is the right one here: *poiesis*, characterized by the externality of the object to be transformed.

What do we see in the practice of production? We may take as our example either the craftsman or the assembly-line worker in modern big industry; the result is basically the same in both cases. We have to do with a process of transformation of a given *raw material* (wood, earth, ore, cattle, wool and so on) by the action of workers (*labour-power*) using *instruments of production* (tools, machines). Raw material, labour-power, instruments of production – these are the three elements so 'combined' (Marx) as to produce the desired result: steel, textiles, or animals for slaughter – in short, products ready to be consumed. Marx calls this the 'labour-process'. It takes place in all forms of society, whether or not they comprise social classes.

Nothing would seem to be more 'concrete' than this process, since all its elements are, in every case, natural and individual, and can be seen and touched. Nothing would seem to be more concrete … were it not for the simple 'fact' that the *combination* of these elements must be realized, must be possible and active; otherwise, the process will not take place, will not produce anything. This idea of a 'combination' does not seem like much at all, because, every time we see a craftsman using tools to do woodwork, or a farmer driving his tractor to plough a field in which he is going to plant wheat, or a milling-machine operator working on a part in a steel factory, we see a 'combination' that has been up and running for a long time: it has already been realized. But things did not always 'run smoothly' this way. Before they could begin to do so, a very long process of trial and error had to occur.

Take the worker: if he had not *previously* acquired the indispensable technical knowledge, he would stand helplessly in front of his machine and the 'combination' would miscarry. Take his machine: if it does not have a source of energy (in the past, the current of a river; later, steam; today, petrol or electricity), it will not run. Take the petrol in the motor: if it has not been properly refined, the motor will not go, and the 'combination' will stall. But it is not the milling-machine operator who chooses all these concrete givens: they are imposed on him in the form of a result by the whole past history of science and technology. This history exists in the form of both known laws and their technical applications in the raw material one chooses and the machines one has. Since the same history teaches that one cannot make just any machine operate on just anything, that one cannot decree the invention of a machine whose principles are unknown, and that one cannot entrust the labour-process to people with no technical experience of it, it appears that this very 'concrete' process does not yield up all its secrets as soon as we lay eyes on the concrete elements making it up: it exists only under the domination of abstract laws.

We are thus led to affirm that no labour-process can 'function' (the 'combination' of its elements cannot become active) unless it is determined *by abstract laws* that are, on the one hand, both scientific and technical (they determine the knowledge of the raw material worked on, the realization of the instruments of production, and the workers' experience) and, on the other hand, historical (at a given point in history, only certain combinations and not others are possible). *Hence no labour-process is possible except on conditions constituted by the abstractions known as the technical relations of production.* The technical relations of production ensure the 'combination' of the concrete elements of the practice of production, and require that the workers acquire the experience needed to put these elements to work.

This conception of the practice of production as a labour-process remains, however, 'abstract'. Why? Because it is not just a question of accounting for the fact that the 'combination' has been realized and 'works'. We must also account for the fact that this combination is *social*, in other words, that it exists in a society which exists: which exists thanks to this production, and which would not exist if it were not reproduced.

Let us take a simple approach to the matter: there can be no labour-process unless there are *workers at the bench, on the construction site or in the factory*. And the wood will not be on the work bench, the cement on the building site or the steel in the factory unless, in previous labour-processes, workers were present in the forests and sawmills, or the mines and foundries. When I say: unless workers were or are present, I mean unless they are *there on time, in sufficient numbers and with the requisite work discipline*. It will be said that that goes without saying. Not at all! For workers are like everybody else: they would rather go fishing or play a hand of rummy or do devil-knows-what, as the fancy takes them. Who is it, then, who makes them show up at work at a set time, all together, and submit to this discipline, in very exacting work conditions?

In class societies, the answer is simple: workers have to work in exchange for their food (slaves) or wages (workers in capitalist society), lest they starve. If they have to work, it is because they own nothing but their labour-power. But if they own nothing but their labour-power, who owns the means of production (land, mines, factories, machines)? A social class that exploits them. There is, then, the class of those who own things and the class of those who work because they own nothing. To say 'classes' is to say 'class relation'. If the workers show up at the start of the working day, it is, in the last instance, because *the class relation* forces them to.

The same remark can be extended to classless societies. Here, it is not the relation of exploitation that forces workers to go work at the appointed place (for example, the hunting ground) at the appointed time. It is *a social relation* nonetheless, governed by a whole set of constraints disguised in the form of myths and rituals, and this social relation too organizes the labour-process.

Thus we see that this simple fact – that the workers who are needed to carry out the labour-process show up at the appointed time and place – that seems to 'go without saying' is, on the contrary, the least 'natural' and least 'obvious' thing in the world. If the workers are present, *it is because the relation of production forces them to be*, whether it is a communal relation (without classes), as in certain pre-capitalist societies called 'primitive', or a class relation.

That is why I could say, a moment ago, that the conception of the practice of production as a labour-process is an 'abstract' conception. For we can, provisionally and for the sake of argument, neglect the fact that the factory is there, that the raw material is there, and that the machines are there. After all, once they have been transported to the spot, they will not get up and leave by themselves. But what of the workers? What makes them keep coming back? *The constraint of the social relation*, whether it is a communal or a class relation (a relation of exploitation). Marx calls this social relation, when what is involved is production, *the relation of production. It is an abstract relation*, since it goes over the workers' heads, and forces them, even if they think they are 'free', to go to work for reasons having to do with either the community's survival or the perpetuation of the exploiting class. It is an abstract relation because it has nothing to do with the concrete movements that the workers make in performing their tasks.

One can, however, ask the same question the other way around. If the labour-process is to take place, if the 'combination' is to become active, it is not enough for workers to have to show up at the workplace at the appointed time. *There has to be a workplace*, that is to say, a certain space where the means of production have already been assembled: factory, raw material, machines and so on. These 'objects' do not transport themselves, nor do they come together all by themselves or by happenstance. Someone has to own them and have a reason to assemble them at the workplace that way. In a class society, the means of production belong to the exploiting class, and its reason for assembling them in a place and a configuration that makes production possible is to extort surplus labour, that portion of the product produced by the workers that *exceeds* the portion they need to subsist: the exploitation of workers.

Due allowance made, the same thing holds for communal societies. When, after the magician sets the day and hour of the hunt, the men all gather in the same part of a forest to track game, it is because this forest belongs to the community and because the people of the community recognize this common ownership of the means of production as a social relation transcending individuals.

Thus, in addition to the 'combination' of the concrete elements of the labour-process, what makes possible the organic encounter of elements at the same time and place is, as far as both the workers and the means of production are concerned, abstract social relations. In class societies, these relations 'distribute' people into owners and non-owners of the means of production, into social classes. In classless societies, they ensure the social conditions for the organization of labour on communal property.

We should perhaps make one point more precise here. For the abstraction of this social relation of production is a rather special one. Observing the opposition between the class that owns the means of production and the class that is deprived of them – in other words, the exploiting and exploited classes – we may be tempted to say that this relation of production is a 'human' relation, since it involves *only human beings*, distinguished by the fact that some are rich and others poor. This would be, in some sense, a *two-term* relation: the rich exploit the poor. To say so, however, would be to neglect the crucial fact that wealth and poverty are determined by a *third term*, the means of production, for the rich are rich because they possess the means of production, while the poor are poor and have to work, that is, to submit to exploitation, because they are deprived of them. But means of production are not human beings; they are *material things possessing* a value. This brings out the specific structure of the abstraction of the relation of production: it is not a two-term, but a three-term relation, in which the relation between classes is determined by the distribution of the means of production between classes.

With that, we glimpse the possibility of a form of abstraction that is utterly disconcerting for idealist philosophy, whether empiricist or formalist. For empiricist or formalist abstraction is always conceived on the model of a 'two-term' or an *x*-term abstraction, where *the objects in question are all on the same level* – horizontal, let us say. What we glimpse here is that the distribution of the same abstraction over 'two terms' does not exhaust it, since it is itself the effect of a relation to a third, material term located 'behind' or 'before' the others and governing their relations.

We shall therefore say that the labour-process is dominated by the technical relations of production. 'The labour-process', however, is a (bad) abstraction, for there is no labour-process that is not dominated by a social relation of production. It is to bring out the presence of this essential abstraction (this relation of production) that Marx, after analysing the elements of the labour-process, speaks of the *'production process'*. He shows that if the labour-process does indeed mobilize the very same elements in every society, *there are as many production processes as there are modes of production* (as there are relations of production). For the social constraints that *force people to work* are not the same in 'primitive' communities, a slave-holding regime, the feudal system and capitalist society. Let us add that the objective of this 'production process' is not the same in classless societies (simple useful products not subject to commodity relations because they are not made to be sold) and class societies (surplus labour extorted from the immediate producers, surplus labour that takes the form of surplus value in capitalist societies, where what is produced is commodities, objects made to be sold).

We could go still further to show that the relation of production not only governs the distribution of the means of production between those who possess them and those deprived of them, but also commands, to a large extent, *the division and organization of labour* in the process of production. Thus the 'immediate and concrete' relation between the worker and his work, far from being immediate and concrete, is concrete only because it is dominated, that is, established and determined, by the all-powerful abstractions known as the relation of production and the social relations flowing from it.

Can we, under these conditions, maintain the Aristotelian conception of practice as *poiesis*, in which the object transformed is radically *external* to practice? To all appearances, what happens is indeed *poiesis*. Nature is there prior to all productive labour, and human beings transform it in order to obtain the products they need from it. There is a sort of brutality in the fact that coal is found in one country and not another, in the fact that, when we discover it, the ore is there, and not man-made, but totally external to man. On closer inspection, however, it appears that the energy utilized in a factory also comes from nature: electricity is produced by waterfalls or coal, petrol comes from oil, and so on. Human beings transform energy, they do not produce it. And are human beings themselves – their force, the force of their muscles or brains – not natural products in their turn? If so, we may say that in the labour-process, at the limit, one part of nature (humankind) utilizes transformed natural forces or transformed parts of nature (energy, tools) to transform another part of nature (raw material). This would tend to show that nature transforms itself. Aristotle's first definition would thus refer us to the second: to the idea of a practice of self-transformation with no external object.

There is, however, something that prevents us from putting matters that way: the difference between the laws of physical nature, which govern the raw material and instruments of production as well as the play of the workers' physical force, when it exists, and the abstract laws governing the existence of labour-power. All these laws are laws, and have the same necessity. The laws governing labour-power, however, are not an extension of the laws of physical nature and do not resemble them. Is there any need to provide some idea of this difference? *The laws of nature are not 'tendential', that is, they are not conflictual and not subject to revolutions*, whereas the laws that govern the relation of production are laws that pit one class against another. As such, they are premised on conflict, and either the perpetuation or the overthrow of the established order.

That is why the practice of production is more accurately depicted, at the limit, as *poiesis* rather than *praxis*: because the laws of nature, even when they are utilized in production, are external to the laws of the social relations governing production. Human societies go through rapid revolutions, classes appear, the dominant class yields to another class, and all this in very short time spans compared to nature's; nature hardly changes at all in the same length of time. It is always there, and always the same, compared to the different forms of society that struggle with it for their subsistence; it is always external to production and the relations governing production.

9 SCIENTIFIC PRACTICE AND IDEALISM

It is plain that, in human existence, the vast majority of practices are comparable to the practice of production, and that their object is external to them. It is hardly necessary to demonstrate this for material production itself. It is more interesting to make the demonstration for scientific practice or theoretical practice (the meaning of the latter is broader, for it takes in ideological practice as well, to the extent that ideological practice is theoretical, and also philosophical practice, which can by all rights be called theoretical). After everything that has been said so far, we already have some idea of what is in question here. But it will doubtless be useful to make our idea a little more precise. For idealist prejudices that have the force of law hold sway in this domain. They present scientific work as, say, the simple product of an intuition or illumination suddenly granted, for more or less mysterious reasons, to an individual who has witnessed an astonishing phenomenon or arrived at a deeper view of things. This is an intuitionist (idealist) conception of scientific work. But there are other idealist depictions of scientific work: for instance, the empiricist description that we have already discussed. In the empiricist view, because truth is contained in the object, the scientist's task comes down to extracting it; he produces the 'abstraction' known as knowledge by adding up parts extracted from each individual object that offers itself to sense perception. Empiricism can be *sensory*, and either *subjective*, if all that is revealed of the object is what is perceived of it, or *objective*, if sensory perception reveals the properties of the perceived object itself. If the object is revealed in intellectual intuition, empiricism is *rationalist* (as in Descartes).

This conception, however, supposes the existence of an object not only independent of the knowledge of it (this thesis is materialist), but also containing in itself, in an immediate way, knowledge of itself, which the scientist need only extract. Let us note in passing that this conception, very frequent in the ideological consciousness of scientists, especially experimental scientists, is not without real substance, inasmuch as it states a truth, albeit in roundabout and therefore false fashion: namely that the knowledge produced by the scientist's work is well and truly knowledge *of* the object, which exists independently of his knowledge of it, outside scientific work. This means that knowledge of any object at all 'belongs' to the object even before that knowledge is produced, even before it is known. Hence one can legitimately situate it in the object in advance, since it belongs to it by all rights.

This conception has just one drawback, but it is a serious one: it brackets out the scientist's work and thus the transformation of which the object is the site during the process of knowledge. If the empiricist thesis were correct, one could not help but wonder why scientists are needed at all, why the truth of the thing cannot be read off 'by simple sight', as in the case of Adam's knowledge in Malebranche's conception of it. The whole of the immense conceptual and material apparatus of science then becomes superfluous: it is an effort out of all proportion to its results, since those results have been attained in advance. What is more, it becomes impossible to understand the absolute condition of all scientific work: constant exposure to the risk of running into dead-ends and errors, hence the risk of refutation (rather than verification) by experience. The British philosopher Popper was right to insist on this condition (the risk of *experimental refutation*), even if he worked it up into an idealist philosophy of the conditions to which a theory must subscribe in advance if it is to be certain of squarely confronting this risk.[1]

It is, however, not sufficient to avoid these idealist conceptions of scientific activity in order to have done with false depictions of it. Today, the most widespread of these false conceptions, which, like all philosophical conceptions, has very old roots, is the one purveyed by *logical neo-positivism*. 'Neo-positivism', because it appeals to the authority of positivism; 'logical', because it renews positivism by subjecting it to the formal conditions of mathematical logic.

Logical neo-positivism has one great strength: it is based on self-evident truths, those of scientific practice itself. It recognizes nothing but *facts*, objective, material facts verified by experimentation. In that sense, it takes its place in the tradition of Kantian idealism: only those objects whose existence and properties can be put to the test of experimental verification, however complex it may be (and it has become very complex in modern times), exist as scientific objects. This means that all 'objects' that are not susceptible of verification by an experimental test that can be repeated at will anywhere at any time (since these conditions are objective, they can be reproduced) do not exist for science, and therefore do not exist at all, or exist in the form of unverifiable discourses that are imaginary, since they cannot be experimentally refuted. The religions, psychoanalysis and Marxism are all examples.

As we have described it so far, logical neo-positivism has not introduced anything really new, but has basically reproduced the Kantian distinction between legitimate sciences, which prove the existence of their object, and 'pseudo-sciences', which are illegitimate and have only imaginary objects (metaphysics, rational theology and the like).[2] Logical positivism displays its originality when it brings *formal logic* to bear to define truth criteria – in other words, criteria of validity applicable to standing *propositions* or propositions established by experimental work. What formal logic 'works on' is the *language* with which scientists (and non-scientists) operate – that is, scientific language and 'natural' language. Here we encounter our first abstraction again, that of language, which neo-positivism does not accept as a given (as all other idealist philosophies do), but interrogates, explores and differentiates in order to discover the laws of its *legitimate* (and illegitimate) use.

For it is clear that when we use awkward or false formulations to designate a real object's properties, or when we casually throw out genuinely contradictory propositions that go unperceived, we lapse into verbal errors that automatically generate scientific errors. There would be no objection to make to any of this if logical neo-positivism did not in fact subordinate, or tend to subordinate, the rules of experimental validation to laws of logical validity *laid down in advance*, thereby lapsing into *formalism*, which, with empiricism, represents the most characteristic dissident variety [*contre-variété*] of idealism.

For *empiricism*, there is nothing that precedes the object and nothing that comes after it; thus there is *nothing that differs from it*, neither rules of validity nor truth. For *formalism*, in contrast, there is no object that is not subjected, before and after the process of its cognition, and in the course of it as well, to formal rules commanding both its existence and its properties. The old Leibnizian dream of a God who 'calculates' the world he creates, subjecting it, in its existence and properties, to absolute, formal laws of non-contradiction,[3] thus has its latter-day version in neo-positivism, which subjects every proposition to the formal laws of non-contradiction and the 'truth tables'. The height of the paradox – but we are getting used to these philosophical paradoxes – is that logical neo-positivism is a formalism only on condition that this formalism is based on an empiricism, that of the 'facts of language': a radical formalism and a radical empiricism.

It would be easy enough to show, by the same token, that an ontological formalism lurks behind the theses of empiricism. What interests us about these two cases, however, is a demand common to both that shapes what we might call *the philosophical guarantee* of the results of scientific practice. For it is as if the scientists who espoused either empiricist or formalist philosophy looked to it to provide them with *a guarantee of their own practice.*

The technique of the guarantee is a very old human technique that no doubt goes back to the earliest commercial exchanges and property forms. It comes into play when someone who lends a sum of money to someone else requires that the borrower furnish him with a guarantee: the material or moral guarantee that he will be repaid when the loan comes due. The borrower provides the lender with this guarantee either by depositing an asset of the same value as the loan with a third party or by obtaining a moral guarantee from a third party who offers assurances that it will be repaid. The guarantee can also take the form of a mortgage, that is, the lender's right to recover his loan by tapping assets owned by the borrower. In all cases, the operation of the guarantee brings three parties or elements into play: a lender, a borrower and a Third Party – either a person or an asset. The role of the guarantor – that is, the Third Party, the person or asset standing *above* the transaction and the contracting parties – is to guarantee the lender, materially and morally, that he will be repaid without fail at the promised time.

Much the same thing happens in idealist philosophies of scientific practice. The scientist is, so to speak, the 'lender': he advances his efforts, work and hypotheses. The 'borrower' is the scientific object that receives all this anticipated expenditure. And the scientist expects to be repaid for his efforts. He therefore demands *a guarantee* that his efforts *will in fact produce what he is expecting*, what he has gone to such great expense to obtain: *scientific knowledge*. The idealist philosophies are the Third Party who provides him with this guarantee. They guarantee the validity of his statements, the conditions and forms of his experimentation, and the accuracy of his results, as long as he carefully follows all the rules. Formally, then, the results – concrete knowledge, truths – are, so to speak, deposited somewhere in advance. They are already known, at least virtually, by someone (God, Being, the philosopher who talks about them), so that the scientist can embark on his operation or (the word nicely sums up the matter) his *speculation*.

It will be asked what purpose this whole operation can possibly serve, since things do not happen this way in any case, and since the scientist can never know ahead of time whether or not he will succeed. One answer is that there are scientists who require this kind of guarantee, either because they have doubts about their hypotheses or the validity of their experimental instruments, or because they feel an inner need to defend themselves against the attacks of other idealist philosophies that, for their part, cast doubt on the titles of legitimacy [*titres*] of scientific research.

These answers, however, fall short of the mark, for it is not just science which is at issue in this philosophy of scientific practice: at issue are all the human practices in their interrelations, and the whole of the order existing among these practices, which is a social order, hence a political order, hence the locus of a class struggle. The allegiance that these philosophies do not succeed in winning from scientists (although they do in fact gain scientific partisans) they win by utilizing the example of science and its prestige *with agents of the other practices*, whom they intimidate by evoking and 'exploiting' the model of science, the immense advantage of which is that it is not open to discussion. For 'science is science': it knows the truth by definition and cannot be called into question.

With that, we begin to see that, in order to understand what a philosophy might be, we must take account not just of the practices about which it explicitly speaks, but also *of the practices about which it does not speak* and, as well, *of the whole set of practices*, for it is their internal relationship that is at stake in philosophical intervention.

For example, the intimidation effect just mentioned is manifest in the case of Karl Popper's philosophy. For Popper has, on his own admission, constructed his entire (rather limited) philosophy for the express purpose of demonstrating that psychoanalysis and Marxism are not sciences, since, as he sees it, their hypotheses can never be refuted by experiment (psychoanalytic experiment and the experiments of the class struggle are indeed incapable of being reproduced in the same form at all times and places) and since they have, as a result, every chance of turning out to be impostures of a religious kind.[4] Matters are not always as clear or as forthrightly stated in other idealist philosophies of scientific practice. Nevertheless, when we take a close look, we always find 'motivations' of the same sort: it is a matter of using the model of science to validate or invalidate other existing practices.

We should not, however, confine our attention to the function of guarantee or validation. Idealist philosophy always has that function, which, however, does not always have the same ideological and political significance. This function can be exercised in a positive and progressive sense as well, as was once the case with bourgeois idealist philosophy.

When the ascendant bourgeoisie was developing the productive forces as well as tools, machines, measuring devices and other instruments, it needed science. It therefore also needed a philosophy guaranteeing that science was indeed science, provided objective knowledge, and had nothing in common with imaginary constructions such as religion or the philosophy of nature inherited from Aristotle, which was incapable of providing a theory of the motion of physical bodies. This desideratum did not reflect a 'psychological' demand on the part of scientists disconcerted by the novelty of their discoveries and wondering 'whether it was really true' that bodies obeyed Galileo's laws. It reflected the necessities of an implacable ideological struggle. For when the bourgeoisie set out to conquer its place, it had to dislodge those in possession of it. When it decided to win recognition for the existence of the sciences, it had to wrestle with the tremendous forces of religious ideology, which occupied the terrain.

Bourgeois idealist philosophy did not, however, enter the lists on behalf of science alone. It had to take into consideration the fact that the fight for science could not be isolated from the ensemble of political and ideological struggles. On the one hand, bourgeois philosophy acted as a *guarantee* for science (against the overpowering claims of feudal religious ideology); on the other, it utilized a certain notion of science *to guarantee the future of the bourgeoisie's political struggles*. The eighteenth century offers, in the guise of Enlightenment ideology, the purest example of this transfer of guarantees under the unity of philosophy. Philosophy guaranteed that the sciences provided knowledge of the world, both natural and social, while the power of scientific truth guaranteed that humanity would one day see the need for the social reforms required to rid the world of inequality and servitude.

In this period, therefore, in which the bourgeoisie was a revolutionary class, the philosophical function of the guarantee encompassed not just the sciences, but the whole set of social practices, and it was progressive. Of course, bourgeois philosophy 'manipulated' the sciences and 'exploited' their prestige. It did so, however, to emancipatory ends: to emancipate the sciences and emancipate humanity.

The same function of guarantee can operate in a completely different way, a reactionary way, depending on class relations and the stakes of the class struggle.

The bourgeoisie needed science even after firmly ensconcing itself in power, as it had by the mid-nineteenth century; and it continues to need it, since the class struggle requires it to develop and incessantly 'revolutionize' (Marx) the productive forces of the capitalist mode of production. After encountering the first major assaults of the workers' class struggle, however, it was forced to reorganize its philosophical system. Philosophy, whether positivist or logical neo-positivist philosophy, still served as a *guarantee* for science. But now it did so in order to *control* scientific workers in the name of an idea of science different from that advocated by the Enlightenment philosophers: in the name of an idea of science that no longer stood in direct relation with the idea of the emancipation of humanity, but, rather, imposed the truth as *Order*, and as a truth possessed by a handful of men who exercised 'spiritual power' (ideological and political power), as in Auguste Comte, or who saw to the general organization of society, as do modern technocrats assisted by their computers.

Just as the idea of Liberty, once associated with the idea of science, did not come to the classical bourgeois philosophers from scientific practice alone, but, first and foremost, from the practice of the class struggle for the liberation of humanity, so the idea of Order did not come to the positivists from the laws of nature alone, or to the philosophers of the technocracy from computer programming alone. It came, first and foremost, from the practice of the class struggle of a bourgeoisie now forced *to impose its Order*, because that order was being challenged by the workers. The bourgeoisie imposed it in the name of a philosophy guaranteeing that Order is necessary, and that the bourgeois Order is the true Order.

In the two cases just mentioned, idealist philosophy 'exploits' science, its results and its prestige. Here, however, we must carefully distinguish the different meanings conveyed by the same words.

In the first case, idealist philosophy 'exploits' science, that is to say, harnesses a certain idea of science to the service of social practices. Since these practices are revolutionary, however, the idea of science thus 'exploited' respects, by and large, the essentials of the values of scientific practice. The struggle for the emancipation of science and the struggle for political emancipation thus effectively tend in the same direction. This averts the more serious deformations, without ruling them out (thus Descartes, Kant and Hegel all deformed the sciences in order to fit them into their systems).

In the second case, idealist philosophy 'exploits' the sciences, that is to say, enlists a certain idea of science in the service of social practices. Since these social practices are reactionary, however – since it is a matter of putting the workers who threaten the reigning (bourgeois) order violently back in their place in that order – the idea of science thus exploited changes in content. Science becomes the model for knowledge of the kind that observes facts, full stop; establishes laws, full stop; and ensures that the order of those laws reigns in phenomena. Everything that it is impossible to range under this reassuring idea (reassuring for the powers-that-be), all the sciences that threaten this idea and this order, are declared null and void and are said to be impostures: Marxist theory and psychoanalysis are examples. In contrast, all of the dominant ideology's theoretical formations – political economy, sociology, psychology – are christened sciences, and it is necessary to submit to their 'laws', which reinforce the established Order. The meaning of the philosophical guarantee of science has changed: instead of serving, by and large, the emancipation of humanity and the sciences, it becomes a principle of authority and order.

Thus nothing is less 'innocent' than the illusions about science known as empiricism and formalism.

10 SCIENTIFIC PRACTICE AND MATERIALISM

Now that we have cleared away the obstacles represented by the empiricist and formalist conceptions of scientific practice, the road is open for a completely different conception, which tries to be materialist.

How, then, should we visualize scientific practice? As a process that begins by putting a given raw material, a definite form of labour-power and existing instruments of production to work. In this process, labour-power (the researcher's knowledge and intelligence) puts the instruments of production (theory, the material experimental set-up and so on) to work on a given raw material (the object on which it experiments) in order to produce definite knowledge.

It will be objected that this schema simply reproduces that of material production, the schema of the 'labour-process' (Marx). That is not wrong, but there are big differences between the two.

The first has to do with the nature of the '*raw material*'. Rather than consisting of raw material in the proper sense (iron ore, coal, etc.) or of already processed material (steel, copper, etc.), the 'raw material' of scientific practice consists of a mix of material objects as well as non-scientific or already scientific representations, depending on the degree of development of the science involved.

But, to make our task harder, let us suppose that we are present at the birth of one of the sciences (we know that we can rather accurately date the moment of their birth) and let us imagine, accordingly, raw material that is as 'pure' – in other words, as untheoretical – as possible. For we know that every already developed science works on raw material that is to a large extent already scientific, that is, theoretical.

In this extreme case, then, we are assuming that the scientist has before him only what is given by his perceptions, unaided by instruments or measuring devices. Let us point out straight away that this hypothesis is unrealistic, for all the examples we are familiar with show that every science had a minimum of technical equipment at its disposal at its origins (Greek mathematics defined its figures using ruler and compass). No matter: let us assume something like a total absence of theoretical determinations. What do we see in such a case? Not the pure contact between a subject who knows and the object to be known that empiricism describes, not the pure concrete, but a whole world of abstractions. The concrete doubtless reveals itself through sensory perceptions, but what they indicate is less what it is (its 'essence') than the mere fact of its existence. Doubtless, for the existence of something to be indicated, something of its 'essence' must be revealed as well. But all this takes place under the domination, precisely, of an imposing layer of abstractions, whose deforming effects seem so natural that we do not so much as suspect their existence.

What abstractions?

To begin with, there are the abstractions of all the concrete practices that exist in the social group under consideration: practices of production, sexual practices of reproduction and (when it is a question of a class society) practices of class struggle. There are also all the abstract social practices that regulate class functions or class conflicts in the society involved: law, morality, religion and, when it exists, philosophy. The function of these abstractions – as is shown by the experience of primitive societies, to say nothing of the others – is not just to regulate the social relations on which they bear; another of their effects is to assign a place and meaning to all possible empirical observations. This means that, in early scientific practice, it is all but impossible to separate factual observations from the abstract generalities which constitute not their basis, but their network of reference and meaning.

Thus it may fairly be said that the raw material on which the scientist works in the most rudimentary form of science is inseparable from certain definite abstract generalities, themselves the results of a very long elaboration of the different social practices. That is why I earlier suggested the term 'Generalities I' to designate this raw material, the plural serving to indicate the complexity of the abstractions condensed in the seemingly unmediated 'facts' with which scientists supposedly deal.[1] Among these Generalities I, I pointed to the presence, alongside generalities deriving from the other material or sexual social practices, of generalities stemming from various ideologies (legal, moral, religious, philosophical, etc.).

What has just been said about the hypothetical science whose conditions we have just examined holds a fortiori for every already constituted, developing science. The raw material on which researchers work comprises, besides the generalities we have mentioned, other forms of abstraction: the abstractions of technical practice and the abstract knowledge that has already been produced by a science. We can, then, consider the limit case of mathematics, in which a science *works only on itself*, that is, on results it has already produced. If, now, we consider science to be a 'subject', it may be said to fall under Aristotle's second definition, since it does not have to do with an external object, inasmuch as it is itself its own object.

Mathematics, however, is emphatically a limit case. In all experimental sciences, there exists an external, objective material element. Even if that element is contained in the framework of the existing theory, even if it is realized in instruments of observation and measurement, it is no less present for that and, as such, is an object of sense perception, direct or indirect. In modern physics, to be sure, one never sees the object as such (this or that particle) with the naked eye. One observes, however, at least a trace of it, direct or indirect, as recorded on a film or as revealed, after analysis, by the shift in the rays of the light spectrum. Yet this sensory element cannot be recorded without this entire experimental apparatus, which represents a considerable mass of abstractions and knowledge, realized in the apparatus itself.

It must be pointed out that such abstractions are not empty, contrary to what ordinary usage of the word 'abstraction' suggests. The opposite is true: they are full of definite knowledge obtained at the end of a long process, and their orderly combination [*assemblage*] defines not an empty space, but, on the contrary, a perfectly mapped space. It is in this space that the scientific event will occur: the scientific 'fact' that will make new discoveries possible or make it necessary to modify either the working hypotheses or the experimental set-up. The greater the progress the science makes, consequently, the more its raw material tends towards the concrete, which is simply a result of the combination of the multiple abstractions or knowledge constituting it. Marx put it this way: science does not proceed, as everyday ideology supposes, from the 'concrete to the abstract', from empirically existing objects to their truth (contained in them from all eternity, so that it is enough to extract it). *On the contrary, science proceeds from the abstract to the concrete*;[2] it gradually refines abstraction, the existing abstractions, moving from ideological abstractions to the abstractions of technical-practical knowledge and, ultimately, scientific abstractions, and, after exactly combining them, to a definite abstraction bearing on a concrete object. This definite abstraction thus becomes the concrete knowledge of a concrete object. It must be said that the majority of philosophers and even scientists are unaware of this fundamental materialist truth; yet, without it, it is impossible to understand what occurs in scientific practice.

From the standpoint of the process of scientific practice, there is little to be said about the *researcher*. For he is wholly defined, certain special aptitudes aside (which can play a decisive role in some cases) by the state of the existing science in which he works. He can invent a theory only on the basis of existing theories, discover problems only on the basis of results already obtained, design experimental set-ups only on the basis of the theoretical and technical means available to him and so on. He is an agent of a process that goes beyond him, not its subject, that is, its origin or creator. The process of the practice – that is to say, of scientific production – is thus a 'process without a subject'.[3] This does not mean that it can dispense with the researcher's labour-power or his intelligence, talent, etc.; it means that this process is subject to objective laws which also determine the agent's – the scientific researcher's – nature and role.

That is something all scientists know. They are very well aware that the gigantic dimensions of modern experimental installations make it obvious that a researcher is merely the agent of a complex process that transcends him. They are even aware that the scientific problems that are posed are posed not by this or that individual acting alone, but for the whole international scientific community, and that all the great discoveries are made 'in several places in the world' 'at about the same time', although those involved have not tipped each other off. They are aware that research is engaged in an impressive adventure which is, moreover, largely determined from without, by the demands of production and the imperatives of class struggle. They are aware that, even if they unite, they can do very little to influence the way scientific research develops. They, or at least some of them, are aware that if they want to do something to influence the course of its development, *they have to 'shift terrain' and get involved in politics*. For, contrary to the assumption of idealist philosophers, it is not science or knowledge that commands politics, but politics that commands the development of science and knowledge.

The fact that the development of scientific practice has the character of a 'process without a subject' marks each of its moments and elements, its raw material no less than its agents (researchers), instruments of production, and results. We shall leave this idea aside for now and come back to it in a different context later.

What has been said about the raw material of production obviously also holds for *the instruments of production*. These are, we said, realizations of scientific abstractions, of theoretical knowledge. This is easy to see as far as the instruments employed in experimentation are concerned. In the past, measuring devices were simple: today, they have given rise to highly abstract theories justifying their nature, the quality of the metal of which they are made, the temperature at which they are used, the vacuum (or not) in which they are put to work and so on. I shall not go into this aspect of things, well-known thanks to a phrase coined by the philosopher Gaston Bachelard: 'instruments are materialized theories'.[4] I would, however, like to underscore a less familiar aspect of the matter: the fact that the current '*theory*' of a science figures among its instruments of theoretical production. We can, moreover, say that this theory is present in a science's raw material as well, since the matter worked on is defined, in a given science, in accordance with the theoretical achievements of that science. Thus Bachelard has shown that scientists experiment on 'pure bodies', although there are no 'pure bodies' in nature, since every 'pure body' is the product of a scientific theory and a corresponding technique.[5] What holds for the instruments of production holds a fortiori for the raw material, for what is of interest about the theory figuring in the instruments of theoretical production is that it figures there not in a form different from itself, as raw material or instrument of production, *but in the pure form of the theory of the existing science*. This no doubt does not mean that the theory figures in the instruments of production in its entirety, for, as a rule, it does so only partially, in the form of a certain number of scientific concepts. The operative significance of these concepts, however, does depend on the theory as a whole. They intervene both directly and indirectly in the work performed on the raw material, in the form of hypotheses to be verified or instruments of observation, measure and experimentation.

The interest of this analysis is that we can, here too, take the example that seemed exceptional to us a moment ago, mathematics, and say that, in a certain sense, science, even experimental science, works only on itself, since it is, regarded from this angle, its own raw material, its own agent and its own instruments of production. If, however, it works only on itself, how does it manage to make discoveries rather than endlessly repeating itself? The answer is that it works on a contradictory object, for the theory that works on itself, at the limit, does not work on a theory that has eliminated every internal contradiction – that has, in other words, arrived at the ultimate knowledge of its object. Quite the contrary: it is an incomplete theory which works on its own incompletion and derives, from this 'play', gap or contradiction, the means with which to progress beyond the level of knowledge it has already attained: in short, the means to develop.

What it then produces is new knowledge. Earlier, I suggested the term 'Generalities II' to designate the complex set of abstractions and instruments that the agent of scientific research 'puts to work' on the raw material (Generalities I). At the same time, I proposed that we call the new knowledge produced by this whole process of knowledge 'Generalities III'.

I am aware that this terminology is open to objection. It can be objected, in particular, that if, as I have claimed, scientific abstractions are distinguished from technical-practical abstractions by their *universality*, the scientific knowledge obtained at the end of the process should be called *Universalities*, not *Generalities*. The reader will recall the distinction we drew above: a generality is always empirical, whereas a scientific abstraction, which is universal, is always theoretical. I admit, therefore, that this criticism is partly justified. Moreover, it could be extended to Generalities II, since, in the case of a well-developed science, scientific and therefore universal abstractions always figure among these Generalities as well. But, precisely, we also find *ideological* generalities figuring among both Generalities I and II, and ideological generalities, we know, are falsely universal.

Moreover, we find ideological generalities even in the knowledge produced at the end of the process, Generalities III. This is the sign that the science is not complete, as it never can be; it is the sign not only that its theoretical problems are never fully resolved, but, further, that it is inevitably subject to the pressure of the surrounding ideology, which contaminates or can contaminate the way it poses scientific problems (although it can sometimes also help it to pose them). That is why I prefer to retain the term 'Generalities' to designate even the scientific abstractions comprising the knowledge that the process produces.

If we now consider the process of scientific practice as a whole, we can see that it is dominated by a set of abstractions that are all *relations*. These relations are not simple abstractions nor even a sum of simple abstractions; they are abstractions which are combined in a specific way, producing a relatively stable structure. Among these relations, we may immediately mention those already discussed, between the existing theory and the technology of the experimental set-up.

A close look reveals that these relations are extraordinarily complex. The phenomena of experimental validation take place under the domination of these relations, which strictly define their conditions. The relations of theoretical production are not, however, the only ones to come into play; philosophical relations and ideological relations do as well. If idealist philosophers' way of depicting the relations between philosophy and the sciences is mistaken, if these philosophers are mistaken, in particular, when they say that philosophy defines the elements of every scientific theory, they are not mistaken when they include philosophical and even ideological relations among the relations of scientific production.

Philosophical relations, usually conveyed, like ideological relations, in natural language, or in abstract language that has become part of natural language, are constituted by certain arrangements of philosophical *categories* and *theses* which play their role at the frontier between what a science already knows and what it is trying to find out, hence in the constitution of its theory.

To take a simple example, it is obvious that scientific physics, which begins with Galileo, would have been unable to come into being without a new concept of causality to replace the old, outmoded concept of causality taken over from Aristotle. What operated to produce the category of causality that put physics on the road to a new concept of causality, if not the philosophy of Descartes and the Cartesians? In this case, we may say that philosophy responded to an explicit demand emanating from physics. Very often, however, philosophy precedes any demand, producing categories that science will utilize only much later. To take, here too, just one simple example, Aristotle had forged in his philosophy, for general theoretical reasons that took theological form, the category of a first cause that was, paradoxically, an 'unmoved mover' and, consequently, operated at a distance. Twenty centuries later, Newton adopted the same category to think the action that bodies exert on one another at a distance in the form of attraction and repulsion – thereby scandalizing the Cartesian mechanists, who could not conceive of physical action without contact and thus without collision.

It is important to understand that, in this phenomenon, which reveals that *philosophical relations* (and ideological relations as well: the distinction does not matter much here) also command the process of the production of concrete scientific knowledge, we do not have to do with linear determination, in either time or space. We have to do, rather, with forms which, while they express philosophical relations necessary for the development of the existing sciences, and thus imposed by the major, dominant theoretical problems of their day, may hold the surprise of either anticipation or insignificance. *The philosophical relations of theoretical production* are not arbitrary, when one considers a given science at a given moment in its history. Obviously, however, they do not exhaust the ensemble of philosophical categories and theses in existence in their time.

For the stake of philosophical battle is not just the sciences; philosophy must defend the whole front on which all the other human practices also figure. In devising categories and theses that will be deployed on the front of scientific practice, philosophy takes into account *the ensemble of the stakes of its combat*; this means that, while respecting the reality of scientific practice as far possible, it has to inflect its 'representation' of it so as to adjust all its interventions to each other on a common theoretical basis. It is because of this inevitable 'distortion' that philosophy is, for reasons of principle, not a science and, likewise for reasons of principle, does not provide knowledge, yet is haunted by one particular practice: that of intervention in the theoretical (and other) relations of scientific practice and the other practices. We shall see the nature of the intervention involved.

Obviously, the thesis that there exist relations of scientific production that are not purely scientific, but also philosophical and ideological, flies in the face of the positivist depiction of science. For positivism, as for all forms of rationalism, everything intervening in scientific practice is purely scientific, even the object which, albeit opaque before scientific experimentation on it began, proves that it already possessed its own 'essence' in itself once its essence has been extracted from it by abstraction.

Positivism derives its thesis of science's absolute scientific neutrality from that notion, together with its thesis about the omnipotence of science, which, as the bearer of truth, has only to reveal itself to people or be taught to them in order to be recognized by them and so serve them as a politics, for their greater good. This rationalist conception of science is the classic form of the bourgeois ideology of science, and it is such because it is part of the ideology of the dominant class, the ideology that is dominant in its turn. This is observable not only among scientists, who are directly influenced by this rationalist ideology of science, but also in very broad strata of both the bourgeoisie and also the working class, whom this ideology reaches directly by way of the science curriculum in primary schools.

In this connection, it is worth noting that the idea that science can be reduced to the restricted sphere of its purely and directly experimental practice is, in the proper sense, a (*bad*) *abstraction*. This is not just because everything found in this sphere (raw material, equipment, instruments, even theoretical problems, etc.) depends on the outside world, but also because scientific practice is not confined to the production of purely scientific results. For these results are the object of technical applications, since that is their basic raison d'être; they are also the object of a curriculum that is an indispensable part of the labour force's education. This curriculum, however, by no means reproduces the whole process of the production of knowledge; it limits itself to expounding its basic results and, given the prevailing balance of power, it necessarily expounds them in the form of the dominant ideology, the rationalist ideology which neglects the role of ideology, philosophy and class struggle. Thus this curriculum contributes in its own fashion to reproducing the ensemble of the conditions of scientific production.

This is a crucial point, which Marx underscored in discussing material production. No production is possible if it does not produce, along with its results, the means of replacing those of its own conditions used up in the process of production: *no production is possible, in other words, sustainable, if it does not ensure the conditions of its own reproduction.* We may say, in this regard, that philosophical and ideological conditions play a determinant role, precisely, in the production of the conditions of reproduction.[6]

What allows an experimental science, which varies the conditions of its experiments, and varies its hypotheses and experimental set-ups as well, to conceive of the possibility of such variations? What if not the existence of *invariant relations*, which make such variations conceivable and realizable? On close inspection, these relations turn out to be *philosophical or ideological relations*. The notion of substance or cause, for example, made it possible for the 'variations' of Aristotelian physics and, later, Galilean physics, to emerge in response to new problems thrown up by the practice of production or military practice. Similarly, the notions of natural law and human nature made it possible for the 'variations' of natural law in its entirety, and thus of the corresponding political theory in its entirety, in its extremely diverse forms (think of what forever separates Hobbes from Locke and even from Rousseau), to emerge and then consolidate itself in response to the new problems posed by the political and ideological conflicts of the seventeenth and eighteenth centuries.

Thus there exist philosophical categories (substance, cause, God, idea, etc.) or ideological ideas or notions (natural law as moral law, human nature as rational and moral, etc.) that have dominated human culture for centuries. This domination was not exercised over the 'ignorant' and 'simple-minded' alone; it also served as a *theoretical matrix* for theoretical, philosophical and scientific constructs of the very highest level of abstraction, the greatest difficulty, and the most far-reaching theoretical and practical import.

This set of (philosophical) categories and (ideological) ideas has thus served *to reproduce the conditions of theoretical production*, ensuring its perpetuation and, consequently, its progress. We must of course bear in mind that as a result [*sous l'effet*] of the combination of the different problems posed by the different practices, this body of theoretical relations of production is transformed in the course of history. But such transformation takes place relatively slowly, and the moments of its mutation are conspicuous enough to allow us to periodize this history. Thus a history of scientific practice in its different branches of production (the different sciences) can be conceived of and written, on condition that we do not lapse into an anecdotal account of the pure events visible in the field of that practice; on condition that we conceive of these relations of theoretical production as the main condition of that history, as that which commands the reproduction – in other words, the existence – of scientific practice.

We have to do here, doubtless, with a form of existence of philosophy that is not easy to discern and define, since it is easily confused with idealism's depictions of it (philosophy's omnipotence vis-à-vis the sciences). It is all the more important to conceive of it clearly, for, as we are beginning to suspect, as soon as there is philosophy somewhere, and ideology as well, there is also struggle: not an arbitrary, but a necessary struggle, linked in the last instance to class struggle. If there is struggle, there must be one party to the struggle that serves the interests of science, and another that exploits them in the dominant ideology's interests. Science is thus not neutral, because this struggle for or against values for which it serves as support or pretext is pursued at the very heart of it. As a rule, scientists are unaware of this, with the result that they succumb, uncritically, to the influence of the dominant ideology's ideas. Non-scientists, as a rule, are also unaware of it, with the result that they succumb to the ideas of the same ideology, which turns science's prestige and efficacity to its own profit, to the profit, that is, of the class which that ideology serves. Only a few rare scientists, materialist philosophers and Marxist political activists are aware of it and conduct themselves accordingly. The scientists are aware of it, thanks to the instinct of their practice; the philosophers, thanks to the principles of their philosophy; and the activists, thanks to the theory of historical materialism (or theory of the laws of class struggle) discovered by Marx.

11 IDEOLOGICAL PRACTICE

Now that we have discussed the practice of production and scientific practice, it is imperative that we also discuss ideological practice, for, without knowledge of it, we cannot arrive at an understanding of what philosophy is.

In my opinion, there clearly exists an ideological practice. Naturally, it is highly disconcerting, for it is not easy to recognize in ideological practice the categories that we have employed in our analyses so far. We should, however, take a closer look at it.

The most disconcerting thing about ideological practice is that we find no trace of the presence of an agent in it. If an ideology is a system of more or less unified ideas, it is clear that they act on 'consciousnesses' without the visible intervention of any agent whatsoever, not even that of the person who propagates them, since it is the self-evidence and power of ideas that acts through him. For we cannot say that the agent, in an ideology, is the individual who invented it. Everyone is well aware that the ideologies which play a real role in world history have no known author, or that, even if one can assign an author to them (Christ, for example), he could have been replaced at the same moment by anyone else at all. Thus it seems as if *ideology acted all by itself*, as if it were itself its own agent. This alone brings it close to the Aristotelian definition to which we have referred.

What continues to disconcert us in ideological practice, however, is the 'nature' of the raw material on which ideology acts as its own agent of transformation. On a rough preliminary approach, we can say that this raw material consists of human individuals insofar as they are endowed with 'consciousness' and have certain 'ideas', whatever they may be. Yet it can be seen right away that human individuals and their consciousness are mentioned here only as *supports* of the ideas they have, and that the raw material on which ideological practice acts is constituted by this system of ideas. Thus we find ourselves faced with the paradox of an ideological practice in which one system of ideas acts directly on another, for, since there is no distinct agent, the instruments of production (Generalities II) are conflated with the sole system of ideas of the existing ideology. On this condition, we can conceive of ideological practice as the transformation of existing ideology under the impact [*sous l'effet*] of the direct action of another ideology, distinct from the first. Otherwise, the question of its transformation would be absurd.

All this may seem mysterious. Things are nevertheless quite simple in principle, but on one condition: that we understand that an ideology is a system of ideas (or representations) only insofar as it is *a system of social relations*. In other words, in the guise of a system of ideas acting on another system of ideas in order to transform it, a system of social relations acts on another system of social relations in order to transform it. And this struggle, which occurs 'in the realm of ideas' or, rather, in that of 'social ideological relations' (Lenin),[1] is merely one form of the general class struggle.

For, between these ideas, there takes place something quite similar to what takes place, as we saw a moment ago, in the relation of production. Do you remember?[2] A three-term relation, and therefore a double-entry relation: a relation between two classes, but with regard to their respective relations to the means of production. In the case of ideology too we have a first relation: between two ideas or two systems of ideas. A second relation, however, immediately comes into play to confer its significance on the first: for the relation between the two systems of ideas intervenes with regard to their *respective relations to a different reality*. Which one? *The stakes* of the ideological class struggle, the relations of the ideological class struggle.

Examples? One can fight at the level of ideas for or against the claim that nature is rational, for or against determinism, for or against political freedom, for or against the existence of God, for or against the freedom of art and so on, ad infinitum. In this case, what happens? We may say the following. The ideology (the ideas) that operates (ideological practice) to transform the existing 'raw material' – in other words, the ideas (the ideology) currently dominating consciousnesses – does nothing other than to make these 'consciousnesses' pass from the domination of the old ideology to that of the new. Thus ideological practice comes down to this *transfer of domination*, this *displacement of domination*. For example, where a religious conception of the world once dominated, ideological practice (ideological struggle) succeeds in imposing the domination of a new ideology: say, a bourgeois rationalist ideology. (This happened in Europe between the fourteenth and the eighteenth centuries.)

Well and good, the reader will say, but these simple statements pose formidable problems: first, the problem of the mechanism of this domination; second, the mechanism of the *constitution* of these ideologies. All that is presupposed by what was just said, but has not been explained.

Let us, then, briefly discuss the mechanism of this domination. How can a 'consciousness', that of a concrete individual, be dominated by an idea and, above all, by a system of ideas? The answer will run: this happens when that consciousness recognizes them to be true. Doubtless. But how does this recognition come about? We know that it is not the mere presence of the truth which causes it to be recognized as true; considerable work is required to make that happen, the work of technical practice or scientific practice.

But it may be that recognition can come about all by itself, as a result [*sous l'effet*] of the presence of the true. When I meet my friend Pierre in the street, I recognize him, and say: 'It's Pierre, all right.' And I really do have the feeling that it is I, Louis, who find myself in direct, concrete contact with the truth that Pierre is there in the street, coming my way, and that I, Louis, recognize him: 'It's Pierre, all right.' Matters are, however, a little more complicated, because, for me to be able to say, 'It's Pierre, all right', I have to know *who Pierre is*, that he is tall, has dark hair, has a moustache and so on. Thus recognition [*reconnaissance*] presupposes cognition [*connaissance*], and I find myself caught in a circle.

Yet, in some sense, *recognition* takes priority over *cognition*, for if the work of cognition takes time, the conclusion of recognition comes about at once, in a fraction of a second, as if recognition were preceded by itself, always and everywhere; as if the idea of Pierre took possession of me in the instant in which I believe it is I who recognize Pierre; as if it were Pierre who, simply by dint of his presence, imposes this self-evident fact on me: 'It's Pierre, all right.' Thus the roles are reversed. It is I who believe that I recognize Pierre, or such-and-such an idea to be true: for example, the idea that God exists. In reality, however, *it is this idea that imposes itself on me through the encounter with Pierre*, or through the manifestation of this idea (in the case of God: a sermon).

If I carry this paradoxical idea to its extreme consequences, I come to an astonishing conclusion, which I can formulate as follows.

It is quite as if, when I believe in an idea or a system of ideas, it were not I who recognized them and, encountering them, said: 'It's them, all right! And they're true, all right!' Quite the contrary: it is as if, when I believe in an idea or a system of ideas, it were this idea or system of ideas that dominated me and imposed on me, by way of the encounter with their presence or manifestation, the recognition of their existence or truth and, simultaneously, my capacity to recognize them as true and to say so in all good faith. It is as if, at the limit, the roles having been completely reversed, it were not I who interpellated an idea in order to say to it: 'Hey, you, let's have a look at you, so I can tell whether you're true or not!' Rather, it is as if it were the idea or system of ideas that interpellated me and imposed its truth on me and, together with its truth, recognition of its truth and, together with that recognition, the function of recognizing – indeed, the *obligation* to recognize – its truth. That is how the ideas making up an ideology forcibly impose themselves on people's free 'consciousnesses': by interpellating people in forms such that they are compelled freely to recognize that these ideas are true – in forms such that they are compelled to constitute themselves as free *subjects*, capable of recognizing the truth where it resides, namely in the ideas of ideology.

That is the basic mechanism operating in ideological practice: *the mechanism of the ideological interpellation that transforms individuals into subjects*. And as individuals are always-already subjects, that is, always-already subject to an ideology (man is by nature an ideological animal), we have to say, to be consistent, that ideology transforms the content (the ideas) of 'consciousnesses' by interpellating subjects as subjects, that is, by making concrete individuals (who are already subjects) shift from a dominant ideology to a new ideology that is struggling to attain domination over the old ideology through individuals.

We could take the analysis of the effects and conditions of this very special mechanism much further, but we shall leave it at that for now. For we must also try to answer another question: why ideologies? Where do ideologies come from?

However far back we go in the social existence of humanity, we observe that people live in ideology – in other words, under the domination of 'ideological social relations'. Why? It is clear that these relations are bound up with the social life that people lead, with the division of labour, the organization of labour and the relations existing between the different social groups. In this respect, it is not such-and-such an idea considered as an individual fantasy that counts, but *only the ideas endowed with a capacity for social action*. That is where ideology begins; short of that, we are in the realm of purely individual imagination or purely individual experience. But as soon as we have to do with a corpus of socially established ideas, we may speak of ideology.

But then the social function of this corpus of ideas appears straight away. We spoke a moment ago about the different social practices. Human beings are so constituted that human action is inconceivable without language and thought. It follows that no human practice exists without a system of ideas represented in words and constituting, in this way, the ideology of that practice. Since the practices coexist in social life, but since some of them, the practices of social unity and social division, of social cohesion and social struggle, manifestly prevail over all the others, inasmuch as they are the condition for them, no ideology – I mean the ideology under whose domination each practice is carried out – stands off in its own corner, isolated and self-contained; rather, each ideology finds itself dominated and restructured by the social ideologies of social unity or social struggle. It is these ideologies (primitive myths, religion, political and legal ideologies) which set their stamp on the local ideologies that they subordinate to themselves.

That is why we can say that, despite their local and regional diversity, despite the diversity and material autonomy of the multiple practices that they dominate and unify, *ideologies in class societies always bear the mark of a class*, that of the dominant class or that of the dominated class. And since there is no getting round the pair dominant ideology/dominated ideology as long as we remain in class societies, we would do better to talk, rather than about a dominant ideology and a dominated ideology, about *the dominant and the dominated tendency in each* (local and regional) *ideology* – with the dominant tendency of ideology representing the dominant class's interests, while the dominated tendency strives to represent, under the domination of the dominant tendency, the dominated class's interests. This stipulation is important, for, without it, we could understand neither how the ideology of the dominated class can bear the marks of the ideology of the dominant class, nor, above all, how elements of the dominant ideology can figure as such in the ideology of the dominated class, and the other way around.

But, if everything that has just been said is true, we must add one stipulation about ideology's forms of existence. For we are too readily inclined to believe that '*ideology is ideas*' and nothing else. In fact, except in an idealist philosophy such as that of Descartes, one is very hard put to say what is an idea and what is not in a person's 'consciousness'. One is even at a near loss to say what, in a human being, is consciousness and what is not. A human being's ideas always have, in that human being, a form of material existence or a material support in the humblest sense of the word 'matter', even if it is just the sound of the voice when it articulates sounds to pronounce words and sentences, or the gesture of an arm or posture of a body making the merest suggestion of a movement to designate an object, hence an intention, hence an idea.

This is a fortiori the case when we consider the social existence of the ideologies. They are inseparable from what we call *institutions,* which have their statutes, code, language, customs, rituals, rites and ceremonies. Even a simple fishing society provides an illustration, as do, a fortiori, a church, or a political party, or the school system, or a labour union, or the family, or the Order of Physicians, or the Order of Architects, or the Order of Barristers, etc. Here too, we may say that ideologies require their material conditions of existence, their material support, or, better, their material forms of existence, since this corpus of ideas is, properly speaking, inseparable from this system of institutions.

We cannot, without making fools of ourselves, claim that each of these institutions was conceived for the *unique* purpose of incarnating the dominant ideology and inculcating it in the popular masses in the service of the dominant class's interests. For it is plain that the school system also serves to educate the workforce, to transmit knowledge that humanity has acquired in its history to children and adolescents. Nor can we say that all political parties or labour unions were conceived for a unique purpose: for a working-class party serves the working class. Nor can we say that the medical ideological apparatus was conceived for the unique purpose of diffusing bourgeois ideology, for it also serves to provide care for the ill, that is, to rehabilitate the workforce, and so on. We cannot even say of the Church, although it does not seem to provide any service related to production, that it is purely and simply an apparatus of ideological inculcation; firstly, because it does not invariably and in all periods serve the dominant class; and, secondly, because it fulfils eminently social and symbolic functions on the occasions of birth, suffering and death, in forms that affect people at the personal level.

Yet the fact is that, under cover of these different social functions, which are objectively useful in terms of production or social unity, these ideological apparatuses are penetrated and unified by the dominant ideology. It is not that the dominant class decided, one fine day, to create them in order to assign them this function: it was able to conquer them (when they were already in existence and served the old dominant class: for instance, the Church, the school system, the family, medicine and so on) or lay the groundwork for them *only in the course of, and at the price of, a very long, very bitter class struggle*. Their existence is thus in no sense the simple result of a decision corresponding to a preconceived plan perfectly conscious of its objectives. It is the result of a long class struggle by means of which the new class constitutes itself as the dominant class and seizes state power and, once firmly settled in power, undertakes to conquer the existing ideological state apparatuses, reorganize them, and lay the groundwork for the new apparatuses it needs.

12 THE IDEOLOGICAL STATE APPARATUSES

I have pronounced the decisive word: the state.[1] For, plainly, everything turns on the state. Except among the idealists of consciousness, who tenaciously defend the idea that ideology is ideas and nothing else, we will in fact find theorists prepared to grant all that has just been said about the ideologies, as long as *the word 'state' is not pronounced*. Even the most conservative bourgeois theorists are prepared to make this concession: yes, ideology is something other than ideas; yes, ideology is conflated with the institutions that 'incarnate' it; yes, one must talk about *ideological apparatuses*. And functionalism (a philosophy which thinks that *the function exhaustively defines every organ*, every element of a whole: that the religious function of pardon defines the Church, the function of teaching defines the School, the function of childrearing defines the family, and the function of 'public service'(!) defines the state)[2] is happy to accept these views. The line of demarcation, however, lies here: it appears as soon as it is a question of the state *as such*, not 'public service', which is just one aspect of the state. I mean in class societies, of course, for the state exists only in class societies.

Why insist so heavily on the claim that the major ideological apparatuses are ideological *state* apparatuses? I do so to bring out the organic relation between their class ideological function and the apparatus of class domination known as the state. It is quite as if the class that seizes state power and becomes dominant has to have the use not just of the repressive state apparatuses (the army, the police, the courts), which 'function above all on physical violence', but also of another type of apparatus, *which functions above all* 'on ideology', in other words, on persuasion or inculcation of the dominant class's ideas: on 'consensus'. Involved here is not a whim, the self-indulgence of a dominant class that would like to dominate not just by force, but also by affording itself the luxury of a gratuitous supplement: persuasion, consensus, consent. For no dominant class can ensure that it will endure by force alone. It has to secure the free consent not only of the members of the class that it dominates and exploits, but also of its own members, who do not readily agree to subordinate their private, particular interests to their own class's general interests, and who likewise do not accept the idea that their class has to rule otherwise than by naked force to ensure its domination: precisely by ideology, and the dominated class's consent to the dominant class's ideas. It is not just that this function of ideological domination can be exercised only by the dominant class and the instrument of its domination, the state; it can, further, be exercised only if the dominant class's ideology is constituted *as the truly dominant ideology*, something which calls for state intervention in the ideological struggle. And if it is true that the state thus ensures that this ideology achieves the relative *unity* which makes it not *one* of the ideologies of the dominant class, but *the* ideology of the dominant class, it is clear that the state's role is determinant in everything involving the dominant ideology and its realization in *ideological state apparatuses*.

The foregoing is intended to make it crystal clear that if we do not bring the concept of the state into play, if we do not designate the better part of a class society's ideological apparatuses as so many ideological *state* apparatuses, we forgo the means of understanding how ideology functions in that society, for whose benefit the ideological struggle is played out, in which institutions this ideology is realized and this struggle is incarnated. That is why there is a real theoretical danger in thinning *the concept of ideological state apparatuses* down to the simple form of a simple *concept of ideological apparatuses*.[3]

Let us take a closer look at this.

When a dominant class seizes state power, it finds itself confronting a number of already existing ideological apparatuses that functioned in the service of the old state apparatus and in it. These ideological apparatuses are themselves products of a prior process of unification intended to subject local and regional ideologies to the unity of the dominant class's ideology. But these local and regional ideologies were not originally forged to help to achieve this unification and thus to help to ensure the functioning of the dominant ideology: they are anchored in the practices corresponding to them, whose diversity is, at the limit, irreducible in their materiality. Thus, when capitalism was emerging in the long period of the decay of feudalism, 'local ideologies' such as those of peasants who were still serfs, others who were tenant farmers or independent farmers, and workers who were employed in their homes all coexisted with regional ideologies such as those of the various schismatic sects (not just the Protestants, but also the Albigensian Cathars), the ideologies that accompanied scientific practices or the discoveries of the explorers and so on. Hence there is *diversity in the materiality of the ideologies*, a diversity which it proved impossible to unify completely in the old dominant ideology, and which can also not be wholly reduced within the unity of the new dominant ideology. That is why it seems to me correct to recognize the dialectic of this process of unification in principle, while inscribing our recognition of it in *the open-ended plurality of the ideological state apparatuses*. 'Open-ended', because there is no predicting how the class struggle will evolve: it can breathe new life and vigour into old ideological apparatuses (for example, in our day, the Church in certain countries, such as the USSR), but it can also create new, completely unforeseen ideological apparatuses (the news and information apparatus is undergoing spectacular developments today with the modern mass media).

The most spirited objections elicited by this sketch of a theory of ideology and the ideological state apparatuses have been political and theoretical. This conception has been accused of lapsing into functionalism and, accordingly, of subjecting every individual to the absolute determination of the system of the dominant ideology. Thus I am supposed to have displaced onto ideology the economic determinism that the economistic interpretation of Marxism treats as primary. If the dominant ideology 'interpellates' every individual as a subject, if the ideological apparatuses are *uniformly* brought under the law of a perfectly unified dominant ideology, it obviously follows that an oppositional political party (for instance, the communist party) is just one part in the system, subject to the law of the system and wholly determined by the system. Such a party would accordingly take its place in, and serve, that system – to be very precise, it would be an instrument in the service of the bourgeois class, destined to hold the working class in check and instil an ideology of submission in it, so that it accepts the exploitation to which it is subjected without rebelling. That can happen. The same applies, according to my critics, to the trade unions, school system and so on: all possibility of political action intended to transform the prevailing order, whether in society as a whole or in one or another social sector, is supposedly foreclosed. Thus, at the limit, all political action would be condemned to reformism – in other words, would in fact go to reinforce the system of bourgeois domination – and any and all revolutionary action would be impossible.

To say so, however, is to misunderstand the Marxist theory of class struggle and classes, as well as the Marxist theory of the determination of the superstructure by the infrastructure and the 'reciprocal action' of the superstructure – thus of ideology and the state – on the infrastructure; it is to espouse the bourgeois theory of class struggle. The struggle of the bourgeois classes does indeed constantly *tend* to impose its ideological hegemony on the working class, to bring the latter's fighting organizations under its own domination, and to penetrate them from within by revising Marxist theory. The theory of the ideological state apparatuses accounts, at all events, for this historical fact, this tendency that the bourgeoisie cannot renounce if it wants to maintain its dominant position. It is an undeniable fact, inscribed in the history of the class struggle, that the bourgeoisie always seeks to win back positions it has had to concede in the course of the class struggle. Not only does it hope to turn the clock back, to 'restore' the old order, but – this is subtler and infinitely more serious – it even proves capable of integrating into its own struggle the concessions that it has had to make to the working class.

Everyone knows, for example, the history of the major working-class gains: reduction of the working day, recognition of the right to organize unions, collective agreements and so on. The bourgeoisie has not granted any of these gains of its own free will, but only after long, bloody class struggles waged by the proletariat and its fighting organizations. Every time, the bourgeoisie has managed to conduct an orderly retreat and, to date, has succeeded in integrating such reforms as it has conceded into its system of exploitation. If it was forced to agree to recognize the workers' right to organize labour unions, for instance, it has cleverly managed to integrate the unions thus created into the legal order of its own institutions, in such a way, that is, as to induce some of them to play the part of 'scabs' or strikebreakers. If it was forced to grant certain 'social advantages' (such as child benefits or socialized health care), it has cleverly managed to get the workers to pay for them, either directly (employee contributions) or indirectly (employer contributions or state subsidies which, directly or, through taxation, indirectly, tap the surplus value of production).

The same 'law' manifestly governs political parties. If the proletariat had to wage long, bloody struggles for the right of political association, the bourgeoisie has proven perfectly capable of turning the result to its advantage by winning the great majority of working-class activists organized in social-democratic parties to the reformist cause. The advent of imperialism has by no means altered these practices. Quite the contrary: in the metropolitan countries, it has accelerated and exacerbated them by creating new forms of organization of the labour-process (Taylorism and Fordism) which, on the pretext of letting workers set up their own work schedules or choose their posts in production, has subordinated them still further to bourgeois ideology. It has achieved the same end with the new forms of exploitation imposed on 'Third World' countries, *on the pretext of* 'emancipating' them politically.

Thus a 'tendential law' (Marx) comes into play in the bourgeois class struggle, operating independently of the consciousness of its agents and victims.[4] The result is there for all to see: *the bourgeois class struggle never disarms. When it has to give up ground, it does so in the intention of winning it back*, very often under conditions more favourable than those that prevailed initially.

The Second World War provides one of the most conspicuous illustrations of this law. Imperialist contradictions had plunged the capitalist world into a form of crisis that the older variety of capitalism had never known, a crisis that was not just monetary and economic, but political and military as well. The contradiction between the international capitalist class and the international working class, as well as the exploited 'Third World' countries, was at the root of this crisis too, but it operated, now, on an infinitely expanded scale. The older variety of capitalism had resolved its 'cyclical crises' by destroying surplus commodities (dumping them into the sea) and temporarily suspending hiring of the labour-force (unemployment). I say *'resolved', because the manifestations of this crisis annulled its causes*: once surplus production had been destroyed, it became possible to start producing again on sounder bases and, thanks to the decrease in the employed labour-force, to start hiring again on a more profitable basis.

With imperialism, everything changed. Because financial and productive capital was no longer national, but international, and because there now existed not just a global market for commodities, but also a global market for capital that governed all investments and their movements and alliances throughout the world, the crisis too was globalized and, pitting states bent on conquest against each other, took on a political and military cast. The globalized crisis accordingly took the form of an inter-imperialist war, entailing mass destruction of goods and people. Here too, *the crisis represented the solution of the difficulties that had precipitated it: it was its own antidote.*

Was there overproduction of capital? The war did away with most of this overproduction by destroying factories and productive plant. Was there a surplus workforce? The terrifying innovation of 'total' war, directed against not just combatants, but all of a country's inhabitants, indiscriminately, eliminated existing surplus labour. And capitalist production, that is, capitalist exploitation, could start up again on (for capitalism) sounder bases. It will of course be said that Russia's revolutionary transition to socialism during the first imperialist war narrowed these bases, as did China's and Central Europe's at the end of the second. But imperialism was able to cut its losses; *it reorganized on this narrower basis* under more favourable conditions, since the war had put an end to the immediate causes of the crisis. Moreover, imperialism has not hesitated to try to win back, ideologically, politically or economically, the ground it has been forced to give up. It has even been fairly successful at this, despite some spectacular setbacks (Vietnam), offset by successes elsewhere around the globe (Chile, etc.).

The most extraordinary thing in this whole unconscious process, however, is the way in which imperialism has succeeded in overcoming its own crisis. To understand this, we must obviously consider the crisis on the scale on which it has in fact occurred: a global scale, not that of one or another country taken in isolation. When we do, we observe the following stupefying phenomenon. In 1929, the imperialist world was struck with full force by a crisis that had existed well before then, in overt but limited form, in Germany, Italy and Japan. What political 'solutions' were mobilized to meet this crisis? They were of two kinds: fascist solutions and popular democratic solutions.

The states that had been affected earlier than all the others, Italy, Japan and Germany, the victims of the First World War, responded with fascism, that is, the constitution of violent, authoritarian states that adopted police measures as well as discriminatory nationalist ideologies to justify their acts. On careful consideration, however, it appears that these political measures were simply means of realizing a class politics faced with a highly threatening situation, the politics of an imperialist bourgeoisie that was vigorously combated by the working class and found the force of a riposte in these very well thought-out political measures. Yet the latter were merely the means of, and cover for, a very precise policy of economic exploitation: monopolistic concentration, a close-knit alliance between the state and the monopolies, central direction of the economy (of production and circulation) in the service of the monopolies, and the like. What occurred in this way in the fascist states' economies – some have called it the beginning of 'state monopoly capitalism' – also occurred in the popular democratic states, *but under the domination of counterposed political forms.*

What the imperialist bourgeoisie of the fascist states managed to impose through its own class struggle was imposed by the workers' and popular forces' class struggle in France, Spain and the United States. The Popular Fronts, much like (important differences notwithstanding) Roosevelt's New Deal, thus served as instruments in the most gigantic process of monopolistic concentration in history – unintentionally, of course. Little matter that Roosevelt had founded his popularity on a struggle against the monopolies:

he had to if he was to succeed in getting them to accept the 'expansion of the state' required to institute social services (Social Security and unemployment assistance, measures that ultimately fostered concentration, even when it took the form of state-capitalist concentration). Establishing social services was, in its turn, crucial to the 'democratic' solution of the very serious 1929 crisis, so that the American economy, stimulated by entry into the war against Japan, could be relaunched on 'sounder' bases. In the long run, the 'social' measures adopted by the Popular Front governments in France and Spain had, after the defeat of those governments, the same effects.

Shortly after the bourgeoisie had taken the step back represented by this necessary retreat, it was able to go on a counter-offensive that was crowned with extraordinarily swift success. Evidently, it could not call a halt in the same way to the imperialist states' life-and-death struggle to divide up the world: war was inevitable. Yet war too played its part in resolving the crisis by destroying capital and labour-power throughout the world. To be sure, the imperialist bourgeoisie had lost still more ground by the time this bloody adventure was over; but, *within the borders* that it had managed to defend, it got bravely back on its feet and set out to win back the part of the world that it had temporarily lost.

I offer this summary of the mainsprings of an essentially economic and political, but also ideological, crisis in order to show the proportions that the capacity of the imperialist system and its state apparatuses to 'co-opt' working-class victories and make them serve its own ends can assume, once the moment in which they hold out the promise of a revolutionary future has passed. What was gained in the ideological domain (the working class's new freedoms and, later, the values of popular struggle in the Résistance) was subsequently 'integrated' by the bourgeoisie's ideological class struggle in the workers' own ranks. Involved here is an irresistible *tendency* of the dominant class's ideological struggle to bring, as far as possible, all existing elements of ideology, the advanced forms of the dominated classes' ideology included, under the dominant ideology's law – and this through not an external operation, but a transformation that operates inside elements of the adverse ideology. Such an operation is obviously unthinkable without the existence and intervention of the institutions known as the ideological state apparatuses.

It is precisely to the extent that the ideological state apparatuses and the dominant ideology that they purvey *are a function and a means of the dominant class's struggle that they escape a functionalist conception*. For the class struggle does not come to a halt at the frontier of the state apparatuses or the ideological state apparatuses. The dominant class's class struggle is not waged in a vacuum. The dominant class struggles against real adversaries: the old dominant class on the one hand and the new exploited class on the other. In its strategy and tactics, it has to take these adversaries' existence, the positions they occupy and their ideological arms into account. Doubtless, it gets the better of its adversary by violent means, defeating the old dominant class by taking state power and defeating the exploited class through the violence of exploitation and the violence of state power. It would not, however, be able to exercise its power on a long-term basis if it did not also exercise an ideological 'hegemony' (leadership) over its adversary that secured, on the whole, the latter's consent to the established order. It must, then, both seize control of the old ideological state apparatuses and construct new ones while taking account of the reality of this ideological balance of power and also, to some extent, respecting its adversary's ideas in order to turn them to its own advantage. In short, it has to wage a lucid class struggle if it is to succeed in establishing its ideological hegemony through the transformation of the old ideological state apparatuses and the construction of new ones.

This struggle is not settled by fiat; nor, a fortiori, is it settled automatically. It took the bourgeoisie centuries to win its struggle. However paradoxical it may seem, and although it contradicts an idea apparently dear to Gramsci, we can say that some national bourgeoisies, such as the Italian bourgeoisie, never have managed to win their struggle and doubtless never will. This is one more argument for the thesis I am defending. For if there can be little uncertainty when it comes to defining the repressive state apparatus or determining in whose hands it is, things can be much less clear where the ideological state apparatuses are concerned. What prevails in this domain is, doubtless, the tendency towards unification of the dominant ideology. This tendency can, however, be 'countervailed' (Marx) by the effects of proletarian class struggle.

For these reasons, I contend that the Marxist theory of ideological state apparatuses is free of functionalism of any kind (and of any kind of structuralism as well, since structuralism defines the places of institutions exercising set functions not subject to the effects of the class struggle). This theory is simply the theory of the class struggle in the domain of ideology, of the conditions of existence and the forms of this struggle, to which the places and functions of the elements are subordinated. Very concretely, this means not just that the state apparatuses themselves are one stake of class struggle among others, as the whole history of the constitution of a class as the dominant and then the hegemonic class shows, but also that class struggle goes on *in* the ideological state apparatuses as well (consider May 1968), where, depending on the conjuncture, it can play a non-negligible role. It is easy to understand that this struggle can become extremely intense if we think, for example, of the struggle that pits working-class parties against bourgeois parties in the political ideological state apparatus. This is doubtless only an electoral and parliamentary struggle, yet it has repercussions well beyond elections and purely parliamentary debates.

Since I have mentioned this form of struggle, I should go into greater detail about it. For it will be objected that it is a political, not an ideological struggle. It will be objected that political parties are part of *the political apparatus*, not of an ideological state apparatus. That is not correct. Or again, carrying things to extremes, my critics will object that every political party is (in my view) an ideological state apparatus and is for this reason integrated, as such, into the dominant class's system of domination. That is not correct, either.

To grasp these nuances, which are important, we have to attend carefully to the distinction between a (repressive) state apparatus and ideological state apparatuses. The repressive state apparatus, which is unified and sharply delimited,[5] includes the chief of state; the government and its administration, an instrument of the executive; the armed forces; the police; and the judiciary and all its agencies (courts, prisons and so on). Let us note, in particular, that the president of the republic (who represents the unity and will of the dominant class), the government that he leads and the administration are all part of *the state apparatus*: the part that directs the state and state policy. Let us further note that the administration too is part of the repressive state apparatus, despite its claims to be 'serving the general interest' and playing the role of a 'public service'. Charged with applying the bourgeois government's policies in detail, it is also charged with overseeing them, and therefore with sanctioning them, and therefore with repressing those who fail to respect them. While it performs functions that may seem to be in the interest of all the individuals in the same social formation (education, the means of communication, the post and telegraph office, the highway department and so on), experience shows that class interests generally dominate these apparently 'neutral' activities, since, to give only three examples, civil engineering usually redounds to the benefit of the trusts, education is subordinated to the requirements of the material and ideological reproduction of the labour-force, and the mass media are in the hands of the dominant class's ideological class struggle. All this amidst multiple contradictions.

That said, let us return to the *government*. Although it is (more or less) 'responsible' before a National Assembly and a Senate elected, in France, by universal suffrage, the government is part of the repressive state apparatus. Its members (and all the civil servants answerable to it) make up what we shall call *the political state apparatus*, an integral part of the repressive state apparatus.

We shall, in contrast, call the 'political system' the political ideological state apparatus; this political system can also be called the 'political constitution' of a given social formation, in view of the fact that it can vary under one and the same class's domination. Thus the bourgeoisie has successively exercised its class dictatorship under the democratic republic with a limited franchise based on tax qualifications; the Empire; the monarchy based on the Charter; the constitutional monarchy; the Republic; Caesarism; the parliamentary republic; and, currently, after passing through a fascist regime during the Occupation, the presidential republic.

The political ideological state apparatus may accordingly be defined by the way the 'popular will' is represented (or not). The government is supposedly responsible before the representatives of this 'popular will'. It is, however, well known that the government has ample means for eluding this 'responsibility', just as the bourgeois state has untold resources for distorting the workings of universal suffrage, when it consents to establish it (census enfranchisement, disenfranchisement of women and young people, indirect elections, a bicameral system, the 'separation of powers', rigged elections and so on). What ultimately justifies treating the 'political system' as an '*ideological state apparatus*' is the fiction, corresponding to a certain reality, that the component parts of this system as well as the principle of its functioning *are based on the free choice of the people's representatives by the people, as a function of the 'ideas' that each individual has about the politics that the state should put into practice.*

It is on the basis of this fiction (for state policy is ultimately determined by the dominant class's interests in its class struggle) that 'political parties' are founded; they are supposed to represent the major opposed alternatives of national politics. Each individual can then 'freely' express his opinion by voting for the political party of his choice (assuming it has not been condemned to operate illegally). Let us note that there is a degree of reality to *political parties*. In a rough way, they represent the interests of antagonistic social classes in the class struggle, or those of social strata seeking to promote their special interests amidst class conflicts. It is by fraying a path through this reality that the fundamental class antagonism ultimately emerges into the light, more or less, notwithstanding the obstacles thrown up by electoral trickery.

If this analysis is correct, it follows, at all events, that no one can affirm, on any grounds whatsoever – as some have tried to make me say, in order to lock me into a 'theory' that would rule out all possibility of class struggle – *that all political parties, the parties of the working class included, are ideological state apparatuses*, integrated into the bourgeois 'system' and therefore incapable of waging their class struggle. If what I have just said is on the mark, we can clearly see that the existence of political parties, far from negating the class struggle, is wholly based on it. And if the bourgeois class constantly strives to exercise its ideological and political hegemony over the parties of the working class, that too is a form of class struggle; the bourgeoisie succeeds in doing so only to the extent that the working-class parties fall into the trap, either because their leaders are intimidated (the 1914–18 *Union Sacrée*) or simply 'bought off', or because the base of the working-class parties is diverted from its revolutionary task by material advantages (the worker aristocracy), or, again, because it succumbs to the influence of bourgeois ideology (revisionism).

All this appears even more clearly when we consider the revolutionary workers' parties – for example, communist parties. Since they are organizations of working-class struggle, the interests of the bourgeois class and its political system are obviously utterly foreign to them. Their ideology (on the basis of which they recruit) is inimical to bourgeois ideology. Their organizational form (democratic centralism) has nothing to do with the organizational forms of the bourgeois parties or even the social-democratic and socialist parties. Their objective is not to confine their activity to the class struggle in Parliament, but to extend it to cover the ensemble of workers' activities, from economic class struggle to political and ideological class struggle. Their ultimate vocation is not to 'participate in government', but to overturn and destroy bourgeois state power.

We must insist on this point, since most Western European Communist Parties today declare themselves to be 'parties of government'. Even if a communist party does happen to participate in a government (and it can be correct to do so in certain circumstances), *it cannot, on any grounds, be defined as a 'party of bourgeois government'*, nor even of a government under the dictatorship of the proletariat.

This point is crucial, for a communist party has no business entering the government of a bourgeois state (even if this government is a 'left' government of popular unity intent on carrying out democratic reforms) in order to 'administer' the affairs of a bourgeois state. But it also has no business entering a government of the dictatorship of the proletariat in the belief that its ultimate vocation is to *'administer' the affairs of this state, whose destruction it should be preparing.* For if it devotes all its forces to such administration, it will be unable to help to destroy the state. A communist party can consequently not conduct itself on any grounds whatsoever as a 'party of government', for to be a party of government is to be a 'party of the state', something that comes down either to serving the bourgeois state or helping to perpetuate the state of the dictatorship of the proletariat – when a communist party's mission is to help to destroy it.

In the last instance, it is the type of political practice characteristic of a communist party which makes this incompatibility intelligible. For a communist party has a 'political practice' altogether different from that of a bourgeois party (Balibar). A bourgeois party can call on the support and resources of the established bourgeoisie, its economic domination, its exploitation, its state apparatus, its ideological state apparatuses and so on. It does not, in order to exist, have to make a priority of uniting the masses that it wants to rally to its ideas: the social order itself sees to this task of persuasion, propaganda and recruitment. Most of the time, a bourgeois party need only properly organize its electoral campaign in order to reap the benefits of this domination, converted into self-interested convictions. That, moreover, is why a bourgeois party does not need a scientific doctrine in order to exist: it need only cultivate the essential themes of the dominant ideology to rally 'partisans' convinced in advance.

In contrast, a revolutionary workers' party has nothing to offer its members: neither prebends nor material advantages. It presents itself for what it is: an organization of the workers' class struggle whose sole strengths are a scientific doctrine and the free will of its members, in agreement on the basis of the party statutes. It organizes its members in the forms of democratic centralism with a view to waging the class struggle in all its forms: economic, political and ideological. It defines its line and political practices not on the basis of the simple revolt of exploited workers, but on that of its scientific theory and concrete analyses of the concrete situation – in other words, of the balance of power in the current class struggle. Hence it takes the broadest possible account of the forms and the force of the dominant class struggle, that of the dominant class. It is on the basis of this 'line' that it may deem it useful and 'correct', at a given moment, to enter a left government that does not challenge the existence of the bourgeois state – for the purpose, however, of conducting its own class struggle in that government, with its own objectives. At all events, it always subordinates the immediate interests and practices of the workers' organization to the working class's future interests. It subordinates its tactics to the strategy of communism – that is, the strategy of establishing a classless society.

Under these conditions, communists are right to talk about their party as a 'party of a new kind', completely different from the bourgeois parties, and to talk about themselves as 'militants of a new kind', completely different from bourgeois politicians. Their political practice – illegal or legal, extra-parliamentary or parliamentary – has nothing to do with bourgeois political practice.

It will doubtless be said that the communist party too constitutes itself the same way bourgeois parties do, on the basis of an ideology, which, moreover, the party itself calls proletarian ideology. That is true. In the communist party as well, ideology plays the role of 'cement' (Gramsci) for a particular social group. In the communist party as well, this ideology 'interpellates individuals as subjects' and is the motor of their subjective and objective action. But what is known as proletarian ideology is not the purely spontaneous ideology of the proletariat. For in order to exist as a class conscious of its unity, and as an active class, the proletariat needs not just experience (that of the class struggles it has been waging for more than a century), but also objective knowledge, with which Marxist theory provides it. It is on the twofold basis of these experiences as clarified by Marxist theory that proletarian ideology is constituted: as a mass ideology capable of unifying and 'cementing' the unity of the working-class avant-garde in its class-struggle organizations. It is therefore a very special kind of ideology: *ideology by its form*, because, at the level of the masses, it functions the way any ideology does (by 'interpellating' individuals as subjects), but *scientific theory by its content* (because it is developed on the basis of a scientific theory of class struggle).

An ideology, to be sure, but not just any ideology. For every class recognizes itself in a particular, by no means arbitrarily chosen ideology, the one that is capable of unifying it and guiding its class struggle. Everyone knows that the feudal class, for example, recognized itself in *religious ideology*, or Christianity, and that the bourgeois class, similarly, recognized itself in *legal ideology*, at least in the period of its unquestioned domination. The working class, for its part, recognizes itself – even if it is receptive to elements of religious and moral ideology – above all in *political ideology*: not in bourgeois political ideology, but in proletarian political ideology, that of the class struggle for the abolition of classes and the construction of communism. It is precisely this ideology which constitutes proletarian ideology: a spontaneous ideology in its earliest forms (utopian socialism) and, later, after the fusion of the Workers' Movement with Marxist theory, an informed ideology.

As one can well imagine, such an ideology did not result from a *teaching* that 'intellectuals' (Marx and Engels) dispensed to the Workers' Movement, and that the Workers' Movement adopted for some mysterious reason. Nor was it, as Kautsky claimed, 'introduced into the Workers' Movement from without', for Marx and Engels would not have been able to conceive of their theory if they had not developed it on class theoretical positions, a consequence of the fact that they belonged, in a concrete sense, to the workers' movement of their day. This ideology, a product of the fusion of the Workers' Movement and Marxist theory, was, in reality, the result of a very long class struggle, with many rough ups and downs. It continues today, despite dramatic divisions commanded by imperialism's class struggle.

This reality raises the question of ideology and ideological practice again. Not, this time, the question of its mechanism, which has now been elucidated, in the main, but that of its 'illusion'. For we have just seen, from the example of proletarian ideology, that an ideology can be ideological in form alone, while being scientific in content. How could that be if an ideology were pure and simple error or even illusion? The fact is that no ideology in the world, not even religion, is purely arbitrary. It is always the index of real questions or problems, albeit invested in a form of miscognition and, therefore, necessarily illusory. It is this double character of ideology that I was trying to bring out when I said that ideology was *knowledge* in the form of *miscognition*, and an *allusion* to reality in the form of an *illusion*.[6]

Do not misunderstand me: I say an illusion, not simply an error. For someone who is mistaken is mistaken, full stop: the day he discovers his error, he acknowledges it and abandons it in order to adopt the truth. But illusions are naturally stubborn, as the saying goes: they persevere and, in a certain sense, could not care less about the truth. The reason is that something in an illusion has an 'interest' in lasting or making the illusion last. There is a cause at work in an illusion which it cannot know (which it necessarily miscognizes) and which has an interest in this persistence in error. Since this cause cannot be in the 'object', since it is in the subject, yet also exceeds the subject, it is plainly social, and the enduring 'interests' it serves are those of certain social 'causes' or 'values'. The reason for the double character of ideology must be sought at their level.

Let us therefore suppose that it is vital for the reigning social order that all members of society, whether they dominate it or are dominated and exploited, freely accept certain 'self-evident truths', such as the existence of God, a transcendent morality, the existence of moral and political freedom and so on – or completely different myths, simpler or more complicated. Once we make this assumption, we see a system of representations materialize, of which no one is the author in the proper sense. It will be simultaneously 'true', to the extent that it takes the realities of people's experience into account, and 'false', to the extent that it imposes 'its' truth on those truths[7] so as to confer their 'true' meaning upon them and confine them to it, forbidding them to leave it in order to go and see from a bit closer up whether this lovely little story is true. There you have ideology: cognition-miscognition, allusion-illusion, a system with no possible outside to which it might be compared, a system which is nothing but 'outside', because it encompasses everything that exists in the world and pronounces the truth about everything in advance of the slightest experience.

Undoubtedly, ideologies are not the only things that answer to this odd definition. Idealist philosophies are also of this type: they do not admit of an outside, and even if, as a rule, they acknowledge the outside world's existence, they wholly absorb it and possess, in advance, the truth of all things, past, present and future. Thus they are nothing but pure 'outside'. And it is not just idealist philosophies that work this way. Even sciences can lapse into ideology, despite the 'break' distinguishing them from it. Marxism itself, in the Stalinist period, also worked this way, in a closed circuit [*en vase clos*] with no outside. That is to say, it reigned over everything outside it without exception, since it was itself sheer, implacable 'outside'.

If ideology presents itself in this fashion, in a double form, cognition but also miscognition, we can readily see that it is not cut off in advance, radically, from all possibility of knowledge, hence from scientific knowledge. History in fact constantly offers us examples of sciences that emerge from the ideology underpinning them as the result of a 'break' – as the result not of a straightforward 'inversion', as Marx and Engels rather too hastily affirmed, but of highly complex conjunctions in which material practices intervene under the domination of the 'relations of theoretical production' that are elements of ideology and philosophy.

Thus ideology occupies a key position in the ensemble of practices and their abstractions:

1 There is no practice except under the domination of an ideology.

2 There are local and regional ideologies.

3 Ideology is tendentially unified as a dominant ideology as a result [*sous l'effet*] of the dominant class's struggle to constitute itself as a ruling, hegemonic class.

4 The dominant ideology tends to integrate into its own system elements of the dominated ideology, which thus finds itself absorbed by the dominant ideology.

5 Ideology operates by interpellating individuals as subjects.

6 Ideology is double: cognition-miscognition, allusion-illusion.

7 Ideology has no outside and is nothing but outside.

8 Ideology commands philosophy from without, in the forms of its struggle.

9 Ideology is among the theoretical relations of production constitutive of all science.

10 A science can be 'practised' as an ideology and pulled down to its level.

11 Proletarian ideology is a special ideology resulting from the fusion of the proletariat's spontaneous ideology with the Marxist theory of class struggle.

We may conclude from the foregoing that there is no class struggle, in other words, no political practice, that does not find itself under the domination of an ideology. That brings us to the question of political practice.

13 POLITICAL PRACTICE

Marx himself said that the essence of political practice was class struggle, but that he had not discovered the classes and their struggle; bourgeois economists and historians had (from Machiavelli to the early nineteenth-century economists and historians).[1]

This remark, which Marx made just once, in 1852, is not insignificant, for it is contained in the same letter in which he points out that his own contribution was to have 'demonstrated the necessity of the dictatorship of the proletariat'.[2] It is also noteworthy because it indicates, *pace* certain Marxists who are far-leftists in theory [*gauchistes en théorie*], that the bourgeoisie knew perfectly well what politics, classes and class struggle were. The bourgeoisie was nevertheless mistaken in that it thought that the forms of political practice (hence of class struggle) were always and everywhere the same (give or take a few circumstances) and thus 'eternal'. In contrast, Marx underscores, in the same letter, the historical dependency of these forms on the existing modes of production.

These seemingly very minor details distinguish the Marxist from the classic bourgeois theory of class struggle. For bourgeois theorists have never managed to discover the 'base' in which class struggle is rooted: the relation of production, class exploitation, in other words, the class struggle in production or 'economic class struggle', which varies with the mode of production. To put it schematically, the classic bourgeois theory of class struggle considers it to be the result of a conflictual encounter between pre-existent classes.

The earliest classical figure of this encounter is war or invasion. That is how feudal and bourgeois theorists pictured the matter in the seventeenth and eighteenth centuries: 'barbarians' had invaded the territory of the former Roman Empire and enslaved its inhabitants, whom they made serfs. The result of this victorious invasion was that the barbarian class dominated the native class, previously dominated by the Romans. This was the origin of feudalism, that 'Gothic regime' (Montesquieu) which had initially reigned in Germania's forests, where the king had been but 'a peer among his peers' in a sort of warrior democracy. The same theorists denounced the bad habits of the degenerate kings who later allied themselves with the 'commoners' [*roturiers*] in order to impose their law on those who had once been their peers.

The theorists of the bourgeoisie retorted that these kings had simply brought the Roman Empire's constitutional law [*droit politique*] back into force in order to gain the upper hand over the turbulent nobles who, with their incessant wars, had been doing serious wrong to the people going about its business. On this interpretation as well, there were two opposing classes: the king and the commoners on the one hand, who governed and produced, and, on the other, an exploitative nobility living off the spoils of a war, the brunt of which was borne by the people alone. In both interpretations, however, a purely *external encounter* was at the origin of these political relations, hence of these conflicts: the encounter of a military invasion.[3]

Machiavelli, the most profound of the bourgeois political theorists and Marx's direct ancestor, went further. He had understood that the political relation was not the product of an accident or an encounter, but was necessarily antagonistic; that conflict was primary; and that domination and servitude governed all political forms and practices. From this, he drew conclusions of crucial importance for political practice: that one has to rely on the people's support to hold the high and mighty in check and so on. Machiavelli did not see, however, or did not clearly say, that this political antagonism was rooted in an antagonism based on exploitation *in production itself*.

To grasp the nature of the bourgeoisie's political practice, it would have been necessary to go on to pose the question of its implantation in the capitalist mode of production. In Machiavelli's day, this mode of production had not been sufficiently consolidated for matters to appear clearly.

What is a *mode of production*? It is a certain way of producing, that is, of coming to grips with nature in order to draw from it the products that people in a social formation need to subsist. This relation to nature, a material and technical relation, brings determinate social relations into play in every mode of production: not just forms of cooperation in the labour-process, forms of the organization and division of labour, but, above all, *relations of possession or non-possession that social groups defined by these relations maintain with the material means of production.* Thus it is the unity of the productive forces (means of production plus labour-power) and the relations of production, under the domination of the relations of production, which defines a mode of production.[4]

It should not, however, be supposed that a mode of production falls from the sky to take hold of people in a given region of the world at a random moment under random circumstances. Nor should it be supposed that a given mode of production engenders within itself, automatically and in definitive form, the mode of production that will succeed it. Nor should it be supposed, certain hasty formulations in Marx's Preface to his 1859 *Contribution* notwithstanding, that the relations of production adapt to the development of the mode of production and that every mode of production is accordingly defined by the degree of development of its productive forces or the degree of adaptation of its relations of production.[5] In these different interpretations, we have to do with a mechanical determinism and a linear dialectic. In reality, things are more complicated. No destiny compels a given mode of production automatically to engender the next mode of production.

Let us take the case of the capitalist mode of production. Everyone knows how wittily Marx ridiculed the capitalist 'theory' of capitalism's origins. For capitalist ideologues, it was none other than the small independent producer who brought capitalism into the world by *abstaining* from immediately consuming the products of his labour! At the origin, the story goes, there was a multitude of small independent producers, who produced enough to feed themselves and their wives and children. Then, one day, one of them started producing more than he needed, and so had a *surplus* on hand, which he used to hire a pauper's labour-power. At exactly the same moment, it occurred to him that he could also *exchange* part of his surplus with other small independent producers and, by convention, assign the units thus exchanged a fixed value in metallic *currency*.

Trade in products and labour-power sprang up as a result. Naturally, employers employed wage-workers out of the goodness of their hearts, to save them from starvation! But employers did not give wage-workers the whole product of their labour: they gave them just enough to feed themselves and their families. *The upshot was the exploitation of labour.* And our small independent producer, now an employer with wage-workers in his employ or a merchant selling the accumulated surplus of his production, watched as his stock of metallic currency grew, and thus became the first capitalist – in sum, by virtue of abstinence, perseverance and generosity! This was, for capitalism's ideologues, the best way of demonstrating: (1) that capitalism, since it was part of the natural order, had always existed; (2) that capitalism, since it was part of the natural order, would always exist; and (3) that it was unnatural to undermine the capitalist order.

Marx showed, documents in hand, that this was not at all how things had happened.[6] He demonstrated that capitalism, as a mode of production, had sprung from a *historic 'encounter'* – which, although it had been necessary [*pour avoir été nécessaire*], had nothing inevitable about it – between (1) *'owners of money'* who had accumulated funds using pre-capitalist methods (usury, unequal exchange or illicit commerce, theft, pillage, appropriation of 'communal land', confiscation of small producers' assets and so on); (2) *'free workers'*, that is, workers who enjoyed freedom of movement and could dispose of themselves freely, but who had been violently dispossessed of their means of labour (land, tools); and (3) important *scientific and technical discoveries* that revolutionized the work process (the compass, optical apparatuses, the steam engine, the spinning jenny and so on).

One usually says, in a schematic overview, that the capitalist mode of production was produced by the feudal mode of production and at the heart of it, since the feudal mode of production contained its 'seeds'. This is, basically, how the idealist philosopher Hegel reasoned, mobilizing a distinction between the 'in-itself' (the seed) and the 'for-itself' (the developed seed). Of course, the capitalist mode of production could only emerge (at least in this period) from within the feudal mode of production. Yet it emerged from it in a strange way that has not always been perceived, perhaps not even by Marx. For the *'owners of money'*, the ancestors of the bourgeois, who were already bourgeois or on the way to becoming bourgeois by virtue of their functions, including their political role in the state of the absolute monarchies, *these bourgeois were not at all bourgeois by virtue of their social origins or even their social position*. A good many were aristocrats who had gone into commerce or banking (think of Germany and the Netherlands). A good many, and this is the most surprising thing, were landed aristocrats, big landowners who, for one reason or another (in Scotland, for example, because they wanted vast hunting grounds!), helped themselves to the small producers' fields, throwing their former owners into the street, or devoted themselves to working the mines on their holdings, or took advantage of the hydraulic energy of the rivers and streams running through them to lay the foundations of metallurgy (as happened in France). Thus these feudal lords participated, *for their own reasons*, reasons that, however, *encountered* the reasons of the bourgeoisie properly speaking, in the 'emancipation', that is, the expropriation of the workers required to constitute capitalist production.

Thus we can legitimately defend the idea[7] that *the capitalist mode of production met up with* [*s'est rencontré avec*] *the bourgeoisie* (and with feudal lords who had become bourgeois), or, more precisely, that it was born at the 'encounter' of these independent processes, which affected, conjointly and simultaneously, *feudal lords* who had enriched themselves or landed proprietors eager to consolidate and exploit their holdings; *bourgeois* whose wealth stemmed from international trade (thus 'owners of money' all); and, finally, *workers* who had been *'freed'* by being dispossessed.

When we look at things this way, we see, to be sure, that the capitalist mode of production was born at the heart of the feudal mode of production, *but as the result of a combination of relatively autonomous processes* that might not have encountered each other, or might have encountered each other under conditions that would not have allowed the capitalist[8] mode of production to appear. The proof is that it is highly likely [*on a toutes chances de penser*] that *the capitalist mode of production was born and died several times in history* before becoming viable: for example, in the Italian cities of the Po River valley late in the fourteenth century, where surprising conditions came together: mechanized big industry (thanks to hydraulic energy), a waged workforce and even parcellized labour. In the framework provided by this conception, we can begin to think the singular social and political role, which continues to intrigue historians, of a bourgeoisie that, paradoxically, was well and truly part of the feudal mode of production, even as it anticipated – here too, thanks to its participation in the state of the absolute monarchy – the advent of the capitalist mode of production.[9]

This bourgeoisie anticipated this advent to the extent that it was, like the pre-capitalist aristocracy, *an exploiting class* extorting surplus value from wage-workers in manufacture, the mines and the ports. We may say that this condition of exploitation marks *the bourgeoisie's political practice* from its beginnings and for all time. There are two reasons for this. First, in its political practice, the bourgeoisie had necessarily to take into account, if only to protect itself against revolts, the exploitation to which it subjected wage-workers. Second, the new, ascendant bourgeoisie was too weak to seize state power by itself and had the greatest possible interest in deflecting the anger of those it exploited towards the feudal state, hence *in concluding an alliance with the very workers it exploited against the feudal lords' dictatorship.* And since the bourgeoisie's class struggle against the aristocracy did not end when it seized state power, but was pursued long afterwards against the reactions of the same adversary, who had not disarmed; since the bourgeoisie long continued to need, in order to get the better of this adversary, an alliance with those it exploited; and since, once this adversary had been defeated, the bourgeoisie persevered in the same practice, this time by dividing the working class in order to ally itself with the segment of it that it had succeeded in winning over, it is easy to understand why the bourgeoisie's political practice was necessarily marked by these very special conditions.

We may therefore say that it has always been, and still is, the characteristic feature of the bourgeoisie's political practice (radically different in this respect from the feudal aristocracy's or the proletariat's) *to act through intermediaries,* very precisely, *by way of the action of the class, or a segment of the class, that it exploits and dominates.* Thus the lower classes in the countryside and the cities furnished the bulk of the rank-and-file forces of the 1789 revolution in France, just as the working class's intervention determined the success of the 1830 and 1848 revolutions there and in the rest of Europe. Every time, after attaining its class objectives, the bourgeoisie put the 'troops' from the lower classes who had fought alongside it back in their place, by fire and the sword when necessary. When the threat became too acute, in June 1848 and again in 1871 under the Commune, the bourgeoisie resorted to the drastic measure of military massacre. Since then, it has not ceased to create allies for itself through the division – which it perpetuates – of the working class.

To see to it that one's own class objectives are achieved, in the main, *by those one exploits* is to succeed in dominating the exploited politically and, at the same time, in subjugating them ideologically from on high: by means of the state. The bourgeoisie's power is thus *state power* par excellence, and its own political practice is therefore the practice of its own class state. That is why it has been at such pains to 'perfect' its state, fit it out with all the requisite apparatuses, be they repressive or ideological, and unify its own ideology as the dominant ideology by all available means. We can sum up the political practice characteristic of the bourgeoisie by saying that it consists of getting maximum use out of the forces of the popular masses it dominates, by dominating them through state repression and the state ideology.

The political ideological state apparatus ranks among the most important of the ideological weapons that the bourgeoisie afforded itself: above all, the parliamentary representative system (when there was one), which brought off the feat of 'freely' subordinating to the bourgeoisie the will of those whom the bourgeoisie exploited. It did so by means of the electoral mechanism, in which everyone is supposed to express his individual will and the 'general will' is supposed to result from a tally of the ballots. Is there any need to show how effective this state system of political and ideological domination proved to be when the big imperialist wars broke out? The people of countryside and city marched off to war, without rebelling, in the belief that they would be fighting 'for the fatherland', when they were in fact marching off to 'die for the industrialists' (Anatole France). They were put back in their place, whenever a rebellion did threaten, with measures of the utmost violence (the 1917 mutinies on the front, which Pétain drowned in blood).

When, at the very beginning of the rise of the bourgeoisie, Machiavelli described its practice, he imagined a prince who could stand up to the feudal class. But, if this prince was to fulfil his appointed role, he would have to rely on the support of the mass of the bourgeois; if his state was to endure, he would have to 'become a multitude', thus securing the people's confidence in his grand design. Machiavelli's Prince already was this man, a symbol of the bourgeoisie, who would ally himself with the bourgeois and those they exploited to construct a state that would dominate them with its armed might and its ideology. Just as the bourgeoisie does not work, but makes others work – that is why it dominates those it exploits – so *it does not act for itself, but makes others act: the others whom it exploits*. An admirable political practice, which, from exploitation and domination, derives the means to secure its own power.

It has not been said emphatically enough that *proletarian political practice is, or should be, utterly different*: 'a new practice of politics' (Balibar).[10] How could it be otherwise? To survive, the proletariat has only the strength of its own hands. To fight, it has only its ideas and its reasoning power. It is by definition unarmed, and constantly faced with the threat of the arms of the bourgeoisie's troops. When it wants arms, it has to conquer them with its bare hands, at the risk of its life. But it is much harder for it to conquer its ideas.

For the proletariat lives under the domination of the dominant class's ideas, a domination that is both direct (the Church, the state) and indirect (the school system, the political system, etc.). When it wishes to gain a degree of independence in its revolt, it can begin only by making use of the ideas to which it is subjected: for example, religious ideas, as in the Peasant Wars under Luther[11] in Germany; moral or legal ideas, as in the earliest forms of socialism; bourgeois political ideas (liberty, equality) and so on. Since all the revolts staged under the banner of these ideas were defeated, they were followed by a period of protracted effort, amidst trials and reflection; the people were looking for other ideas that would allow them to take the bourgeoisie at its word. Eventually, they realized that such ideas were misleading, that these ideas were meant to mislead them, and they went to work looking *for ideas of their own, ideas specific to them* and capable of freeing them from ideological servitude to their class adversary. They finally 'found' these ideas in the work of intellectuals, full-fledged members of the militant Workers' Movement of the day, first in Owen, then in Proudhon and Bakunin and, finally, in Marx and Engels: in *Marxist theory*. A long combat, a long experience, which was not without its setbacks. Here too, nothing was inevitable; but without this *encounter* (comparable, due allowance made, to the 'encounter' between the bourgeoisie and the capitalist mode of production), the 'fusion' or 'union' of the Workers' Movement and Marxist theory would not have taken place. That it is an always precarious union proves, even today, the relatively contingent character of this 'encounter'. At the same time, however, the fact that its effects have lasted is proof of the rightness of this 'encounter' [*prouve la raison de cette 'rencontre'*].[12]

Unlike the bourgeoisie's political ideas, which are divorced from its practice, since they are above all *ideas for others*, the proletariat's ideas, since they were born of *struggle*, could not but be translated into acts (lest they perish), and from acts into organizations of struggle: organizations of economic struggle to begin with, the predecessors of the *labour unions*, which had been formed even before the 'fusion' and, later, *political parties*. Again, unlike the bourgeoisie's political practices, the practices of the organized proletariat were always direct practices, without intermediaries. If the proletarians unite, the reason is that they know that they 'can count only on their own strength'.[13] They are the ones who stage strikes to defend their living and working conditions. They are the ones who stage insurrections to take state power. Thanks to long, harsh experience, *putschism*, in which a specialist organizes a smash-and-grab operation, remains foreign to the proletariat's political practices, as does *spontaneism*, the dream that a general strike will put power in the people's hands without a political battle. Contrary to bourgeois political organizations, dominated by a caste of politicians or technocrats, proletarian political organizations tend towards the greatest possible democracy of discussion, decision and action, even if this tradition too can be lost. On the basis of this extensive mass political experience, a new ideology arises and gradually gains strength, an ideology in which history is no longer made by individuals or ideas, but by the self-organized masses.[14]

Obviously, proletarian political practice is also distinguished from bourgeois political practice by its *perspectives*: not its *subjective* perspectives (the bourgeoisie wants to perpetuate exploitation, while the proletariat wants political and social revolution), but its *objective* perspectives. For the bourgeoisie, albeit aware of the forms of its own practice, *does not have a scientific theory of the laws of class struggle and does not want to acknowledge the existing theory of them*. It continues to preserve something of the myths about the nature of class struggle that we have examined. In its estimation, there is no reason that its domination should disappear and that classes and their struggle should disappear along with it. In its estimation, the exploitative order that it imposes on wage-workers is natural and normal: there have to be bosses, lest people stray into misadventure and stumble from misfortune to misfortune. To maintain its domination, the bourgeoisie need only hold them at a respectful distance, by force or with clever promises. It does not for a moment suspect that it is the representative of a transitory order; or, if it suspects it (and, increasingly, it does), it is only to defend its order with redoubled force. At all events, it does not care to know the objective reason for the threat haunting it.

Thanks to Marxist theory, the proletariat knows that class struggle makes history. Thanks to Marxist theory, it knows that what purports to be Political Economy is merely a theoretical formation of bourgeois ideology, intended, together with the reigning forms of psychology and sociology, to mystify the exploited and 'adapt' them to their exploited condition. Thanks to Marxist theory, it knows that the bourgeoisie will surmount the crises of imperialism, its 'global' crises included, unless the masses invade the stage of history and overthrow the bourgeois order. Thanks again to Marxist theory, it knows that the whole order of a class society hinges on the dominant class's dictatorship and, consequently, that bourgeois dictatorship must be overthrown by the dictatorship of the proletariat in order to alter the course of history and clear a path for communism, of which socialism is merely the 'lower stage' (Marx).[15] This knowledge of the necessary laws of history, far from condemning the proletariat to political passivity, provides it, rather, with the means of intervening in history through its organizations and alliances. The proletariat knows that these perspectives are not utopian, for communism is not a dream, but a necessity, a tendency, inscribed in the history of the present. Yes, communism already exists in our midst and has for a long time now, not just in embryo, but in actual fact: for example, in communist organizations and other communities (even religious communities) or activities – on one absolute condition: *that no commodity relations reign in them, but only the free association of individuals who desire the emancipation of humanity and act accordingly.*

That is what puts so distinctive a stamp on communists' practice: they are people who are 'not like everyone else'. Even when they are active in a parliament or municipal government, communists are not people 'like everyone else'. The reason is that their vision is not restricted to the closed horizon of these assemblies, or even to that of their voters: they act on behalf of the broad masses, not just for today, but for tomorrow and the future of communism. That is why they can, on these bases, find common ground with many other people of goodwill, who may – in the case of those with religious convictions, for example – espouse completely different ideologies, while acting in the same sense.

What confers one last distinctive feature on the practice of communists, the best and the most conscious of proletarians, is that the goal they pursue in their political practice is, fundamentally, *the end of all politics*, including the end of all democracy, which is necessarily limited by its rules. For they know that *every form of politics* is, like it or not, *bound up with the state*, and that the state is nothing other than the exploiting class's machine of domination, since it is a product of class struggle and serves the dominant class struggle by ensuring that the conditions for the reproduction of class society as a whole are maintained. Hence communists act politically *to bring about the end of politics*. They make use of politics, of class struggle, so that, one day, politics and class struggle will end. *That* is the dialectic. As Hegel put it: learn to make use of gravity against gravity. If you do, you will be able to build a house with vaults[16] that stay up all by themselves.

Communists also know, as Lenin said and as everyday experience proves, that the most difficult moment to negotiate is socialism, that river full of eddies and cross-currents, where the boat of socialism can capsize if the dictatorship of the proletariat does not firmly defend the helm against the capitalists. For socialism is no longer capitalism, but is not yet communism. It is a *transition* in which capitalist relations (surplus value, wage-work, money, the state and its apparatuses, the regime of political parties)[17] coexist with communist relations (collective property, the party and so on). During this transition, the class struggle continues, albeit in new, often unrecognizable forms, threatening the progress of the crossing. Yes, it is possible to lapse back into capitalism, if one follows an economistic, idealist line. The vestiges of prophetic ideology in Marx himself notwithstanding, the transition to communism is never guaranteed in advance, even if one proclaims, as does the USSR, that one is already establishing its 'material bases'. (This is a concept that makes little sense in Marxist theory, which, for its part, talks about *the* base, that is, the infrastructure, not about 'material bases', which might then be distinguished from the relations of production.) Hence there is a need for the kind of political vigilance that never loses sight of the prospect of communism and never sacrifices its long-term future for the sake of immediate reforms, albeit well aware that that future is aleatory.

Is it necessary to add that proletarian ideology, so profoundly inspired by so original a practice of politics, can have significant effects on most other practices? We can expect it to produce surprising results, if only the lessons of this practice are extended to the practice of production, the organization of the labour-process, the democracy of the party and other organizations, and even the natural sciences. However, just as Marx preferred not to 'write recipes for the cook-shops of the future', we too shall refrain from anticipating. What counts is to be attentive to everything that may be born and is already being born around us.

What lessons shall we draw from this rapid analysis of political practice? That it displays *a specific relationship to abstraction*. Political practice can no more forgo abstractions than can the practice of production, technical practice or ideological practice. Firstly, because the absolute condition for its existence is constituted by relations – economic, political and ideological relations – that mark it in all its determinations. Secondly, because, under the domination of these social relations, *it produces abstractions in its turn*, practical to begin with, then abstract and theoretical abstractions, which modify its own field of action and field of verification. Lastly, because these abstractions eventually 'encounter' those of a science, forged, it is true, by intellectuals who were armed with all the culture of their time, yet who were able to develop this science only on the theoretical (philosophical) positions of the proletarian class.

There is, however, one difference here, which becomes increasingly pronounced as time goes on. We have already mentioned it in our discussion of ideological practice. It is that this whole social process of political practice, even when it takes the form of the antagonistic division of class struggle (as is always the case in class societies), *bears less on an external object than on the process itself*. We have perhaps succeeded in showing that, in the case of bourgeois political practice, it was a matter of letting others act in the bourgeoisie's stead, hence of 'manipulating' those exploited by the bourgeoisie in order to act on the situation of the class relation. It was at all events a matter, in keeping with the general schema of practice, of using means of action to transform the existing social order (or maintain it by defending it). Even in this case, however, the 'subject' of the process – that is, the bourgeoisie – was implicated in it, and thus not acting on a situation from without. On the contrary, the situation of class relations was in some way acting on itself, through an intermediary, the bourgeoisie, which, it is true, arranged for those it exploited to act in its stead and for its benefit. Hence this practice, *considered as a whole*, corresponds much more closely to Aristotle's second definition (transformation of the self by the self) than to his first (production of an external object).

The same holds a fortiori for proletarian political practice. For, here, there is no longer any intermediary at all. It is a peculiar feature of proletarian political practice consciously to assume this condition, and to *realize the unity of transformation of the objective situation with self-transformation*. Marx came up with the earliest formulations of this identity in his 'Theses on Feuerbach', where he speaks of revolutionary 'praxis' as the identity of the transformation of the object (the balance of power) and the subject (the organized revolutionary class). Here, what subsists of externality in bourgeois political practice, between those who lead and those who act, or between ideas and action, disappears in favour of a dialectic of unification and reciprocal transformation of the objective situation and the revolutionary forces engaged in the combat.

This new relation, this new concrete abstraction, confers, this time, its full significance on the Marxist-materialist thesis of the primacy of practice over theory. It clearly shows that the schematic opposition between a practice that is exclusively material, on the one hand, and a theory that is exclusively intellectual and contemplative, on the other, is one of the oppositions of idealist philosophy, since, here, political practice is sustained by theory, while political theory is inspired throughout by the 'lessons of practice'.

The relation between practice and theory and the primacy of practice over theory must be conceived of in terms of content: every transformation of already existing theory may well stem from practice, but what is involved is never a pure practice devoid of all theory. Theory, in turn, grounding its development on the transformations of the political struggle, gives back to practice, in the form of fruitful scientific abstractions, what it has received from it in the form of concrete experiences. The unity of theory and practice thus constitutes a circle, or, if one prefers, something comparable to the wheel of a locomotive, which always carries the ballast of a *balance weight* to conserve and accelerate its rotation – namely *practice*. The weight that conserves and relaunches the movement is, however, itself firmly attached to the wheel. The analysis of political practice thus confirms what the preceding analyses have taught us: abstract relations are the condition for every practice, and they depend, in the final analysis, on social relations, hence on class relations. From this standpoint, political practice occupies a privileged position, since its raw material, its agent and its instruments of production are, directly, these class relations themselves.

Can we now turn to philosophical practice and the forms of abstraction peculiar to it? We cannot, for we must first examine two other practices of great importance for our discussion: psychoanalytic practice and aesthetic practice.

14 PSYCHOANALYTIC PRACTICE

Only since the last world war can psychoanalytic practice, founded by Freud at the dawn of the century, be said to have begun to gain recognition, and only since then have we begun to suspect its ideological and political import. For Freud's discovery represented a sort of scandal.

Freud set out to show that it was necessary to have done with the bourgeois idealist representation of man as an entirely conscious being, as a sentient, juridical, moral, political, religious and philosophical subject, as a transparent being 'without a backside'. Freud's aim was not to say what biologists, neurologists and physiologists had already been saying for a long time: that human beings have *bodies* as well as brains, and that, when they think, they do not know what is going on in either their body or their brain. Philosophers had always said that. Freud's aim was not to say that when man thinks, since most of his ideas are merely products of the social activity outside him, he does not know what mechanism is producing his ideas: historians, sociologists and others had been saying that for a long time. Those 'outsides' were not what Freud was talking about: he was talking about an outside *inside thought itself*.

Freud said that thought is in the main unconscious, yet is thought, and that the conscious part of thought is limited. Hence he no longer talked about consciousness or the conscious subject, but about a 'psychic apparatus' that thinks by itself, without a subject, and imposes its 'unconscious thoughts' on that part of itself endowed with preconscious and conscious thought. François Mauriac tells us that he was persuaded, as a child, that grown-ups 'did not have rear ends'. In sum, humanity did not believe, until Freud (although it had suspected it before him) that thought had a 'rear end'; that behind consciousness, attached to it as its truth, is an 'unconscious' which, in its fashion, 'thinks'. This unconscious consisted not of biological or social reality, but of a very special kind of immaterial reality.

The Christian philosopher Malebranche had already said, albeit with reference to God, 'he acts in us without us'.[1] Due allowance made, the Freudian unconscious behaves the same way. Something, an 'id', unnameable, without a subject, acts in our 'psychical apparatus', and thus in us, without the sanction of our conscious will, governing even our conscious thoughts and acts.

Concrete examples of this reality were not far to seek: they could be found in dreams, everyday life or the strangest instincts. Diderot discerned, in the *enfants sauvages*, the same story that Sophocles had put on stage, about a son who kills his father and marries his own mother: left to themselves, these children would try to kill their fathers and sleep with their mothers![2] A strange 'instinct' indeed, for it was a stranger to all reason; it had the character of an impulse, like hunger, but had no comparable motivation. For what was to be gained by this murder and this incest that could not be had at no risk in other sexual relations? In this case, every individual, or at all events every child, is 'acted' in himself and independently of his will by a force stronger than he is.

And what shall we say about these 'slips' of everyday life, these acts that are without reason, yet are stronger than any reason; that are seemingly meaningless, yet testify to an unconscious desire to forget some detail or reactivate some memory – in short, to 'fulfil' one or another unconscious desire? Freud deciphered them with disconcerting ease, just as he deciphered dreams. An ancient human tradition had attributed powers of divination to dreams; this recognition reflected people's unconscious desire to control their future. When one went into detail, however, how many unconscious desires were revealed by analysis of the strange narrations that people in the waking state produced about what they had 'dreamed' while asleep and had saved from oblivion so that it might be recounted! Freud discussed the 'realization of desire' in the same terms (*Wunscherfüllung*) that the German philosopher Feuerbach had used fifty years earlier to discuss religion![3]

The task, then, was to explain all these facts, there for all to see, and draw the lessons they had to teach. This was the accomplishment of Freud, who came round to presupposing the existence, behind these acts and their consciousness, of an *unconscious apparatus* in which unconscious desires were at work, propelled by 'drives', forces located on the border-line between the psychical apparatus and the biological, and invested, in accordance with laws of economic and dynamic distribution, in very specific formations known as fantasies, few in number and very strange.

By fantasies [*fantasmes*], Freud meant 'fancies' [*fantaisies*], imaginary but unconscious representations that were autonomous and powerful. They existed thanks only to the way they were arranged on a certain 'stage', where they figured one beside the other in *relations* of affinity or antagonism. They seemed to represent, in the element of the unconscious, configurations similar to real situations stemming from earliest infancy. In real infancy, there is the child, its mother (its first love object) and its father (plus brothers and sisters). Among these real personages, there exist relations of dependency, love, fear, rivalry and so on, of which the infant gradually acquires an experience that is either gratifying or disappointing. It seems that one finds, in the unconscious as well, *but in the form of fantasies*, equivalents of all these personae, represented in the form of unconscious images (imagos) that are in most cases condensed: the fantasy of the mother can occasionally represent the image of the father, the fantasy of the child itself can also represent the image of the father or mother and so on.

The most remarkable thing, however, is that the relations between these fantasized 'personae' appear on the 'scene' of the unconscious, that 'other scene' (Freud), as linked to one another by sexual desires. The infant does in fact desire to 'sleep with' its mother, whose 'persona' is gradually put together from 'partial objects' such as the breast, face and so on, the sole objects apprehended in the first moments of a child's existence. Let us note that Freud discovered the existence of 'infantile sexuality' less by setting out from concrete observations, although that too is possible, than by analysing adults' fantasies in the psychoanalytic cure. Declaring that infantile sexuality existed, in defiance of a culture that had always fiercely censored it, created no mean scandal. It was, however, necessary to hypothesize its existence in order to explain all the facts offered by the experience both of everyday life (dreams, etc.) and of the analysis of the unconscious of adults in psychoanalytic treatment. In the absence of such a hypothesis, all these facts would have remained unintelligible.

Freud's work on these facts led him to forge specific abstractions to account for them: the well-known 'topographies'.[4] The term 'topography' designates a certain arrangement in an abstract space, in which there figures a certain number of defined realities that play a particular role as a function of their properties and, above all, their interrelations. Thus Freud initially put the 'unconscious'[5] (so designated in order to break with all notions of consciousness and the subject) in place in the first 'topography'. Above 'the unconscious', the site of unconscious thoughts (or drives and fantasies), he put the '*preconscious*', the site of thoughts that are not conscious, but can become conscious at will (ordinary memories). Above the 'preconscious', he put not consciousness, but the '*conscious*', the organ of perception and action. Between the group conscious-preconscious, on the one hand, and the unconscious, on the other, he introduced the bar of *repression*, an unconscious force that prevents unconscious thoughts from emerging in consciousness and maintains their effective force at the heart of the unconscious. 'The unconscious' was a general reservoir of energies whose forces were distributed, in accordance with a strict economy, in the preconscious and conscious, where they induced the strange phenomena that are frequently observed.

This abstraction seemed sufficient to account for the facts. However, new facts bearing, above all, on the nature of the 'ego', which Freud had supposed to be wholly conscious, forced him to modify his abstract configuration. This led to the second 'topography', which extended the domain of the unconscious into the 'ego' itself. The upshot was a new distribution. At the base was the 'id', now no longer confined to its own field of activity. Above it was the '*ego*', which corresponded to conscious 'consciousness-perception', the function of vigilance and action. Next came the 'superego', an unconscious instance that represents prohibition and represses unconscious thoughts into the 'id'. Finally, there was the 'ego-ideal', the conscious-unconscious representation of the idea pursued by the conscious-unconscious psychic personality in its striving to identify with this representation.

Among these different instances, Freud invariably put economic and dynamic relations of distribution, allocation and the cathexis/anti-cathexis of an unconscious energy situated in the 'id' and connected – he did not say how – to the individual's underlying biological reality, his drives and instincts. With this economy (Freud's inspiration here was classical political economy's theory of production-allocation-distribution-investment, but also the energetics developed by Ostwald, a German chemist who had constructed a gigantic philosophical system in order to reduce everything to energy), Freud could account for all the facts observable in both everyday experience and the clinical experience of the cure.

The most remarkable, the most extraordinary thing about this theory is the fact that Freud developed it in its entirety without making systematic observations of the objective phenomena of infantile sexuality: he based it on observations of adults and, above all, the psychoanalytic treatment of adults. Hence he was open to the charge of reckless extrapolation. The facts observed in infantile sexuality, however, validated his hypothesis: observations of infants revealed that they were endowed not only with an undeniable sexuality, but even with a 'polymorphous perversity' (their sexuality, unlike that of adults, could take all sorts of forms and be fixated on all sorts of sexual objects, indiscriminately).

But the most stupefying feature of Freud's work was and remains the *absolutely autonomous* character of the whole of this theory and mechanism. Everything happens in the mechanisms of the unconscious as if they led a life completely independent of *both* their biological condition of existence, although it underpins them, *and* their social condition of existence, although it indirectly commands them.

This thesis caused a theoretical scandal and, at the same time, incomprehension. People could not reconcile themselves to the idea that all these mechanisms, manifestly conditioned by the biological and the social, could be independent of their conditions of existence. Yet, all their resistance notwithstanding, they had to face up to the facts. Freud's theory, as isolated as an island that has surged up in the middle of a vast uncharted sea, did indeed account for the facts, and did so 'without a hitch', with no need for help from the realities on which it was based, but was not dependent.

Freud's disciples would propose additional hypotheses to explain this paradox. Jung appealed to a 'collective unconscious' with social or biological origins; Reich appealed to familial structures projected onto the superego, and so on. Freud remained fiercely opposed to all these extrapolations, sticking to the facts and the explanations that he had advanced. The result was crises and splits in the psychoanalytic movement that have yet to be overcome.

Was the task, in this conjuncture, to attach psychoanalytic theory at all costs to the realities on which it seemed to depend, such as neurobiology or the theory of social and familial structures, and thus to Marxism, at the risk of lapsing into the arbitrary, dangerous constructions just mentioned, and, accordingly, to deduce Freud's theory from biology or historical materialism? Experience showed that this was to lapse into intellectual adventurism, as is proven, in particular, by the attempts of Reich and his disciples, who, despite their ambition, had no political purchase on the realities that they claimed to grasp.

Was it preferable to put the accent, as Lacan is doing today in France, on the real autonomy of psychoanalytic theory, at the risk of its temporary scientific isolation, but also at the risk of its solitude? This attitude appears to be more correct,[6] at least for the moment. One sometimes has to agree to leave a theory in a prudent state of scientific *incompletion*, without anticipating the discoveries of neighbouring sciences. For experience also shows that one cannot decree the completion of a science.

At all events, the experience of the history of psychoanalytic theory demonstrates that objective abstractions which are not ideological, but are not yet scientific, can and must remain in this state for as long as the neighbouring sciences have not reached a level of maturity that makes it possible to re-unify neighbouring scientific 'continents'. Just as it takes time to bring the class struggle to its term, it also takes time to bring the constitution of a science as a science to its term. Moreover, it is by no means certain that psychoanalytic theory can ever take the form of a science in the proper sense of the word.

But, whatever its theoretical destiny, the most noteworthy feature of psychoanalytic theory is *its relation to practice*. We should here note the crucial point that Freudian theory could only be developed on the basis of a specific practice: that of the cure, or the transformation of the fantasy relations in an individual's unconscious, and that it could advance only by producing a practice constantly adjusted in the course of the psychoanalytic experience, that of the cure.

What is the cure? It is an experimental situation that is in many respects comparable to the experimental set-ups and montages of the well-known experimental sciences. At the same time, however, it is a practical situation that precipitates transformations in its object thanks to instruments of a particular kind used to produce such effects. The cure brings together, in the seeming solitude of a tête-à-tête that is in fact dominated by a Third Party, the psychoanalyst, the laws of the unconscious and the patient, whom some (Lacan) call the 'analysand' to emphasize the fact that he is, ultimately, the driving force behind his own transformation: in a sense, the 'physician healing himself' discussed long ago by Aristotle. The psychoanalyst is only there to 'punctuate' (Lacan) and inflect the analysand's discourse, fraught with unconscious meanings. In the beginnings of psychoanalysis, treatment was basically reserved for neurotics (patients who, unlike psychotics, that is, madmen, maintain contact with the outside world, yet have a profoundly perturbed relation to it). Today, especially after Melanie Klein's work, psychoanalysis is also making a start on psychotics, or the 'mad' properly so called.

In the psychoanalytic cure, we again find, *mutatis mutandis*, our categories of practice. The 'raw material' is the patient himself, his unconscious, and the effects that the 'pathological' configuration of his fantasies has on his conscious and his practical attitudes in life. The instruments used to produce the effect known as the cure are, firstly, unconscious identification with the psychoanalyst through *transference* and, secondly, *the working-through* (*Durcharbeiten*) of unconscious fantasies by the analysand and psychoanalyst. The transference 'takes' (if it takes) only after some time, when, at the end of a certain number of sessions, the patient succeeds in identifying with the psychoanalyst, 'treating' him as a surrogate for a parental personage (father or mother). He then projects his own unconscious desires onto the psychoanalyst, that is, attributes them to him as if they emanated from this real personage, who listens while saying nothing, or almost nothing.

Since the patient can and 'must' say everything without restraint, he manages to express his unconscious desires in this strange situation. He thinks he is saying one thing, that he is expressing a *demand* (help me! love me!), and gradually comes to see that he is saying something quite different, since he is expressing an unconscious desire (I want to kill you! I want to die! I want to be all-powerful! I want to be loved!). Little by little, this contradiction becomes active and, by comparing his conscious thoughts to his unconscious desires, the patient eventually puts the former to work on (*durcharbeiten*) the latter and the other way around. Ultimately, this brings about a redistribution of his 'affects' (profound, unconscious emotional attachments to certain unconscious fantasy images) and a re-equilibration of his conscious and unconscious psychical apparatus as a whole.

It is at this point[7] that the 'cure' intervenes, the final moment of which is the dissolution of the counter-transference. For the psychoanalyst, contrary to the approximative idea that makes him an 'unmoved mover' akin to Aristotle's distant and impassive God, invests the patient with unconscious desires of his own, in the sense that he wants to keep the patient with him or else wants to be rid of him too soon. The psychoanalyst must, therefore, with the help of the analysand, who never ceases to play an active role, *analyse his own counter-transference* in order to terminate the psychoanalysis. When neither the transference nor the counter-transference is dissolved, the cure can become the 'interminable psychoanalysis' that Freud described in his last texts. If the counter-transference is successfully dissolved, the cure can be brought to an end and the patient can return to his private life under favourable conditions.

The reader will have concluded, from the basic configuration of the psychoanalytic cure and its practice, that psychoanalysis represents a concrete experience with virtually no equivalent. In this experience, the psychoanalyst is by no means a physician, that is, an authority invested by society with scientific *knowledge* giving him the *right* to treat others, that is, the right to respond to a *demand* to be healed addressed to him by a patient who knows where it hurts and goes to see the doctor to be cured of his illness. Psychoanalytic practice is the most serious questioning of, and challenge to, *medical practice* that has ever existed – indeed, of *any* practice involving 'a subject supposed to know' (Lacan)[8] capable of healing and counselling by virtue of the authority of his knowledge and social power. *The psychoanalyst is not a physician, moral or practical counsellor, confessor or priest; he is not even a friend.* He is simply the mute agent of a process without a subject in which fantasies (his own) confront, silently but concretely, someone else's fantasies (the analysand's) in an effort to re-equilibrate them until they are in a state that puts an end to the troubles affecting his psyche.

By thus introducing a new practice into the world of the practices, psychoanalysis produced phenomenal effects in ideology and philosophy. Amid the massive domination of bourgeois legal, moral and religious ideology and philosophy, amid the massive domination of the philosophy of consciousness and the subject (Husserl was Freud's contemporary), psychoanalytic theory proceeded to stage a veritable 'Copernican revolution'. Before Copernicus, people thought that the sun revolved around the earth. Copernicus imposed the objective truth that the earth revolves around the sun. Before Freud, it was thought that everything in man revolved around his consciousness, that the essence of man was consciousness. Freud imposed the truth that consciousness is merely a derivative effect, and that human consciousness 'revolves around' the unconscious. This dealt moral, legal and religious ideological prejudices a blow that might well have been mortal, had they not been shored up by the entire traditional bourgeois order. This Freudian critique of *homo psychologicus* (man, an essentially psychological being), comparable, in the history of ideas, only to the Marxist critique of *homo economicus* (man as defined by his economic needs), had major repercussions on all of philosophy. Lacan has played an important role in France in compelling recognition of these effects, even if he was to interpret them in a disputable way.[9] A certain junction between Freud's and Marx's materialist *philosophies* appeared, producing certain interesting results that bore no relation to the adventuristic enterprise of a Reich in an earlier period.[10]

What lessons should we draw from the sudden emergence of this unprecedented practice of Freud's? Firstly, that practices can surge up on the basis of millennial experiences left unexplored and can completely transform a field of experience. Secondly, that these practices always irrupt under the domination of determinate abstract relations, even if they are constituted in an altogether paradoxical way: it is enough if they turn out to correspond to the nature of the unprecedented object that has surged up in knowledge. Finally, that even when these relations are as unusual as the relations of psychoanalysis (relations of transference between unconsciouses), they are decisive for both the theory and the practice in question. To this it must be added that psychoanalytic practice further enriches Aristotle's ancient intuition about *praxis*, for it is the subject himself who produces his own transformation through the intermediary of the psychoanalyst. In this respect too, psychoanalytic practice is similar to revolutionary practice, with the difference that the two practices obviously do not have the same object, inasmuch as psychoanalysis changes only the internal configuration of an individual's unconscious, whereas revolutionary practice changes a society's class structure.

This last comparison is not without consequences that are theoretical and practical alike. For Freud himself had already noticed something like a parallelism (compare the Spinozist thesis)[11] between unconscious imagos and the social figures of the familial personae, between the *mise-en-scène* of the unconscious and that of the family, between social censorship and unconscious repression and so on. Yet Freud was careful not to go beyond this simple suggestion. Had he not been, he would have fallen into the sociologistic error of treating unconscious imagos as straightforward reproductions or images of the social personae of the family. Someday we may be able to go beyond the present state of this rough analogy, which, albeit suggestive, has led no further – on the day, perhaps, when new discoveries are made in what would seem to be the 'neighbouring' sciences (neurophysiology? the theory of the structure and ideology of the family?). We cannot, however, anticipate these future developments without running great risks, which Reich vainly confronted in his time, and which are today being pursued by the champions of a spontaneist far-leftism [*gauchisme*].

A science, if it wishes to safeguard its independence and simply endure, must sometimes be willing to remain for a very long time, and perhaps indefinitely, in the solitude of its own defined abstractions, without trying to conflate them with the abstractions of the other existing sciences.

15 ARTISTIC PRACTICE

[Its isolation from existing sciences notwithstanding], psychoanalysis has not failed to produce far-reaching effects on another practice and its theory: aesthetic practice and theory.

Human beings have in every day and age produced strange objects distinguished by the fact that they are of no material use, in that they meet none of humanity's vital needs: the need for food, for sex and so on. Originally, these objects were invariably endowed with social significance – religious significance, for example – but had no direct practical significance. Peculiar to all of them was the fact that they were appreciated for their *uselessness* as long as they gave *pleasure* to those who 'consumed' them through sight, hearing, touch and so on. In these singular objects, we find the earliest evidence of what would later become objects of art. But we also find in them, from the outset, the double character that was to be their hallmark. They were *useless*, to be sure, but they were *social*: to be beautiful objects, they had to be recognized as such by the social group. Yet the social group saw not only the beauty of forms or sounds in them, but also, by way of this universal recognition, recognition of a common essence, its own, that of its own social unity. Yet this unity was already guaranteed by other relations and functions, to which artistic social objects added the function, apparently necessary for the human community, of being useless and beautiful, and therefore invested with *pleasure*.

The result of this singular attribution is to produce *a new form of abstraction*. All objects of art are produced materially, like any other product, by labour that transforms a certain raw material. The result of this material transformation, however, is to produce not a useful object with the capacity to satisfy people's vital needs, but an object with the capacity to procure them a special pleasure, *a pleasure that costs nothing and involves no danger*, a 'fictive triumph' (Freud) produced by their consumption of it – visual, auditory and so on.[1] In a word, the abstraction of the production of objects of art presents itself in the paradoxical guise of the production (exhibition, presentation, representation) of a certain, apparently raw, material (stone, wood, sound) invested with form. *Abstraction* thus presents itself in the form *of a concrete object* in which matter is, as it were, proffered completely naked in the aesthetic form enveloping it. *The necessary abstract exists in the form of a useless concrete.*

The characteristic feature of this concrete, however, of this work of art – sculpture, painting, music and so on – is *to please*, even when it represents the horrors of a tragedy for its spectators. Why do works of art move us? Marx said, about ancient tragedy, that it moves us because it is the childhood of humanity, and people take pleasure in their childhood.[2] Aristotle said, more profoundly, that a spectacle is like a purgation which imaginarily frees men of their terrors and allows them to feel, in the face of something terrible, the pleasure of a relief that frees them from an action that they can watch and thus need not accomplish.[3] It is all profit at no cost: they desire a forbidden or impossible act, and it unfolds before their eyes without danger.

Taking up this intuition, Freud sees the fulfilment of a desire in the work of art, a fulfilment that is imaginary, as in dreams, and thus objectively without effect, but subjectively pleasant to contemplate.[4] That people feel a need to experience, in the form of an imaginary pleasure, the satisfaction of a desire that they cannot fulfil (because, as in utopia, the conditions for its fulfilment have not been met, or because a social taboo prohibits fulfilling it) would appear to be a fact that is both undeniable and seemingly indispensable to the functioning of social relations. Just as there are '*incidental expenses*' of production in every mode of production, products that serve to produce certain effects, while *serving no purpose* in and of themselves, so there seem to be, in the reproduction of social relations, aesthetic '*incidental expenses*', of use in the production of other effects while serving no purpose in and of themselves – no purpose other than to produce an imaginary pleasure.

What purpose can this imaginary pleasure possibly serve? Unquestionably, it helps to sustain the existing practices and ideologies. It is a fact that, while experiencing the pleasure of *playing*, a child engages in a veritable apprenticeship that prepares it to engage in practices of production or social relations. It is a fact that *games and festivals, public spectacles* and the like strengthen the social bond by bringing people together in one place and offering all of them the same object of pleasure to consume, an object that extols idealized social relations or 'plays' with prohibitions. Works of art, which are not purely ideological, since they are objects comprising matter and a form directly accessible to the senses, thereby enter ideology's sphere of influence and take their place in it, in the fundamental political division of ideological confrontation.

They do so with all the ambiguity familiar to us by now, since ideology is ultimately organized in relation to [*ordonnée à*] the state: thus they serve either the dominant ideology or the 'values' for which the dominated class is struggling. Doubtless the history of aesthetic forms always concerns the *matter* that the artist works on and offers to the eye or the ear; and this history, carrying the ballast of materiality, doubtless depends on the objective possibilities of the matter in question, whether it is marble, wood, fabric, colours and sounds, or the 'themes' of drama and the novel. The choice of these possibilities and their combination in properly aesthetic forms nevertheless falls within the province of ideology and the struggle separating ideology from itself. This paradoxical condition explains the illusion of both the artist who believes that he is engaged in purely artistic work, and the consumers of his product, who believe that they are engaged in an act of purely aesthetic consumption, whereas what is essential takes place 'behind their backs' (Hegel),[5] in an ideological confrontation that constantly seeks to enlist works of art in the service of its cause.

It follows that, like the other practices, aesthetic practice too, far from being a pure act that creates beauty, unfolds *under the domination of abstract social relations,* which are not just norms defining the beautiful, but also ideological relations of class struggle. It also follows that, since ideology is what it is and always presents things falsely, art can, in addition to the marvels of pleasure that it procures, foster the ideology of purity, beauty and absolute autonomy that serves intellectuals of the dominant class as an alibi. That is why, traditionally, *idealist philosophers have always been fascinated by art and the beautiful,* as if by ideas above the fray of ideas and well suited to persuading people that there exists, at all events, a solution to social conflicts: in culture and beauty, where all can 'commune'.

This 'flight to the front' and into the ideology of art, a leitmotiv of all spiritualist and idealist philosophies, may be observed, in our day, in a country that calls itself socialist, the USSR. There may well be no other country in the world that devotes so many books and philosophy courses to aesthetics (despite the distressing poverty of its aesthetic productions). A professor of aesthetics from Leningrad once gave me a disarming explanation of this. They offer the workers who are reluctant to work, he said, the opportunity to earn more money by doing piecework. That doesn't interest them, because they can do nothing with their money. So, after personal *interest*, they bring socialist *morality* into the picture: they tell them it's their duty to socialist society to work harder. That doesn't seem to interest them, either ... So they roll out their ultimate argument: work harder, because your labour isn't just labour, *it's a work, it's a work of art*: you're artists. They pay no mind. But, so that they can make the workers such speeches, they create more and more jobs for aestheticians and try to awaken a taste for the fine arts in the people.

The 'flight into art' can also be the equivalent of a 'flight into religion': the aim is to find in art an imaginary solution to the real difficulties encountered by society. If art does indeed procure pleasure for people, it is also, all too often, a flight into art, that singular abstraction, which is nothing, in that case, but a bad abstraction.

Can we draw a few tentative conclusions from this long analysis of abstraction?

We may say, firstly, that *people live in abstraction, under the domination of abstract relations* that command all their practices. We may say, secondly, that there is no *abstraction in general*, but that there are different types and levels of abstraction, depending on the different practices and different types of practices. We may say, thirdly, that while there is no abstraction in general, *there are general abstractions* that command the ensemble of the different practices and more or less profoundly influence their specific abstractions. These *general abstractions are the social relations*: relations of production, circulation and distribution, political relations and ideological relations – all of them organized in relation to [*ordonnées aux*] class relations and the class struggle.

Lastly, we may say that all these abstract relations are abstract only insofar as they are, and remain, *rooted in the materiality of the social practices*, and that they are abstract only to the extent that they make possible the *final production of the concrete*, whether it is a matter of the production of objects of consumption, the transformation of political, ideological or fantasy relations, or the production of works of art and so on.

The whole of this gigantic cycle of social production, with its different turnover rates and its complex interconnections, operates under the primacy of the real-concrete over the abstract, and therefore under the primacy of practice over theory. There is no moment in the cycle, however, at which we can observe a pure distinction between practice or the concrete, on the one hand, and theory or abstraction, on the other. At every moment, all the practices exist only under the domination of abstract relations, relations that can be elevated to the level of theory. At every moment, all abstract relations, theoretical relations included, exist only on condition that they are rooted in practice, in the concrete. It is the contradictions of this immense cycle which produce, in the form of class struggle, that which is called human history and which makes this history *human* – makes it, that is, not a disembodied history, but one fraught with weight, materiality and finitude, with human suffering, discoveries and joys.

16 PHILOSOPHICAL PRACTICE

We had to make this long detour through the practices and their abstractions in order to come, at last, to philosophy. To come to the question: but what sets philosophy apart, if it too dwells under the domination of abstraction and in abstraction? And what is the nature of philosophical practice? This question can be put differently: what is the object that philosophical practice transforms?

This long detour was also necessary for an essential reason that we shall here state without delay: *what philosophical practice transforms is the ideologies under the domination of which the various social practices produce their specific effects.*

We shall approach the question of philosophy from a convenient angle: the nature of philosophical propositions.

When I say, 'The kitten is dead', I state a fact that can be confirmed by examining the animal itself or by first-hand testimony, in which the abstraction of language is already present. When I say, 'All falling bodies obey a law described by a simple equation', I also state a fact, but it is the fact of a different abstraction, the abstraction of scientific concepts, since I am not talking about this particular body (the body of the kitten that fell off the roof), but about all bodies that exist in our Euclidean space. Whenever I utter a proposition of this type, I no doubt change something in my knowledge: earlier, I did not know that the kitten was dead; I did not know that all falling bodies obeyed a simple law. I do not, however, change anything in my 'objects': I do not bring the kitten back to life or prevent cats from falling off roofs.

In language, however, there exist propositions of a different type that can change something in their object. When I say to Pierre, standing ten yards off, 'Come over here!', it may happen that Pierre, who has heard me, obeys and comes my way. In this case, my summons has changed something in the order of things, since Pierre has moved from one place to another. When someone knocks on my door and I say, 'Who's there?', I invite the person standing at my door to answer, and he may. But he may also remain silent. Involved here are propositions that can be active, but their action does not depend on me alone.

Let us turn to another domain. When, in court, the presiding judge takes his seat and declares, 'the court is in session', he utters a sentence the result of which is that the court is indeed in session, whatever the opinion or opposition of those present. The English linguist Austin calls such propositions 'performative', in other words, directly operative, producing their effect simply by virtue of being uttered.[1]

To acquire some notion of the nature of philosophical propositions, at least those in which every philosophy sums up its essential ideas, we can set out from this idea of 'performative' statements. When a philosopher (Descartes, for instance) writes, 'God exists', he acts somewhat like the presiding judge of a court who declares that 'the court is in session' – with the difference that his declaration does not bring about the existence of God, except in the world of his philosophy: in some way, Descartes 'inaugurates' a world, that of his philosophy. His sentence makes God exists for him, for he immediately sets about reasoning as if God really did exist, without once doubting it, given that all the other propositions of his philosophy are premised on God's existence.

Thus a philosophical proposition does not resemble the *'passive'* propositions that merely convey knowledge of a fact (the kitten is dead) or a law (the law of falling bodies: $[D=] \frac{1}{2} gt^2$). A philosophical proposition is an *active* proposition which produces a certain effect of existence – which, consequently, makes something called God pass from nothingness to being, with the proviso that what is in question is not this God's *real* existence, but only his *philosophical* existence, his existence in the philosophy of his author and the latter's disciples. This give us the converse of this property as well: the same philosophical proposition provides us with no objective knowledge, although it constitutes an undeniable piece of knowledge for the philosopher who states it. From this, we can see straight away that if philosophy acts, it does so only in philosophy, not in the real world.

These simple remarks are enough to turn all our naïve beliefs topsy-turvy. We thought that philosophy provided us with the highest kind of knowledge, the knowledge of all things, of their 'essence', but we have just seen that it merely provides us with knowledge that is undeniable, but only for the philosopher who states it. We thought that philosophy was 'contemplative', that is to say, passive before its object, but we have just seen that it is active. Finally, we thought that philosophy had to do with real objects, but we have just seen that it produces before our eyes, for itself, something that has nothing to do with real objects! We are in a state of utter disarray.

The fact is that we cannot help but conceive of philosophical practice in the mode of either scientific practice (which furnishes knowledge) or the other practices we have analysed: ideological practices and so on (which produce practical transformations, not knowledge). We must therefore revise our point of view.[2]

Let us go back to the Cartesian proposition that 'God exists'. This is an active proposition, granted. Yet it produces nothing real, except in the world of Cartesian philosophy. Does this mean that what it states is purely illusory? By no means. We shall say, for we can do so without exceeding the limits of philosophical 'fact', that Descartes 'posits' God's existence and thereby changes something in what existed before Descartes, in the mind of an atheist, for instance; yet this *position*, albeit active, remains purely philosophical, confined to its author's system. To designate philosophical propositions which thus 'posit' the existence of a being that, albeit unreal, is essential to the philosophy in question, we shall use the term 'Thesis', a word translated from the Greek that can mean, precisely, *position*.

We may therefore say: *philosophy does not produce knowledge of a real object, but posits Theses* which state the existence of a philosophical 'object' or properties of that object. We shall say, consequently, that *philosophy has no object* (in the sense in which scientific practice and productive practice have objects), but has something else in view: *objectives or stakes*.[3] Would you like examples of philosophical theses? 'I think, therefore I am'; 'God exists'; 'God is infinitely perfect'; 'I doubt, therefore God exists'; 'Bodies are extended in space'; 'The "I think" accompanies the diversity of my representations'; 'To be is to be perceived'; 'The world is my representation of it'; 'Consciousness is intentional'; 'Matter has primacy over thought' and so on. As can be seen, our definition of the nature of philosophical propositions applies to idealist and materialist theses alike. It seems to follow that there is a 'nature' of philosophy as such that encompasses the oppositions observable in philosophy.

What is a philosophical thesis made up of? Of abstract terms, which we shall call 'categories' to distinguish them from scientific *concepts*. A category has no object, in the sense in which a scientific concept is said to have an object. It is assigned its meaning by the ensemble of the categories constituting a philosophical system. A category can play the role of a thesis if it sums up, on one precise point, the *position* of the philosophy in question. A thesis can play the role of a category if that category is summed up by it.

Just as each category takes its meaning from the whole system of categories, so each philosophical thesis refers, for its part, to the whole system of philosophical theses. Thus there exists a rigorous internal bond among all of a philosophy's theoretical elements: the bond of a 'system' or, more precisely, a 'structure'. The grouping of certain categories in the form of a thesis expresses the position taken by that philosophy on controversial questions. Thus when Descartes writes, 'I think, therefore I am', he takes up a position against Thomist philosophy, for which thought is not identical to existence.

Here the practical, active meaning of philosophical propositions begins to come into focus. If a philosophical thesis has no object, if the object it posits is not a real object, but one purely internal to philosophy, *this object becomes, for this thesis, a means of occupying ground held by a philosophical adversary*. This philosophical object represents the 'military' array [*dispositif*] by means of which the philosophy in question occupies defined positions held by a defined adversary in the philosophical war. For a thesis is only posed against another thesis, an adverse, that is, a different or an opposed thesis: *every thesis is thus by its nature an anti-thesis*. Every philosophy accordingly appears to be a kind of theoretical army on the march, deployed on the field of battle, preceded and constituted by its theses, which are its offensive detachments; their mission is to occupy the contested ground that the adversary already occupies, or intends to occupy. Thus we can see why philosophy has no object and does not procure knowledge in the strict sense of the word: it is because its purpose is not to produce knowledge, but to wage a strategic and tactical war against the adversary's theoretical forces, a war that, like all others, has *stakes*.

For we should envision philosophy, that is, the ensemble of the different philosophies in each particular period, as a theoretical battlefield. Kant, who wanted to make the 'perpetual peace' of critical philosophy reign over this battlefield (with the victory of his own philosophy, which would disarm all the others), called previous philosophy, or 'metaphysics' (his word for it) precisely a 'battlefield' (*Kampfplatz*). It should be added that it is an irregular, uneven battlefield, scarred with the trenches of old combats, bristling with abandoned fortifications that have been occupied and reoccupied time and again, studded with the names of places where the fighting was particularly fierce, and forever exposed to the resurgence of fresh battalions that can loom up out of the past and join the new forces on the march. It should be added that it is a battlefield on which, in any given period, a main front can, despite all, take shape alongside the secondary fronts; and all the opposed forces as well as all the secondary fronts can coalesce around this main front and find themselves centred on it. It should be added that it is a battlefield where the fighting has been going on ever since the emergence of the first philosophy in history, and that it is the same battle that is still going on there, under new, provisional names: the battle between idealism and materialism.

Idealists have often made fun of Engels' thesis that the whole history of philosophy comes down to idealism's perpetual struggle against materialism. Idealism has in fact rarely come forward under its own name, whereas materialism, which did not have the advantage, did not advance masked, but declared itself to be what it aspired to be, even if it did not always quite live up to its aspirations. Idealists have criticized Engels for his schematism. It is true: *this thesis is schematic* – but only when it is misinterpreted.

For it is certainly easy to deform it, and say: show us, in history, in which we see realism opposing nominalism, mechanism opposing dynamism, spiritualism opposing positivism and so on – show us the conflict between idealism and materialism, if you please! But that is to assume that philosophies are all of a piece, that some are wholly idealist and others are wholly materialist; it is to assume that the front has remained stationary in history; it is to go looking for chimeras. In fact, and even if we shall have to refine this distinction some day by making studies of each system, *every philosophy is simply a more or less complete realization of one of the two antagonistic tendencies, the idealist or materialist tendency.*

What is realized in every philosophy is not the tendency, but the antagonistic contradiction between the two tendencies. This is not so for reasons of convenience, such as those that once inspired the policy of the princes whom Machiavelli condemned for hiring foreign mercenaries and incorporating them into their own armies.[4] It is so for reasons stemming from the very nature of philosophical war. If a philosophy wants to occupy the adversary's positions, it has to rally the bulk of its adversary's forces to its cause by, among other things, turning his arguments against him. If you want to know your enemy, according to Goethe as cited by Lenin, go to your enemy's country.[5] If you want to defeat your enemy, capture not just his territory and troops, but *above all his arguments*; for, with his arguments, you will control both his troops and his territory. It should be understood that, by vocation, every philosophy intends to occupy *the whole battlefield*, and must therefore arm itself *preventively* with an eye to occupying the adverse positions; that is, it must put it itself, in advance, in a state of readiness to capture positions currently in the enemy's hands. It must therefore seize the enemy's arms and arguments in advance.

Every philosophy accordingly carries its own enemy inside it, so to speak, defeated *in advance*; responds *in advance* to all his counter-attacks; takes up a position *in advance* in his battle formation, modifying its own so as to be capable of this takeover. That is why every idealist philosophy necessarily includes materialist arguments in itself, and the other way around. There is no pure philosophy in the world: read, there is no wholly idealist or wholly materialist philosophy. Even what is called Marxist materialist philosophy will never be able to lay claim to being wholly materialist, for to do so would be to abandon the fight by renouncing the idea of preventively occupying positions held by idealism.

'Well now,' it will be said, 'there's a lovely explanation for you! We understand, of course, how adversaries might fight each other that way. A battlefield, we're told. But, after all, there are many playing fields where the goal is to occupy the adversary's positions in order to take possession of the whole field. In a game, however, everyone at least knows what the stakes are: winning. And everyone knows it's just for fun. Once the game is over, the players leave the field. Do philosophers only pretend to fight, like dedicated amateur sportsmen? Do they fight simply for the sake of winning, or the pleasure of competing and showing off their talents to the spectators? But what pleasure do men as serious as philosophers are take in playing? And where are the spectators?'

This argument must be taken seriously, for, after all, we have so far done nothing more than to define the *formal* conditions of a general, perpetual war, very much like the one waged by the men of the state of nature as described by Hobbes in *Leviathan*. At least we understand, in Hobbes, what people fight for: 'goods', their motivation in the last instance, which sustains the other motivations, rivalry and prestige. But *where are the material stakes of this philosophical war*, which, if it has none, stands every chance of being conceived of in the idealist terms of a struggle for pure prestige?

Moreover, if we take another look at the history of philosophy, we will observe strange changes in the way the theoretical battlefront is traced. Sometimes the fight is over politics and morality (Plato), sometimes – a very serene fight in this case – over mathematics, biology, rhetoric and virtue (Aristotle), sometimes over falling bodies (Descartes), sometimes over substance (Spinoza, Hume), sometimes over the pure sciences (Kant) and so on. If the front shifts this way, if a desperate battle is engaged for this or that unexpected salient, if the same combat is endlessly restaged for such diverse objectives, the reason is that *the philosophical war shifts this way and that on its own battlefield* in obedience to a course of events which, albeit absent from that field, have so profound an impact on it that they can precipitate such shifts: events in the history of scientific discoveries, events in the history of politics, morality, religion and so on. Thus there are *real stakes* in this make-believe war, serious stakes in this semblance of a war. We do not see them as such on the battlefield, however, because *they are found outside it.*

We must therefore examine these stakes in order to discover what they are. When we do, we find that they consist of the ensemble of the social practices that we have analysed. In the order of the historical events which, from afar, affect the philosophical battlefield, the practices and ideologies do not always hold the same place or play the same part. A scientific event, such as the discovery of mathematics in the sixth and fifth centuries in Greece, can suddenly surge up in the midst of the contradictory unity existing among the practices and ideologies, producing a disorder there that it is necessary to overcome at all costs, as Plato so ably did – but there was also the (democratic) 'decadence' of the City that Plato, the politician Plato, wished to reform. Some other scientific event, such as the discovery of Galilean physics or the discovery of universal attraction, can put a 'tear' in the tissue of the reigning ideology and trigger the philosophical reaction of a Descartes or a Kant. As a general rule, however, scientific events do not play the main role in the great ideological upheavals; that role falls, above all, to social and political events that modify the relations of production and political relations, drawing ideological relations in their wake. Such massive mutations in ideology call for a response. Philosophy intervenes at this point in order to modify its previous configuration and confront the upheavals touched off in this way.

But, our indefatigable interlocutor will object, why should philosophy get mixed up in this business? Are philosophers not people who have withdrawn from the world and have nothing but the 'search after truth' at heart? And if they do get involved, who in the world can explain to us *why*, and *in the name of what*, and *with what effect in view*? Here too, we have to take the objection seriously, and respond to it. To do so, however, we must make a long detour – through the state.

17 DOMINANT IDEOLOGY AND PHILOSOPHY

We have said that ideology was structured, in the last instance, by a major contradiction that traverses it, marking it throughout: the one that opposes the dominant ideology to the dominated ideology. But what is the dominant ideology? It is 'the ideology of the dominant class' (Marx).

We know that the function of this dominant ideology is to enable the social class that has taken state power and exercises its dictatorship to become the 'ruling' class, in other words, to acquire the free consent (consensus) of those it exploits and dominates by offering them an ideology which, forestalling their revolt, induces them to submit to this class of their own free will. We also know, however, that the subjection [*assujettissement*] of the exploited and the unification of society under the domination of the class in power is not the dominant ideology's sole function. Its primary function is to unite this class; to fuse, in a unified political will, the various social strata that have aggregated to form it in a given historical period; and, in the most favourable case, to ensure the development of its relations of production, of its production – in short, of its history. The dominant ideology is thus not only for the consumption of others, those exploited by the dominant class; it is first and foremost for that class's own consumption and, *on occasion*, for the consumption, by way of its 'fallout', of the dominated classes.

One term has recurred in this explanation: unity, unify, unification. Every class that comes to power after a social and political revolution has to modify the whole of the previous social and political configuration in order to consolidate its domination. It has to unify itself as a class, constituting a unity with the allies it needs; it has to transform the state apparatuses that it has inherited in order to overcome their contradictions; it has, in particular, to unify the state or reinforce its unity. Naturally, it also has to constitute, *by dint of a unifying operation of a peculiar kind*, the dominant ideology that it needs in order to rule, which must be *one* to be effective.

It is here that the dominant class butts up against the material diversity of the practices, as well as that of the ideologies which these practices inspire, and which govern them. Remember Hesiod: it is the sailor's work that gives the sailor his ideas, the farmer's work that gives the farmer his ideas, the blacksmith's work that gives the blacksmith his ideas. There is something irreducible here. It has its source in the practices of the transformation of nature and the long struggle against winds, sea and earth, against iron and fire. Remember, however, that, from the moment human beings live in society, none of these 'local' practices or the corresponding 'local' ideologies remain isolated. 'Regional' ideologies form above them, uniting them to produce the widely shared ideologies of religion, morality, political and aesthetic ideas and so on. Remember, finally, that this ensemble of 'local' and then 'regional' ideologies are ultimately grouped together in two grand political tendencies that stand over against each other: the ideology of the dominant class (or classes) and that of the dominated classes. It is all too clear that the former crushes the latter, reduces it to silence and distorts it past recognition, except when it gives it the floor the better to refute it. Yet it exists nonetheless, as does the tendency to rebellion among all the exploited and all the enslaved. It is not the peace reigning among the slaves that can deceive anyone, when one knows that it is the peace of servitude.

If this counter-power of rebellion and revolution were not there in the world, it would be impossible to understand all the fantastic precautions taken by the class in power. Hobbes put it well: look at your doors, there are locks on them; why is that, if not because you are already afraid of being attacked by burglars or the poor?[1] Similarly, we may say: look at your dominant ideology; it too bolts all the doors and arranges for God to mount the main guard so that everything will remain firmly in place. Why is that, if not because *you are already afraid of being attacked by your adversaries*, precisely those whom you hold in servitude and reduce to silence? The gigantic ideological apparatus that reigns in this fashion – at the limit, amidst an intimidating silence broken only by a few rare cries or, more seriously, a few rare rebellions – bears witness to the threat hanging over the established ideological power.

It is therefore a matter of the utmost necessity and the utmost urgency that the dominant class *unify its ideology as a dominant ideology*. To do so, it must first take stock of the state of the front and of the ideological arguments, laying hands on whatever may be of use to it: it doesn't much matter who has come up with such-and-such an argument, provided it can serve my cause! What the dominant class finds this way, however, it finds scattered here and there; as for the previously prevailing unity, which no longer suits it, the dominant class has to break it up or reorganize it from within to *make* this unity suit it. This does not happen automatically. Just try to adjust so many disparate elements and arrange for them to cohere well enough to make a unified ideology, one adapted to the dominant class's political objectives! This is all the harder to do in that the adverse classes, the old dominant class and the new exploited class, do not afford the dominant class the leisure to 'slap its dominant ideology together' in its spare time, or let it construct it on a plan carefully laid out in advance. In short, the whole of this long labour of unification goes on in the confusion of struggles and amidst class struggle, and is itself one element or episode of the class struggle.

Consider Plato: this aristocrat, who despised Athenian democracy and looked back nostalgically to the day when the big landed proprietors had ruled Greece, Plato, who was grappling with the irruption of mathematics and the hair-splitting of the Sophists, men rather like the technocrats and demagogues of their time – this aristocrat had to draw himself up to the lofty height of philosophy, his philosophy, to combat the 'Friends of the Earth' and send a giant war-machine out onto the field of battle. Plato discussed everything, every practice, every trade, every idea. Do you suppose he did so just for fun? But this was a man who was to offer his services to chiefs-of-state (in Sicily). At the same time, he offered them his philosophical work, which he was counting on to produce very precise effects. What did Plato do? He *proposed* to the politicians of his day, in revolt against the course that things were taking, his modest personal contribution to patching up the dominant ideology, torn and tattered by the great events of the times: his personal attempt at restoring (but only after recent developments had been taken into account) the old aristocratic ideology, tailored to the tastes of the day – an *aggiornamento*. An individual philosopher can do no more. He cannot take the place of the chief-of-state and impose his own philosophy; he contents himself with producing and proposing it. However, *to produce it, Plato put himself, in a sense, in the place of the chief-of-state or the social class* whose interests the chief-of-state represented, and crowned himself 'king' in philosophy. It was on behalf of that social class that he performed the immense task of philosophical patching up: in short, the task of unifying the old aristocratic ideology on new foundations, those that the changing times had forced on it.

This state of affairs explains the relationship that philosophers as individuals have to philosophy. They are not philosophers unless they feel responsible for this historical and political task and undertake to carry it out. Hence their extraordinary gravity, even when they are bitterly ironic, like Nietzsche, for they all feel they have been invested with a truly historical mission that is within the realm of possibility. Things accordingly take a curious course: no one commissions anything from them, yet they behave as if they had a mandate, as if they considered themselves to be representatives of the dominant class or the dominated classes. They go, as it were, to the market of philosophical wares to offer their theoretical merchandise to anyone who might care to acquire it. Sometimes they find the buyer they were expecting; sometimes they find a completely unexpected buyer who needs this merchandise in order to adapt it, in his own fashion, for the consumption of his clientele; and sometimes they head back home without making a sale. In the last-named case, they keep at their little task until the occasion finally presents itself, or presents itself long after their death, thanks to one of those historical encounters that shall have to be explained some day, or never presents itself. Thus there exists, in history, an incredible *mass of leftover philosophies* that are like so much theoretical waste. This waste is, however, waste associated with finished products that *do* find takers on the market. Thus there are, in philosophical no less than in material production, enormous 'incidental costs' of production.

Doubtless there exist, amidst all this production, theoretical artisans who fabricate a philosophy out of their personal fantasy or delirium, or their subjective preferences, or the sheer pleasure they take in theorizing. Yet directly, or even very indirectly, all these productions fall, in one way or another, under the law of the opposition between idealism and materialism. This is because no philosopher can elude the implacable law of the philosophical battlefield, which has it that, in the last instance, straightforwardly or obliquely, every philosophy will range itself in one of the two camps or its margins (of error or manoeuvre). This adherence does not have to be explicit, nor does every philosopher have to repeat the materialist or idealist theses verbatim. It is enough that what he produces be organized with regard to the general perspective of the battlefield, that it take the adverse parties' positions and arguments into account. It does not even have to take *explicit* account of them: certain silences are sometimes quite as eloquent as certain declarations. Take Descartes: he discusses mathematics, physics, medicine (morality, in his view, is simply an application of medicine) and, of course, God. He says, however, virtually nothing about politics, whereas his contemporary Hobbes discusses it amply and scandalously, as do Spinoza and Leibniz. Yet Descartes' silence about politics, taken together with what he says elsewhere about his God, 'lord and master, like a King in his realm',[2] shows well enough what his party in politics was: the party of the absolute monarchy, which accommodated the interests of a bourgeoisie well served, in the field of the sciences and the ideology of truth, by Descartes' philosophy.

For example – to take a case anterior to Descartes – a man such as Machiavelli, who talks about nothing but history and political and military theory, utters not a word about philosophy. His way of talking about history and politics betrays, however, with blinding clarity, philosophical positions radically antagonistic to the whole moralizing political tradition inherited from Aristotle's commentators and prevailing Christian theory. Thus silence can represent a political position under certain conditions in which silence is a political imperative (Machiavelli could not declare himself to be philosophically opposed to the dominant philosophy). But it is only the balance of power among the ideas reigning over the philosophical battlefield that confers this value on his silence, a value established in spite of it, for this silence is itself one of the forces in the field.

The task of unifying the existing ideological elements as a dominant ideology is, therefore, a task for the dominant class's class struggle, and it is carried out in forms derived from the struggle of the classes. It is here that philosophy plays its irreplaceable role. For it intervenes in this combat to accomplish a mission that no other practice can.

18 PHILOSOPHY AS THEORETICAL LABORATORY

We shall again have recourse to a likeness in order to depict philosophy's mission: that of the adjustor.[1] Our adjustor could have any specialty, but, to clarify our ideas, let us make him a machinist – a worker who has to turn out a complex part for use in a machine. He has a number of material elements to hand: parts made of steel, iron, copper and so on. He has to shape and then adjust them so that they fit together and work the way they are supposed to: this calls for a great deal of work of finishing and adaptation. Now suppose, as I have just done, that these parts are not all made of the same material, iron, but that the state of production and the type of mechanism to be constructed require that the machinist also use copper, a recently discovered metal that has become indispensable on account of the advantages it offers. The machinist has to take the existence of copper and its properties into account in order to adjust all the parts and fit them together in a new way. He will not combine them the way he used to combine parts when all of them were made of iron, because copper is more malleable and less resistant than iron. In making his adjustment, he will make allowances for the fact that this new part is made of copper, and the result will be *a new way of fitting* parts together. A new way of adjusting and combining them and, at the limit, a new adjustor: for it is quite possible that someone good at assembling iron parts will find himself at sea when a copper part suddenly pops up among them.

Things happen much the same way in philosophy. Or, rather, philosophy itself becomes necessary with the discovery of a new metal that suddenly appears among the old, familiar metals.

For philosophy was not always needed to unify the ensemble of ideological elements. In the history of the great majority of societies, religion played this unifying role for a very long time. The grand myths about the existence of God, the creation of the world and final salvation sufficed: all human activities and the corresponding ideologies could find their place in them, thus constituting the unified ideology that the dominant class needed to ensure its domination.

The day came, however, when a new type of knowledge irrupted in history, not technical or ideological, but scientific: *scientific knowledge*. It represented a real danger for the established order, because it offered people proof that 'absolute' knowledge of things could be provided by their own scientific practice rather than divine revelation. The hierarchy of powers in which religious knowledge went hand-in-hand with political authority risked being undermined as a result. It was necessary to meet this materialist threat that was undoing established authority, the men invested with it, and the submission they had obtained from those they exploited. It was necessary to take possession of the new practice and its power and subordinate them to the established order. But men of a kind different from priests were needed to restore the jeopardized order of things, other 'adjustors' who could line up the old parts and the new end to end and set the machine back in motion – an overhauled machine, yet basically the same machine as before. These men could only come from the ranks of those who had mastered the new scientific practice. They had to be well versed in mathematics.

Philosophy was born of this rupture and the political conjuncture in which it emerged.[2] As far as its function was concerned, it simply succeeded religion in the role *of the unifier of ideologies as a dominant ideology*. By virtue of its content, however, it was supposed to get the upper hand over the new elements that the new practice had introduced into the world of men.

But what new thing did mathematical science introduce? The following revelation: to acquire demonstrable knowledge, one had to reason about pure, abstract objects using pure, abstract methods. Those who failed to take this novelty into account were condemned (or risked being condemned) to fall behind the times by an ideology originating in mathematical practice. It was therefore necessary to make the tremendous concession involved in adopting the principles of mathematical demonstration, while pressing them into the service of the dominant classes' ideological objectives, so as not to expose oneself to the danger of being '*outflanked*' on one's *left*. It would not be easy, but no matter: the experiment could be made and might well prove conclusive. It *was* made and it *did* prove conclusive. Witness the work of Plato, who inscribed on the lintel over the door of his Academy: 'Let none who is not a geometer enter here', while – this is telling – subordinating mathematics, demoted to second place, to philosophy itself in his system and, in the last instance, to politics. Every peasant knows that he need only catch a dangerous dog and train it for it to obey him and guard his doorstep. *To domesticate one's adversary by stealing his language*: that is the whole secret of ideological struggle, even when, for determinate historical reasons, it takes the form of philosophical struggle.

Whether or not Plato founded philosophy is a question that may never find an answer. For Plato was preceded by others, such as Parmenides, who had also taken the existence of mathematics into account in the way they reasoned. Parmenides, however, was an idealist like Plato, and it is convenient to suppose, since the dominant ideology was at stake, and since, as the dominant class's ideology, it was necessarily idealist, that philosophy began with idealism. This would make idealism a gigantic idealist *aggiornamento* intended to respond to the irruption of mathematics. Yet it is not certain that that is how things happened. For we find in Plato's works a sort of spectre, that of the materialist Democritus, whose eighty treatises (an immense oeuvre!) were destroyed, in strange circumstances which suggest that they were deliberately destroyed, in a day and age in which it was hard to produce multiple copies of a work.

Thus philosophy may have commenced with Democritus. In other words, it may have commenced with materialism, which would accordingly have expressed philosophically, and positively, without theoretical reservations, 'values' sustained by the conjunction of its time with the discovery of mathematical science. If so, it would have been to ward off this threat, already philosophical and already discussed in philosophical terms, that Plato fabricated his war machine, directed explicitly against the 'Friends of the Earth', in whom we can easily make out Democritus's followers. Whatever the fact of the matter, it is not Democritus who has survived, but Plato – a vivid example of the kind of implacable choice that a dominant ideology makes; and, with Plato, idealist philosophy has dominated the whole history of class societies, repressing or obliterating materialist philosophy. (It is no accident that we have only a few fragments of Epicurus, that reprobate.)

We should not, however, conclude from the conditions surrounding the beginnings of philosophy (the birth of which was precipitated by the irruption of mathematical science) that it has always been a response to events in the history of the sciences alone. While philosophy[3] provided, with the abstract form of its objects and its demonstrative method, the absolute condition for the discourse needed to neutralize the threat that science posed, it has in the course of its history reacted to very different and far more dangerous events. It can even be said that the great social upheavals, the revolutions in the relations of production and in political relations, have exercised the decisive influence on the history of philosophy. Not immediately, for the transition from an economic revolution to a revolution in politics and then in ideology takes time; but on the condition represented by a certain interval, either after the fact (Hegel's famous phrase: philosophy always takes wing at dusk, like the owl of Minerva)[4] or, paradoxically, before the fact. Yes, before the fact: for the social revolution gestating in society's depths can long be prevented from exploding by the thick concrete walls of established authority, the repression exercised by the state apparatus and the ideology in place.

But changes occurring in the base can also have repercussions under the domination of the old dominant class, and can even affect the established ideology. The history of the rise of the bourgeoisie illustrates this thesis: capitalist relations began to take shape in Western Europe as early as the fourteenth century, yet it took from three to five centuries for the bourgeois political revolution to sanction them with a new law corpus, a new state apparatus and a new ideology. In the interval, however, the changes in the base had frayed a path through the existing institutions. The absolute monarchy, a transitional state form associating the *bourgeois de robe* and the capitalist bourgeois with the nobility, was already a manifestation of this. Throughout this period, moreover, audacious bourgeois began to lay the foundations of an ideology that would later become dominant: bourgeois ideology, grounded in legal ideology.

In the same way, proletarian ideology has developed under the bourgeois class's domination, in the course of a struggle that has been going on for 180 years now, without reaching its true term. Here too, ideology has a lead on the revolution. It is, however, no accident that it has been able to take this lead; it is because the bourgeois mode of production already contains elements corresponding in advance to proletarian ideology. This is so because it has increasingly socialized production and educated the exploited about class struggle as a result not only of industrial concentration and work discipline, but, as well, because of the enforced enrolment of the exploited in a political struggle that saw them fighting side by side with the bourgeoisie against the landed aristocracy in the nineteenth century, or thanks to their participation in the bloody struggle that the bourgeoisie waged against avant-garde working-class organizations and the whole working class.

If, however, we wish to understand the surprising phenomenon of the ideological anticipation of history, we must also take into account the fact that the avant-garde ideology which develops under the domination of the class in power can initially only express itself under the conditions imposed on it by the dominant ideology. Not even the most radical bourgeois philosophers and ideologues could throw God overboard. That is why they were all Deists even when they were atheists. They believed not 'in the God of the believers', but in 'the God of the philosophers and scientists', or in Spinoza's Nature-God, or in Hobbes's dumb-animal God, all of whom made the believers among their contemporaries shudder. Avant-garde bourgeois philosophy had to make outward compromises with feudal ideology's 'values', while actually using these 'values' against feudal ideology. '*Larvatus prodeo*,' said Descartes; 'I advance masked.' Feudal power had to fall before the masks could. The case of proletarian ideology is no different. It too had to cloak itself in categories borrowed from bourgeois ideology and even religion (the bourgeoisie of the *Belle époque* was not religious); later, from moral ideology; and, still later, from legal ideology. The first working-class fighters fought under the banner of the Brotherhood of the Sons of God; later, under the banner of the Liberty and Equality of 1789; and, still later, under the banner of Community, before they succeeded in endowing themselves with an ideology of their own: that of socialism and communism.

Philosophy played its silent role, a contradictory but effective role, in these tremendous social and political mutations and their ideological extensions. But just what role did it play?

To forge an image of it, let us return to our example of the adjustor, while taking into account, this time, the imperative just analysed: the one to which all ideology is subject as a result of the class struggle. This is *the imperative that existing ideology be constituted as a dominant ideology*, hence the imperative that *all the ideological elements existing in a given period of human history be unified as a dominant ideology*.

We now have a firm grasp on one point: from the moment that sciences exist in human culture, it is no longer possible for any ideology, even religious ideology, to accomplish, or even, indeed, presume to accomplish this historical task of unification, for it is dangerous for the dominant ideology to let the sciences produce their effects without interference, effects that can only be materialist. The task of unification must accordingly be carried out by a 'theory' capable of bringing the sciences to reason, that is, of putting them in their subordinate place, that is, of subordinating them by means of a 'theory' capable of mastering the existing forms of scientific demonstration and those forms' inevitable, predictable effects. It is not a matter of choice: it is a matter of the balance of power. Here too, what is involved is a preventive solution: philosophy has to 'pre-empt' developments, for, if it fails to step in in time, the risk is that the entire ideological order it wishes to safeguard will collapse.

It is incumbent on philosophy, then, to participate in a very specific way in this work of ideological unification in the dominant ideology's service. Do not misunderstand me: I say 'participate'. For there can be no question, for the dominant class and dominant ideology, of delegating all power to philosophy. The bourgeois or far-left ideologues of our day who equate philosophical knowledge with power mistake the power and knowledge that philosophy *subjectively* attributes to itself for the power and know-how that are *delegated to it within the dominant ideology by the determinant ideology.*[5] We shall see in a moment what the *determinant* ideology is in each of the known modes of production. But, whatever the determinant ideology, philosophy has its role to play in this ideological unification on which the fate of the dominant ideology depends. What is its role?

I would say that philosophy may be likened to an artisan's workshop, one in which a *theoretical adjustor* turns out parts made to measure for the purpose of connecting the various elements (more or less homogeneous, more or less contradictory) of existing ideological forms, in order to produce the relatively unified ideology that the dominant ideology must be. Of course, the material and form of these newly made parts cannot be totally foreign to the elements to be connected. Yet what are involved are new parts that should be utilizable for all possible connections. On this subject, the philosopher Duns Scotus made the most judicious remark that anyone ever has: 'Entities should not be multiplied unnecessarily.'[6] Let us translate: *connecting parts should not be multiplied unnecessarily.* Effectively to unify an ideology, the connecting parts, those that unify it, must themselves be unified. To say so is to indicate exactly the need for 'serial production' of multi-purpose parts that should be utilizable in all cases in which an ideological connection is called for. We need only think of the joints serially produced by modern industry: they can serve in an infinite number of cases.

Of course, since it is a question not just of unifying an ideology by producing interchangeable connecting joints, but also *of unifying the parts* to be connected, this being the only efficient, economic solution, the philosopher-adjustor's work consists in *forging categories that are as general as possible, capable of unifying the different domains of ideology under their theses.* This is where idealist philosophy's old aspiration to know 'the whole' or 'know and cognize [*savoir et connaître*] everything' finds its first meaning (we shall see in a moment what its second meaning is). Philosophy must establish control over, that is, impose its categories on, the ensemble of what exists – not directly, on the ensemble of really existing objects, but on the ensemble of ideologies under the domination of which the various practices operate and transform their real objects, whether nature or social relations. Philosophy thus forcibly establishes its theoretical rule over all that exists not for pleasure or out of megalomania, but for a completely different reason: in order to overcome the contradictions in existing ideology, in order to unify this ideology as the dominant ideology.

Let us consider, for just a moment, what goes on in bourgeois philosophy between the fourteenth and seventeenth centuries. One and the same category is imposed everywhere in order to account for a considerable number of local and regional ideologies and the corresponding practices. This category is that of the *subject*. Originating in legal ideology (the ideology of the law of commercial relations, in which every individual is the rightful subject of his legal capacities, as the owner of property that he can alienate), this category invades, with Descartes, the domain of philosophy, which guarantees scientific practice and its truths (the subject of the 'I think'). With Kant, it invades the domain of moral ideology (the subject of 'moral consciousness') and religious ideology (the subject of 'religious consciousness'). It had long since, with the natural law philosophers, invaded the domain of politics, by way of the 'political subject' in the social contract. It is true that this splendid unity would later suffer mishaps, to which other philosophers (Comte *et al.*) endeavoured to respond. In the form in which it very impressively presents itself in the long history of the rise of the bourgeoisie, however, it provides a demonstration of the thesis we are defending.

For, in this long history, we see philosophy '*working on' a category capable of unifying the ensemble of ideologies and the corresponding practices*, and we see it successfully applying this category, thereby forcing the agents of these practices to recognize themselves in it. For, after all – and not only philosophers, moralists and politicians were involved here, but also authors of mass-market literature and, beneath all of them, those among the exploited who could hope to become bourgeois some day – the corresponding practices were altered by this category, once the ideologies dominating them had been altered. This unity was not confined to the realm of ideas, for, in the end, it triggered a political revolt that was to culminate in the English and French revolutions.

Doubtless, we must take care not to lapse into an idealist conception of philosophy's role here. Philosophy does not do whatever it likes with the existing ideologies. By the same token, it does not fabricate, by decree, just any category capable of unifying the ideologies, in the absence of all material support. There are objective material constraints which philosophy is clearly incapable of getting around and must therefore respect. The work of ideological unification accordingly remains both contradictory and forever unfinished. There always are insurmountable problems. Because he wanted to unify knowledge too quickly, Descartes quite simply forged an imaginary physics that left force out of account. To take account of this problem, however, Leibniz, who had clearly discerned it, introduced a still more imaginary unity.[7]

As for the famous philosophers who are aware that they 'advance masked', and who are forced to think, in the dominant categories, truths that have nothing to do with them, it must not be supposed that the operation leaves them unscathed. If Descartes said nothing about political power, it is also because he shared the illusions of the political ideology behind which this uncriticized, unknown power presented itself. If Spinoza discussed political power in terms of the concepts of natural law in order to criticize them, his critique was too shallow to allow him to get beyond a simple rejection of morality as the foundation of all political power, or to get beyond an abstract conception of force as the foundation of that same power.

Finally, we must also include in the present inventory, here drawn up from the standpoint of bourgeois ideology, bourgeois philosophy's anti-wage-worker front in addition to its anti-feudal front. Here too, the task of unifying ideology as the dominant ideology encounters obstacles that philosophy can undoubtedly skirt, but cannot really surmount. For just try to make an exploited wage-worker believe that he is of the same race as the bourgeoisie and has the same rights; that he too is a free moral, political, legal, aesthetic, scientific 'subject', when virtually all these rights are denied him in practice! The dominant philosophy goes as far as it can in its function of unifying ideology, but it cannot leap out of its time, as Hegel said, or out of its class character, as Marx said.

At any event, we can here grasp the reason for which philosophy has traditionally presented itself in the form of a system. What is a system? It is a set of *finite elements*, or elements that come under a number of *finite categories* (including the category of the infinite), which are interlinked for one and the same necessary reason, by one and the same bond, identical throughout; and it is a *closed* set, such that no element can elude the control exercised over it. The system thus confirms the existence of the unity that is the product of its unification; it is unity exhibited and demonstrated by its very exhibition – visible proof that philosophy has truly encompassed and mastered 'the whole', and that there is nothing in existence that does not fall under its jurisdiction.

Let no one here point, by way of objection, to the existence of philosophies that present themselves as a rejection and a negation of all systems (Kierkegaard, Nietzsche). For these philosophies are, as it were, the underside of the systems they reject; they would not exist if those systems did not. Obviously, to arrive at this conception, we must have an idea of the philosophies that does not consider them in isolation, but relates them all to the philosophical 'battlefield' as their condition of existence, one that is not satisfied to regard them as personal testimony or as a subjective quest for truth. Let us say that the paradoxical form of such philosophies (it is no accident that we observe their existence in periods of historical crisis, such as the Greek fifth century of the Sophists or the German nineteenth century) represents the battle formation, as it were, of philosophical guerrilla warfare, reflecting conditions in which this or that philosopher feels he lacks the force to wage generalized frontal war. He therefore attacks here and there, by surprise, by aphorisms, in an effort to hack the enemy's front to pieces. We shall see, however, that there can be other reasons for this form of philosophical existence.

19 IDEOLOGY AND PHILOSOPHY

We must, however, if everything we have just said is correct, beware of an illusion: the illusion that *philosophy has a natural right to exercise the function of theoretically unifying ideology*. For it is merely the agent of this unification and, as such, may be said simply to carry out a plan that comes to it from elsewhere. What plan? And what is this elsewhere?

This plan is usually (not always) unconscious. We, however, know it: it is a matter of unifying the existing elements of ideology as the dominant ideology. Yet that is a formal plan, lacking, so to speak, the accompanying instructions and even the essential raw material. I do not use the latter term casually, because it will bring us back to ideas that we have already analysed. For we must not forget that the task that philosophy performs is a long process of (class) struggle 'in theory' (Engels),[1] hence a process without a subject (work of which philosophy is not the absolute creator). This task is imposed on philosophy from without by the class struggle as a whole – more particularly, by the ideological class struggle. It is the balance of power in the class struggle that, at a given moment, makes a class in power, or aspiring to take power, feel the objective but also more or less 'conscious' *historical 'need'*, in order to unify itself and mobilize its partisans even in the classes it exploits, for a unified ideology that will allow it to carry its class struggle to a successful conclusion.

Formally, then, it is from the dominant class engaged in conquering power or consolidating its power that philosophy receives the 'order' to constitute a unified philosophical system making possible the gradual unification of all the elements of existing ideology. But that is not all: *this 'order' is accompanied by very precise 'instructions'*, which are likewise not arbitrary.

For history shows that an exploiting class's power is wholly based on the forms of exploitation it exercises, hence on the forms taken by the relation of production in the possession and alienation of the means of production or of labour-power. As Marx says, the whole secret of power, the secret of the state, resides 'in the relationship between the immediate producer and the means of production'.[2] In the bourgeoisie's case, this immediate relation is expressed in the form of the *legal relation*, which is inseparable from *legal ideology*. For legal ideology, every individual is a subject of law, master and owner of his body, will, freedom, property, acts and so on. This legal ideology does not concern commercial exchange relations alone, but extends to political, familial, moral and other relations. Thus bourgeois society as a whole is based on law and legal ideology. A kind of ideological unification is already at work here in practice itself, traced in dotted lines, as it were: an almost universally recognized form, pre-adapted to the majority of existing social practices. The imperative to generalize this form emanates from the bourgeoisie's economic and political practice: the bourgeoisie wants the free circulation of goods, the free circulation of labour-power and even, at least in its beginnings, the free circulation of ideas and texts. Thus philosophy is charged with the historical mission of *universalizing this form* by finding the modalities appropriate to each ideological element and the corresponding practices. Philosophy must therefore make a priority of taking this form (the subject form) and no other as its raw material, and working on it until it is utilizable in every area of social practice. It must make it abstract enough to serve all possible purposes and in all possible cases; it must confer upon it the modalities required by each local or regional ideology; it must, finally, derive from it the higher abstractions that will bring about unity and guarantee this unity.

The illusion of philosophy's omnipotence is thereby dispelled. It is not just the example of bourgeois philosophy which proves it. It has been shown often enough that, in feudalism, philosophy was merely the 'handmaiden of theology'. We might equally well say that the materialist philosophy that the proletariat needs is the 'handmaiden of *its* politics'. For the 'order' for a 'new practice of philosophy'[3] does indeed come from the practice of proletarian class struggle, a practice of philosophy that the proletariat needs in its struggle and for its struggle. A moment's reflection will show that the proletariat is not an exploiting, but only an exploited class. The relations of production to which it is subject are imposed on it from without by the capitalist bourgeoisie. They do not constitute its strength; rather, they would seem to constitute its weakness. No power accrues to the proletariat from the existence of such relations or their supreme consecration by the state. Just as the proletariat can count on nothing but its own two hands to get by, so, to fight, it can count on nothing but its own ideas and forces. It needs an ideology of its own to unify its forces and pit them against those that bourgeois ideology musters. To unify such ideological elements as it may have at its disposal, which are in part the legacy of the long history of the struggle of the oppressed, the proletariat too needs a philosophy of its own that *adjusts* the ensemble of its ideological arms for class combat.

In no case, then, is philosophy an omnipotent power that determines the destination and direction of its own combat. In no case is philosophy autonomous, although it makes a show of founding its own origin and force. Philosophy is simply *the delegation, in the theoretical domain, of the economic, political and ideological class struggle. As such, it is, 'in the last instance, class struggle in theory'.*[4]

20 PHILOSOPHY AND THE SCIENCE OF CLASS STRUGGLE

One last question remains, a question of the greatest importance. All past philosophies known to us were subject to the mechanism just described; all of them acted 'on command' in the dominant class's (or classes') service, working on the 'raw material' of the ideology determinant for that class. This condition, however, made them dependent on the dominant class's (or classes') objectives, *hence on its subjectivity*. If every philosophy unfolds on class theoretical bases and unifies the existing ideological elements as the dominant ideology, for the dominant class's benefit, it is easy to see why philosophy produces not knowledge, but only a weapon in a fight. A weapon is a weapon: it produces nothing but the power of victory. At the same time, it is easy to see why philosophy has always been able to do without the experimental set-up indispensable to every science that produces knowledge. Better, it is easy to see why such an experimental set-up is totally alien to it. We never come across one in philosophy's own practice.

But if this is so, does it not mean that philosophy, which depends on the ideology determinant for the dominant class, *is merely an ideology*? Is it not to expose oneself to the classic jibes of all those who, beginning with the Sophists, have mocked philosophy's pretensions to utter the Truth about all things? In other words, how can we ensure that philosophy is not the theoretical delirium of an individual or a social class in search of guarantees or rhetorical ornament? How can we reconcile this class connection, which we seem to have arrived at, with philosophy's pretensions to produce objective knowledge, or with the assurances that a revolutionary class has a right to expect from the materialist philosophy that should guide it in its combat?

These questions deserve serious examination. For if all that we have said so far has an objective result, it is the one we have attained by showing that every philosophy occupies class positions in theory and, consequently, that it stands in a necessary relationship with the class relations prevailing in a given society. Whether or not this objective link is conscious and controlled depends on another question: the question of the positions that a class occupies in the balance of power in the class struggle. When the class involved is an exploiting class, an *unconscious* necessity governs the whole dispositive that culminates in political and ideological domination. The owners of the means of production do not exploit wage-workers intentionally, but as the result of a mechanism mobilizing class relations that govern and go beyond them. They do not seize state power intentionally and intentionally constitute the ideology from which they will derive effects of domination and subjection; that is the effect of a dialectic that necessitates construction of a state apparatus in order to guarantee the conditions of exploitation. Everything in this mechanism is geared to exploitation and the domination that sanctions it; the dominant ideology, like the philosophy which adjusts that ideology's categories in order to unify it, is driven by the dynamics of class exploitation. In these conditions, it is understandable that the limits of the dominant ideology and the philosophy that unifies it should be determined by the limits of the dominant class's objectives – in other words, by its subjectivity – and that the 'knowledge' philosophy attains should be conditioned by those limits and, consequently, subjective.

Imagine, however, a class that exploits no one and is struggling for its emancipation and the abolition of classes. Imagine that, in its combat, this class undertakes to *unify itself by unifying its class ideology and that it unifies this ideology by forging a philosophy* that can bring this unification about. In that case, if this class is armed with a scientific theory of class struggle, the conditions under which *its* philosophy is elaborated change completely. For the dependency on the proletariat's political ideology in which this philosophy necessarily finds itself will be not blind servitude, but, quite the contrary, conscious determination ensured by scientific knowledge of its conditions, forms and laws. *This scientific knowledge of the ideology commanding the philosophy charged with unifying proletarian ideology will make it possible to create the conditions for a philosophical adjustment that is as objective as can be* – by adjusting this philosophy to the conditions governing the existence of both proletarian class struggle and proletarian ideology in the class struggle against the bourgeoisie.

The term *adjustment* finds its ultimate consequence here: in the Marxist category of correctness [*justesse*].[1] We said some time ago that philosophical propositions do not produce knowledge, since they have no object in the sense in which science has an object. This amounts to saying that philosophical propositions cannot be called 'true'. We may now advance the thesis that they can be called 'correct' [juste], if this adjective, 'correct', designates the effect of an adjustment that takes into account all the elements of a given situation in which a class is struggling to attain its objectives. In that case, 'correct' is the adjective corresponding not to justice [justice], a moral category, but to correctness [justesse], a practical category that refers to the adaptation of means to ends as a function of the class character of the one pursuing those ends. We do not claim to escape class subjectivism by invoking, as Lukács does in History and Class Consciousness, the 'universal' nature of the proletarian class; we do not claim that the 'correctness' of the proletariat's philosophy is the equivalent of truth by virtue of this universality, which supposedly does away with the particularism of subjectivity.[2] Quite the contrary: we shall say that *the 'correctness' of the philosophy of the proletariat escapes subjectivity because it is under the control of an objective science, the science of the laws of class struggle.*

We have enough historical examples to hand to demonstrate the fruitfulness of this 'control', its existence and, at the same time, its shortcomings. It is, precisely, a subjectivist 'class' interpretation of the 'correctness' of Marxist philosophical theses which has, in the crisis of Marxist philosophy that we are currently undergoing, very nearly precipitated the definitive bankruptcy of Marxist theory. When Stalin, in the famous fourth chapter of his History of the CP(b), presented a positivist version of Marxism and the dialectic, he in fact rallied to a (bourgeois) subjectivist conception of proletarian philosophy.[3] As he presents it, the dialectic states 'the most general truths' of practice; it is a form of knowledge, the science of the sciences. As for method, it is an appendage of the dialectic. Setting out from such fragile premises, it was easy, especially in the prevailing circumstances, to lurch, while maintaining this basic subjective determinism, into another type of class subjectivism, *proletarian* class subjectivism. This was the period of 'bourgeois science and proletarian science', of the class character of scientific knowledge, the history of which is well-known, as is the havoc it wrought (see Dominique Lecourt, Lysenko).[4] But, in this case, the most striking thing is the fact *that this conception of philosophical 'correctness' was based on a false theory of the science of the laws of class struggle.* As interpreted from on high by Stalin, Marxist theory was reduced to an economistic evolutionism without surprises, one intended, like any vulgar ideology you care to name, to justify the accomplished fact of the reigning order, [here that of] the USSR, supposedly in the name of the dictatorship of the proletariat, but in fact for the sake of Stalin's personal dictatorship. A scientific 'theory' of this sort was clearly incapable of 'controlling', in any respect whatsoever, the 'correctness' of the philosophical theses it upheld. On the contrary, Stalin provided it with the philosophy it needed, which, unfortunately, the majority of Marxist philosophers, as Stalin's faithful emulators, have yet to abandon.

One can, however – we have historical examples here too – propose a completely different conception of the relationship of scientific 'control' of the 'correctness' of the theses of the proletariat's philosophy by the theory of the laws of class struggle. One surprising feature of the examples we have, those of Marx, Engels, Lenin, Gramsci or Mao, cannot fail to strike us: the great modesty of their philosophical constructions.

I do not just mean Marx. Everyone knows that, once he had 'settled accounts' with his 'erstwhile philosophical consciousness' in *The German Ideology* (1845), Marx basically produced no philosophy at all, a few lines aside. Yet no one today doubts that he profoundly thought and practised his philosophy, or that, in his theoretical and political works, he was a materialist and a dialectician. And when Engels showed him the manuscript of *Anti-Dühring*, a scathing polemical reply to the works of an anti-Marxist socialist, Marx approved of it: yet this book was neither a philosophical treatise nor a philosophical system. Everyone also knows that Lenin too, aside from *Materialism and Empirio-Criticism* and his reading notes on Hegel's *Logic*,[5] neglected to work on a grand philosophical text, in order to devote himself wholly to political practice. Yet, as with Marx, no one doubts that the philosophy at work in that practice was one of exceptional force and solidity. Gramsci likewise devoted nothing of importance to philosophy, and the same is true of Mao, who dedicated only a few occasional interventions to it.

Thus we find ourselves confronting a sort of paradox. It is inconceivable that the proletarian class position in philosophy should not be stated, in order to help unify proletarian ideology with a view to proletarian class struggle. It is, however, surprising that that position in philosophy, with the aberrant exception of Stalin and his emulators, has been so modest and intermittent, and has not afforded itself the advantages of the classical exposition of systems, of their rigour and exhaustiveness. For does the proletariat not, after all, have to 'raise itself to the position of the ruling class', as the 'Manifesto'[6] puts it, and, to that end, provide itself with a dominant ideology, which is inconceivable in the absence of a specifically proletarian philosophy? Once the proletariat has come to power, will it too not need that philosophy to unify the different ideological elements in existence and, in this way, transform the social practices under the dictatorship of the proletariat?

I think that this paradox is, precisely, constitutive of the *Marxist position in philosophy*.[7] I think this for the following reason. We have also seen that the unification of ideology as a dominant ideology is linked to the existence of the dominant classes. We have even seen that philosophy's systematic unity, which serves this unification, is linked to this process of unification as to its condition of possibility. We may now add that this entire 'system', which goes beyond the 'system' of philosophy as such, *is directly bound up with the state, with the unity of the state.* Engels once said, in a memorable phrase, that 'the state is the first ideological power',[8] brilliantly highlighting the relationship that binds the unity of the state to the unity of the dominant ideology and the philosophy which, in its 'systematic' form, serves that ideology. Despite what Engels also said, in an unhappy phrase this time, philosophy does not construct 'systems' in order to satisfy 'an imperishable desire of the human mind', which cannot bear 'contradictions' (an astonishing phrase in the mouth of a dialectician).[9] It constructs them in order to force unity upon the ideological elements that it must furnish with the categories of their unification. But, in so doing, it reproduces the form of the state within itself: its unity, stronger than all diversity.

Did the proletariat have to bow to this form, compulsory for the dominant bourgeois ideology, and this means, also compulsory for that philosophy – *the system*? The easy solution was there for the taking, and the first 'socialist' philosophers – the utopian socialists, Saint-Simon, Fourier, Proudhon and others – took it; they set about fabricating, as Dühring too would later do, proletarian 'systems' that vied with the bourgeois systems. Their 'systems' seemed to offer all the advantages of any system: an exposition of the ensemble of things, each in its proper place, their internal relations, prediction of the future and so on. At the same time, however, they produced the effect of illusion and imposture that an exploiting class needs to assure itself of its future: by taking possession of it in advance, in orderly form, in a systematic exposition.

On a profound political instinct, Marx and Engels refused to go down this easy road. Just as the proletariat could not, in their view, constitute itself as a dominant class unless it invented a 'new practice of politics', so it had, in order to sustain this new practice of politics, to invent a 'new practice of philosophy'. It is still the strategy of communism that is at work in these perspectives, which are philosophical and, equally, political. It is a matter of preparing, here and now, the revolutionary communist future; it is therefore a matter of putting in place, here and now, completely new elements, without yielding to the pressure of bourgeois ideology and philosophy – on the contrary, by resisting it. And, since the question of the state commands everything, it is necessary to break, here and now, the subtle, yet very powerful bond that binds philosophy to the state, especially when it takes the form of a 'system'.

Marx neither revealed nor discovered the existence of this bond. Philosophers had long been aware of it, even if they did not know its exact nature. Plato was well aware, and not just out of personal ambition, that philosophy stood in a direct relationship to the state. At the other end of the history of Western philosophy, Hegel said so even more clearly. In both philosophy and the state, it is a question of power. In philosophy, ideas are in power over other ideas and 'exploit' them. In the state, classes are in power over another class and exploit it. And the power of ideas over ideas sustains, from afar, but concretely, the power of one class over another. If we want to pave the way for a different kind of philosophy, one that will no longer be an expression of class power and will no longer wall a dominant class up in the forms of its own class power, we need to break the bond that subordinates philosophy to the state.

In this perspective, the relationship between the ideologies and the philosophy to come (and now we understand the great Marxist leaders' and authors' relative silence) appears completely different. I have shown (in *Philosophy and the Spontaneous Philosophy of the Scientists*) that idealist philosophy spends its time 'exploiting' scientific practice so as to produce the greatest possible benefit for the bourgeoisie's moral, religious and political 'values'. This exploitation of the practices by philosophy is the rule, and it is inevitable as long as philosophy stands in the service of an exploiting class's politics and is incapable of scientifically controlling the effects of that politics. For the practices have to submit to the stranglehold of ideologies subordinated to the dominant ideology, while philosophy, which unifies this ideology, has to take advantage of certain practices in order to put pressure on others.

In the revolutionary perspective of Marxism, however, we can imagine a completely different relationship between philosophy and the ideologies and practices: a relationship that is one not of servitude and exploitation, but of emancipation and freedom. This substitution will not do away with every contradiction, of course, but it will remove, at least in principle, the greatest of the obstacles standing in the way of the freedom of the practices: those thrown up by class struggle and the existence of classes. We cannot anticipate this future, but we have enough experience, positive and also negative, to imagine the possibility of it and think the fertility of it.

21 A NEW PRACTICE OF PHILOSOPHY

But if the foregoing is true, we can perhaps answer the well-known, much-debated question about 'Marxist philosophy' and the possibility of Marxist philosophy. Marx and Lenin chose to relegate this question to the shadows, but their silence was itself an answer to it, since they insisted so heavily on the Marxist science of the laws of class struggle and, at the same time, the new philosophy whose irruption was occasioned by it. After them, interpretations of all sorts appeared. For the revisionists, such as Bernstein, Marx had founded a science that could adapt to any philosophy at all; the most effective (for example, Kant's) was the best. For the early Lukács, Marx had founded a philosophy that absorbed, à la Hegel, what is mistakenly called the science of history. Labriola and Gramsci were rather tempted, in this period of reaction against the Second International's economism, to share these views. Stalin was too, in his dogmatic way, which made philosophy a science that incorporated the Marxist theory of history.

All these interpretations, even the most discerning of them (Gramsci's), were inspired by the existing model of bourgeois philosophy – by the idea that philosophy can exist only in certain defined forms, in particular, in the form of a system or 'meaning' that encompasses all beings, assigning them their place, meaning and end; in the best of cases, in the form of a 'theory' distinguished from science. I admit that I, for my part, was not always able to escape the influence of this conception, and that, in my first philosophical essays, I modelled my description of philosophy on science; while I did not conflate them, I did go so far as to say that Marx had produced, in a 'double break', both a science (historical materialism) and a philosophy (dialectical materialism).[1] Now I think that we have to forgo expressions of this sort, which can lead us astray.

While every science is indeed inaugurated by a 'break', since it must 'change terrain', abandoning the old terrain of pre-scientific notions, most of which are ideological, in order to develop on new theoretical bases, a new philosophy does not proceed that way. It is not marked by the same discontinuity, since it simply takes its place in the continuity of a millennial struggle which opposes adversaries whose arguments vary, but whose objectives remain more or less the same through the variations in the conjuncture. If a new philosophy wishes to represent a revolutionary class's conception of the world in philosophy, the conception of a class which, since it exploits no other class, seeks to abolish all classes, it has to do battle on the existing philosophical battlefield, and it has to accept the rules of the battle; or, rather, it has to impose its own rules, but on the same battlefield, *without mistaking its adversary*. Imposing its own rules of battle, it can disconcert its adversary by rejecting most of the standing rules, since they only serve the domination of the class in power: for example, the rule of the 'system', and a considerable number of others, those of the Truth of Meaning, End, Guarantee and so on. In short, it must, seizing the initiative, impose a new practice of philosophy on its adversary.

If this is so, I would, for my part, prefer to talk about not 'Marxist philosophy', but a *'Marxist position in philosophy'*[2] or a 'new practice, a Marxist practice, of philosophy'. This definition seems to me to be in keeping with both the thrust [*sens*] of the philosophical revolution brought about by Marx, and the thrust of his and his successors' political and philosophical practice. If it is taken seriously, it should make it possible to begin to emerge from the profound crisis in which Marxist philosophy has been plunged since the Second International and since Stalin. May I briefly clarify one point? I would not describe Marxism as a 'philosophy of praxis', as does Gramsci, who may have been forced to by the censorship of his jailers. This is not because I consider the idea of praxis (transformation of the self by the self) to be out of place in Marxism – quite the contrary – but because this formulation can commit us to the old idealist form of the 'philosophy of . . .', which enshrines a particular determination, here praxis, as the essence or 'meaning' of the ensemble of things. If I may speak my mind, such a formulation can lead to an idealist interpretation of Marx's position in philosophy, in the style, for example, of a return to Kant or Husserl (in Italy, we see this even in the work of Enzo Paci).

22 THE DIALECTIC: LAWS OR THESES?

One more big idealistic obstacle stands in the way of this 'new practice of philosophy' based on proletarian class positions in theory. It is constituted by the old idealist distinction *between theory* (or science) *and method.* This distinction comes from scientific practice. Once a scientist has arrived at a body of objective knowledge that he can unify in a theory, he pursues his experimentation by 'realizing' this theory, in whole or in part, in a practical set-up that puts its object 'to the question' (Kant). To do so, he 'applies' his theory; thus applied, it becomes scientific method. Spinoza translated this practice into materialist terms by saying that the method is nothing other than the 'idea of the idea', that is, the reflection and application, in new experimentation, of already acquired concrete knowledge. Thus the method adds nothing to the concrete knowledge that has already been acquired; it is not a (transcendent) truth which exceeds that knowledge and would make it possible to acquire knowledge with a magic formula.

But this distinction between theory and method has naturally been exploited by idealist philosophy, which has put the accent on the difference between them, and has been tempted to regard method as a Truth prior to all truth, capable of making possible the discovery of every new truth. Thus method in Descartes, albeit a reflection of truth, is by rights prior to it, since the order of the 'search after truth' precedes the order of its exposition. Thus Hegel spoke, in Leibniz's wake, of an absolute method, the dialectic, superior to any truth content. We have to do, in this conception, with a view of the process of the production of knowledge that abstracts completely from its historical presuppositions; it implies that the result of the past history of experimentation exists as an absolute given which one need only apply to any object at all in order to extract knowledge of it. This is to reduce the scientist to the state of a child who, presented with the rules of research by an adult, is amazed to see them produce results. Leibniz, on a good day, criticized the Cartesian conception of method by saying: 'Take what you must, act as you are supposed to, and you will obtain the result you are after.'[1] In sum, a magic act.

Marx and Engels unfortunately inherited this distinction and this fantasy description of method. To think their own relationship to Hegel, they used an unhappy formula: in Hegel, the content was reactionary, but the method was revolutionary. The method was the dialectic. Engels went on to develop this distinction in *Dialectics of Nature*, where he said that, in the new 'philosophy', materialism (or the theory of matter and its properties) was the theory and dialectic was the method; and he came close to affirming the primacy of the dialectic over materialism, begging the question as to how materialism managed to elude the law of change and universal relativism without contradicting the dialectic.[2] By proceeding in this way, let us add, Engels merely abstracted, and called method, an essential property of matter, *movement*, whose laws he then studied (the famous 'laws of the dialectic'), applying this property, movement, to all forms of matter and their transformations.

Stalin took up this distinction and rearranged it and, naturally, it wrought havoc. As can be seen, it was wholly based on the idea that philosophy was a science with an object of its own (matter and its properties), and it inevitably led to a systematic theory of philosophy as the science of the whole or of Being. Hence the 'ontological' conceptions of 'Marxist philosophy', which, coupled with the inevitable 'methodological' conceptions, were and still are defended by those Soviet philosophers who have not thrown off the Stalinist legacy. Hence, too, the strange, paradoxical problem as to why there are *'laws' of the dialectic*, when there are no 'laws' of materialism, unless we assume that the 'laws' of the dialectic are the 'laws' of matter in motion; but then why speak of materialism (that is, of philosophy) rather than matter (that is, of objective reality)? Hence, too, the vexing problem as to *how many laws* of the dialectic there are: there are sometimes three and sometimes four, when they might just as well be reduced to only one (movement in Engels or contradiction in Lenin). Hence, too, the following shocking consequence: since we already know the 'laws' of matter, we need only 'apply' them to any object at all to produce knowledge of it. In sum, we can 'deduce' any particular piece of concrete knowledge from its 'general laws'.

In all these problems, this ostensibly Marxist concept does more than just 'come within a hair's breadth' of bourgeois philosophy; it submits to bourgeois philosophy, and finds itself caught in the insoluble contradiction of submitting to a philosophy from which it claims to be emancipating itself. We have to put an end to this absurdity once and for all by recognizing that this way of posing these problems has nothing Marxist about it, but wholly corresponds to bourgeois idealist philosophy.

This may, moreover, be a good occasion to address this distinction between materialism and the dialectic.

What might it mean, considered from *Marxist positions*? Nothing other than the diversity of philosophical theses. We shall therefore say that there are not 'laws' of the dialectic, but *dialectical theses*, just as there are materialist theses, since 'materialism' is by no means the theory of a definite object, but the ensemble of theses commanding and guiding scientific and political practice.

What is more, we realize, when we examine the matter closely, that this distinction cannot consist in ranging, in one column, theses supposed to be purely materialist and, in the facing column, theses supposed to be purely dialectical. It appears, on the contrary, that *every thesis is at once materialist and dialectical*. Indeed, this conclusion is implicit in the very idea of a 'thesis', since, as we have seen, a thesis cannot stand by itself, confronting an external object whose knowledge it supposedly provides; rather, *it stands in opposition to another thesis*. Every thesis is thus by its very nature an anti-thesis; every thesis exists only under the primacy of contradiction, which is the primacy of contradiction over its opposed terms.

It might even be said that this proposition, which is itself a thesis, is Thesis No. 1 of the Marxist materialist conception in philosophy, and it can be shown that this Thesis No. 1 is both dialectical (since it affirms the primacy of contradiction over the contraries) and materialist, since this thesis is a thesis about objective existence which affirms the primacy of conditions of existence over their effects (Lenin: 'everything depends on the conditions'). The same holds for every other thesis, whether it is said to be materialist or dialectical. Because, as we have seen, it is characteristic of every thesis, in its extreme form, to affirm or posit the primacy of one 'reality' over another, every thesis includes dialectical contradiction in itself; but since this contradiction always points back to its conditions of existence, this thesis is at the same time a materialist thesis.

Under these circumstances, the question as to how many dialectical theses (called 'laws') there are, or how many materialist theses there are, is, properly speaking, meaningless. Philosophical theses are 'posed' to answer questions posed by the development of the practices, which is infinite. We may conclude that *there is an infinite number of theses*, as is proven even by the 'research' of those 'Marxist' philosophers who claim that there exists a finite number of 'laws' of the dialectic.

In the light of these important differences, we can see, in outline, the future of a practice of philosophy which, acknowledging the existence of the conflictual field of philosophy and its laws, sets out to transform it so as to provide the proletarian class struggle, if there is still time, with an 'arm for the revolution'. We can also see that this task can be neither the business of a single individual nor the task of a limited period; it is an infinite task that is constantly posed anew by the transformations of the social practices, and it must constantly be taken up anew, the better to *adjust* philosophy to its unifying role, but with constant vigilance so as to avoid the traps of bourgeois ideology and philosophy. We can see, finally, that, in this task, the primacy of practice over theory is constantly re-asserted, since philosophy is never anything other than the detachment of the class struggle in theory, and since it is therefore subject, in the final analysis, not only to the practice of the revolutionary proletarian struggle, but to the other practices as well.

By the same token, however, we recognize that philosophy is something altogether different from a simple 'handmaiden of proletarian politics': namely an original form of existence of theory, turned wholly towards practice and capable of enjoying genuine autonomy if its relation to political practice is constantly controlled by the concrete knowledge produced by the Marxist science of the laws of class struggle and of its effects. Doubtless the most extraordinary thing about this conception is the profound unity which inspires all its determinations, even as it liberates the practices that are the stakes of its struggle from all the forms of exploitation and oppression exercised by bourgeois ideology and philosophy. Thus Lenin could call Marxist theory a 'block of steel': a 'block' that has nothing to do with a system, since the firmness of its principles and positions in fact aims not to enslave the practices, but to emancipate them.

When one is aware that this 'theory' is itself subordinated to the practice of class struggle, hence to its errors and failures, and its deviations as well; when one is aware that it is wholly caught up in the class struggle, since it constitutes, simultaneously, one of its means and stakes, one understands better how it can escape the idealist image of bourgeois philosophy, that closed system in which everything is thought out in advance and nothing can be called into question without undermining the whole edifice. One understands that a Marxist philosopher can and must be something poles apart from an individual cut off from the world: he must be a militant who thinks, in philosophy, the theoretical conditions for the theoretical development of the class struggle, and a theorist who acts as a militant not just in philosophy, but in political practice as well.

There remains, perhaps, one last question, which brings us back to the beginning of this essay: the question as to the sense in which everyone is a philosopher. This proposition is paradoxical, if we are prepared to acknowledge the highly abstract nature of every philosophical thesis, which presupposes thoroughgoing knowledge in the field of all the social practices. It will be readily conceded that all human beings are 'ideological animals', inasmuch as they can only live and act under the domination of ideas, those of their own practice or the practices dominating their own practice. But as for being a philosopher! It will doubtless be granted, after all that has been said, that if everyone is not a philosopher in the sense of the philosophy of the philosophers, is not consciously a philosopher, everyone at least receives, by way of the dominant ideology or the *philosophically elaborated form* of the dominated class's ideology, something like philosophical 'fallout', to the extent that this fallout ends up permeating everyone's spontaneous ideology.

Yes, in this sense, everyone is, virtually, a philosopher, in that all human beings could, if they had the time and means, become conscious of the philosophical elements that they experience in this way, spontaneously, in their individual and social condition. Yet really to be philosophers, they must, we would suggest, undertake a study of the philosophy of the philosophers, since that philosophy is contained in the philosophers' works. This solution, however, is in large measure artificial, for books are just books and, without concrete experience of the practices of which they speak, the risk is that our apprentice philosophers would not grasp their meaning, trapped as they would be in the closed circle of the books' abstract universe, which does not provide the key to its own meaning.

In this sense, the great philosophers, even the idealists, from Plato to Kant, were right to defend the idea that philosophy is not taught by either books or teachers, but is learned from practice, if one reflects on the conditions of this practice, the abstractions that command it and the conflictual system that governs both society and its culture. One must, of course, have recourse to books, but, to become a philosopher, and the equal of professional philosophers, as Lenin was, although he had received only rudimentary training in philosophy, one has to learn philosophy in practice, in the different practices and, above all, in the practice of class struggle.

If I were asked: but what, finally, is a philosopher?, I would say: *a philosopher is a man who fights in theory*. To fight, he has to learn to fight by fighting, and to fight in theory, he has to become a theorist through scientific practice and the practice of ideological and political struggle.

In a time in which the bourgeoisie has given up all notion of producing even its eternal philosophical systems; in a time in which it has given up the guarantee and the perspectives held out by ideas and entrusted its destiny to the automatism of computers and technocrats; in a time in which it is incapable of offering the world a viable, conceivable future, the proletariat can take up the challenge. It can breathe new life into philosophy and, in order to free the world from class domination, make it 'an arm for the revolution'.

NOTES

1 What Non-Philosophers Say

1 The present and the following chapter are in many respects similar to the first chapter of a posthumously published book-length text that Althusser wrote in 1969–70: 'On the Reproduction of Capitalism', trans. G. M. Goshgarian, in *On the Reproduction of Capitalism: Ideology and Ideological State Apparatuses*, ed. Jacques Bidet, trans. Goshgarian and Ben Brewster (London: Verso, 2014), pp. 10–17. See Chapter 12, n. 1. (This and all subsequent footnotes are the editor's, unless otherwise indicated.)

2 In France, one takes a mandatory class in philosophy in one's last year at *lycée*.

3 Plato, 'Letter VII', in *Plato: Complete Works*, ed. John M. Cooper and D. S. Hutchinson (Indianapolis, IN: Hackett, 1997), 341 c–d, p. 1659; Immanuel Kant, *Critique of Pure Reason*, ed. and trans. Paul Guyer and Allen W. Wood (Cambridge: Cambridge University Press, 1998), p. 694: 'One cannot learn any philosophy . . . One can only learn to philosophize.'

2 Philosophy and Religion

1 Althusser develops the theses advanced in the next few pages in a posthumously published 1982 manuscript, 'The Underground Current of the Materialism of the Encounter', in *Philosophy of the Encounter: Later Writings, 1978–87*, ed. François Matheron, trans. G. M. Goshgarian (London: Verso, 2006), pp. 163–207. He presents them more briefly in the first of a series of five lectures for scientists delivered in 1967: 'Philosophy and the Spontaneous Philosophy of the Scientists (1967)', trans. Warren Montag, in *Philosophy and the Spontaneous Philosophy of the Scientists and Other Essays*, ed. Gregory Elliott (London: Verso, 1990), pp. 82–3. See also n. 24, below.

2 Blaise Pascal, *Pensées and Other Writings*, ed. Anthony Levi, trans. Honor Levi (Oxford: Oxford University Press, 2008), p. 178.

3 Plato, *The Republic*, VII, 517 b–c.

4   Aristotle, *Metaphysics*, II, 1072 a–b.

5   René Descartes, 'Reply by the Author to the First Set of Objections', in *Philosophical Essays and Correspondence*, ed. Roger Ariew (Indianapolis, IN: Hackett, 2000), pp. 151–2.

6   Baruch Spinoza, *Ethics*, Part 1, Definition 6; Part 2, Proposition XXIX, Scholium.

7   G. W. Leibniz, *Theodicy: Essays on the Goodness of God, the Freedom of Man and the Origin of Evil*, trans. E. M. Huggard (Eugene, OR: Wipf and Stock, 2001), §8, p. 128; 'Dialogue', in *Philosophical Essays*, trans. Roger Ariew and Daniel Garber (Indianapolis, IN: Hackett, 1989), p. 270, n. 323: '*Cum Deus calculat et cogitationem exercet, fit mundus*' ('When God calculates and exercises his thought, the world is made').

8   Leibniz, 'On the Ultimate Origination of Things', in *Philosophical Essays*, p. 149.

9   Kant, *Critique of Pure Reason*, p. 386: 'Transcendent illusion . . . does not cease even though it is uncovered and its nullity is clearly seen into by transcendental criticism (e.g., the illusion in the proposition: "The world must have a beginning in time").'

10 Cf. Louis Althusser and Étienne Balibar, *Reading Capital*, trans. Ben Brewster (London: Verso, 2009), p. 48: 'The Marxist theory of the production of knowledge' means that 'we are . . . obliged to renounce every teleology of reason, and to conceive the historical relation between a result and its conditions of existence as a relation of production, and not of expression, and therefore as what, in a phrase that clashes with the classical system of categories and demands *replacement* of those categories themselves, we can call the *necessity of its contingency*'.

11 Nicolas Malebranche, *Treatise on Nature and Grace*, ed. and trans. Patrick Riley (Oxford: Oxford University Press, 1992), p. 117. See also Malebranche, *Dialogues on Metaphysics and on Religion*, ed. Nicholas Jolley, trans. David Scott (Cambridge: Cambridge University Press, 1997), pp. 166–70.

12 René Descartes, 'Early Writings', in *The Philosophical Writings of Descartes*, Volume 1, trans. John Cottingham *et al.* (Cambridge: Cambridge University Press, 1985) [213], p. 2: 'Actors, taught not to let any embarrassment show on their faces, put on a mask. I will do the same. So far, I have been a spectator in this theatre which is the world, but I am now about to mount the stage, and I come forward masked.'

13 Karl Marx, 'A Criticism of the Hegelian Philosophy of Right', in Marx, *Selected Essays* (Rockville, MD: Serenity Publishers, 2008), p. 10.

14 First version: 'Even when it takes the form of a "lay religion", as in the socialist countries.' Second version: 'Even when it takes the form of a "lay" religion (the religion of Reason, cultivated by Free-Masonic sects, which were progressive in the eighteenth century).'

15 Epicurus, 'Letter to Menoeceus', in *Letters, Principal Doctrines and Vatican Sayings*, ed. and trans. Russell M. Geer (Indianapolis, IN: Bobbs-Merrill, 1976).

16 Plato, *Phaedo,* 67 e, 81a. Althusser borrows this formula from Montaigne: see Michel de Montaigne, *The Complete Essays*, trans. Donald M. Frame (Stanford, CA: Stanford University Press, 1958), p. 56: 'That to philosophize is to learn to die.'

17 Baruch Spinoza, *Ethics*, trans. W. H. White and A. H. Stirling (London: Wordsworth Classics, 2001), Part 4, Proposition LXVII, p. 212: 'A free man thinks of nothing less than of death, and his wisdom is not a meditation upon death but upon life.'

18 Plato, *Cratylus*, 400 c; *Phaedo*, 66 a–67 b.

19 Plato, *Protagoras*, 320 d–321 c.

20 Immanuel Kant, 'Lectures on Pedagogy', trans. Robert B. Louden, in Kant, *Anthropology, History, and Education*, eds. Louden and G. Zöller (Cambridge: Cambridge University Press, 2007), p. 460: 'The human being is the only animal which must work.'

21 Cited by T. Bentley, *Letters on the Utility and Policy of Employing Machines to Shorten Labour* (London: William Sleater, 1780), pp. 2–3: 'Man has been defined [as] . . . *a tool-making animal*, or *engineer* (Franklin).'

22 Karl Marx, *Capital*, Volume 1, in *Marx and Engels Collected Works*, Volume 35 (London: Lawrence and Wishart, 2010), p. 331, n. 4: 'Strictly, Aristotle's definition is that man is by nature a town-citizen. This is quite as characteristic of ancient classical society as Franklin's definition of man, as a tool-making animal, is characteristic of Yankeedom.'

23 Giambattista Vico, *On the Most Ancient Wisdom of the Italians*, trans. Lucia M. Palmer (Ithaca: Cornell University Press, 1984), §331, p. 96. Marx refers to Vico's aphorism in *Capital*, Volume 1, p. 375, n. 2: 'Does not the history of the productive organs of man, of organs that are the material basis of all social organization, deserve equal attention? And would not such a history be easier to compile since, as Vico says, human history differs from natural history in this, that we have made the former, but not the latter?'

24 Althusser outlines an answer similar to the one proposed here in 'Du côté de la philosophie', his fifth, posthumously published lecture on philosophy and the spontaneous philosophy of scientists. See *Écrits philosophiques et politiques*, ed. François Matheron, Volume 2 (Paris: Stock-Imec, 1995), pp. 259–62. See also n. 1, above.

25 Plato, *The Republic*, VII, 527 e, 533 d; Spinoza, *Ethics*, Part 5, Proposition XXIII, Scholium.

26 According to an ancient tradition, the first witness to this seems to be John Philoponus (sixth century of our era). See his commentary on Aristotle's *De Anima*, in 'Commentaria', in *Aristotelem graeca*, Volume 15, ed. M. Haydruck (Berlin: Reimer, 1897), p. 117, 1ine 29.

27 The rest of this chapter is based on 'The Transformation of Philosophy' (trans. James Kavanaugh, in *Spontaneous Philosophy*, pp. 243–65), the text of a lecture that Althusser gave in Granada and Madrid in March–April 1976. Released in Spanish the same year, it went unpublished in French in Althusser's lifetime, as did a book expanding on its main theses, most of which was probably written in summer 1976: *Être marxiste en philosophie*, ed. G. M. Goshgarian (Paris: Presses universitaires de France, 2015), forthcoming from Bloomsbury under the title *How To Be a Marxist in Philosophy*.

28 Plato, *Sophist*, 246 a – 249 d.

The Big Detour

1 Aristotle, *Politics*, I, 1254 b – 1255 a.

2 G. W. F. Hegel, *Natural Law: The Scientific Ways of Treating Natural Law, its Place in Moral Philosophy, and its Relation to the Positive Sciences of Law*, trans. T. M. Knox (Philadelphia, PA: University of Pennsylvania Press, 1975), p. 93.

3 Baruch Spinoza, *Ethics*, trans. W. H. White and A. H. Stirling (London: Wordsworth Classics, 2001), Part 3, Definition 2, Scholium, pp. 100–4: 'For what the body can do no one has hitherto determined, that is to say, experience has taught no one hitherto what the body, without being determined by the mind, can do and what it cannot do from the laws of nature alone, in so far as the nature is considered merely as corporeal.'

4 For, in our day, Foucault's and Rancière's work, for example, testifies to a concern with these issues [author's note].

3 Abstraction

1 Baruch Spinoza, 'Treatise on the Emendation of the Intellect', in *Spinoza: Complete Works*, trans. Samuel Shirley (Indianapolis, IN: Hackett, 2002), pp. 27–8.

2 G. W. F. Hegel, *Science of Logic*, trans. George di Giovanni (Cambridge: Cambridge University Press, 2010), pp. 532–3 and 590–5.

3 Plato, *Phaedrus*, 265 e.

4 René Descartes, *Meditations*, in *Discourse on the Method and Meditations on First Philosophy*, trans. Donald A. Cress (New Haven, CT: Yale University Press, 1996), Meditation 1, p. 60.

5 'To call a cat a cat' is the French equivalent of 'to call a spade a spade'.

6 Plato, *Cratylus*, 390 e, 435 a–e.

7 The allusion is to 'The Baptism of the Neophytes', a fresco that Masaccio painted in 1426–27 on a wall of the Brancacci Chapel in the Church of Santa Maria del Carmine in Florence. The painting depicts St Peter christening an unidentified man.

8 Ferdinand de Saussure, *Course of General Linguistics*, eds. Perry Meisel and Haun Saussy, trans. Wade Baskin (New York, NY: Columbia University Press, 2011), p. 67: 'The bond between the signifier and signified is arbitrary. Since I mean by sign the whole that results from the associating of the signifier with the signified, I can simply say: *the linguistic sign is arbitrary*.'

9 Jean-Jacques Rousseau, 'Discourse on the Origin of Inequality', in *Basic Political Writings of Jean-Jacques Rousseau*, ed. and trans. Donald A. Cress (Indianapolis, IN: Hackett, 1981), p. 51: 'I leave to anyone who would undertake it the discussion of the following difficult problem: which was the more necessary: an already formed society for the invention of languages, or an already invented language for the establishment of society?'

10 The French saying, in which the two occurrences of *son* are exact homonyms, means 'he's playing the idiot to fish for information'.

11 *Vache* means both 'cow' and, metaphorically, 'bastard'.

12 G. W. F. Hegel, *Phenomenology of Spirit*, trans. A. V. Miller (Oxford: Oxford University Press, 1976), pp. 59–61.

4 Technical Abstraction and Scientific Abstraction

1 Plato, *The Republic*, IV, 419 a – 434 c.

2 Immanuel Kant, *Critique of Judgment*, ed. Nicholas Walker, trans. James C. Meredith (Oxford: Oxford University Press, 2007), pp. 8–9.

3 Niccolò Machiavelli, *The Prince*, ed. and trans. Peter Bondanella (Oxford: Oxford University Press, 2005), p. 6: 'To know the nature of the people well one must be a prince, and to know the nature of princes well one must be of the people.'

4 Karl Marx and Friedrich Engels, 'Manifesto of the Communist Party', in *Marx and Engels Collected Works*, Volume 4 (London: Lawrence and

Wishart, 1976), p. 483: 'The history of all hitherto existing society is the history of class struggles.'

5 Sigmund Freud, 'Five Lectures on Psycho-analysis', trans. James Strachey, in *The Standard Edition of the Complete Psychological Works of Sigmund Freud*, ed. Strachey, Volume 11 (London: Hogarth Press, 1957), pp. 3–58.

6 Francis Bacon, *The New Organum* (Cambridge: Cambridge University Press, 2000), pp. 41–6.

7 Spinoza, *Ethics*, Part 2, Proposition XL, Scholium 2.

8 There is a handwritten annotation, underlined three times, in the margin of the manuscript here: 'The body!'

9 Baruch Spinoza, *Ethics*, trans. W. H. White and A. H. Stirling (London: Wordsworth Classics, 2001), Part 2, Proposition XLVIII, Scholium, p. 87: 'There exists no absolute faculty of understanding, desiring, loving, etc. These and the like faculties, therefore, either are altogether fictitious, or else are nothing but metaphysical or universal entities.'

10 Carl Wilhelm Scheele (1746–86) produced the gas that Antoine Lavoisier (1743–94) identified as being not 'phlogistic', but oxygen.

11 Gaston Bachelard, *The New Scientific Spirit*, trans. Arthur Goldhammer (Boston, MA: Beacon Press, 1984), p. 13: 'And once the step is taken from observation to experimentation, the polemical character of knowledge stands out even more sharply. Now phenomena must be selected, filtered, purified, shaped by instruments; indeed, it may well be the instruments that produce the phenomenon in the first place. And instruments are nothing but theories materialized. The phenomena they produce bear the stamp of theory throughout . . . A truly scientific phenomenology is therefore essentially a phenomeno-technology.'

12 Karl Marx, *A Contribution to the Critique of Political Economy* (Marston Gate: Forgotten Books, 2014), p. 294.

13 Immanuel Kant, *Critique of Practical Reason*, trans. Werner S. Pluhar (Indianapolis, IN: Hackett, 2002), pp. 154–5: 'On the Primacy of Pure Practical Reason in its Linkage with Speculative Reason.'

5 Philosophical Abstraction

1 Plato, *The Republic*, VII, 537 c.

2 Kant, *Critique of Pure Reason*, pp. 692–3: 'The systems . . . are rather all in turn purposively united with each other as members of a whole in a system of human cognition, and allow an architectonic to all human knowledge, which at the present time . . . would not merely be possible but would not even be very difficult.'

3   G. W. F. Hegel, *Phenomenology of Spirit*, trans. A. V. Miller (Oxford: Oxford University Press, 1976), pp. 10–11.

4   Jean-Paul Sartre, *Critique of Dialectical Reason*, Volume 1, trans. Alan Sheridan-Smith (London: Verso, 2004), p. 817: 'This means that History is intelligible if the different practices which can be found and located at a given moment of the historical temporalisation finally appear as partially totalizing and as connected and merged in their very oppositions and diversities by an intelligible totalisation from which there is no appeal.'

5   G. W. Leibniz, *Theodicy: Essays on the Goodness of God, the Freedom of Man and the Origin of Evil*, §225, p. 271, and Leibniz, 'Monadology', in *Discourse on Metaphysics and Other Writings*, ed. Peter Loptson, trans. Robert Latta and George R. Montgomery (Ontario: Broadview Editions, 2012), §43 ff., pp. 124–5.

6   Galileo, 'The Assayer' (1623), in *The Essential Galileo*, ed. and trans. Maurice A. Finocchiaro (Indianapolis, IN: Hackett, 2008), p. 183: 'Philosophy is written in this all encompassing book that is constantly open before our eyes, that is the universe . . . It is written in mathematical language, and its characters are triangles, circles, and other geometrical figures.'

7   Descartes, *Rules for the Direction of the Mind*, Rule 4, p. 10.

8   G. W. Leibniz, 'On Universal Synthesis and Analysis', in *Philosophical Papers and Letters*, trans. Leroy E. Loemker (Dordrecht: Kluwer Academic Publishers, 1989), pp. 229–35; 'Mathesis universalis', in *Mathematische Schriften*, Volume 7, ed. Carl I. Gerhardt (repr., Hildesheim, Germany: Olms, 1962), pp. 49–76.

9   Manuscript I ends here (see 'Note on the Text', p. 16). The next two paragraphs are the conclusion to the chapter on 'abstraction' in Manuscript II, where they are followed by what has here become Chapter 6, 'The Myth of the State of Nature'.

6   The Myth of the State Of Nature

1   Nicolas Malebranche, *Elucidations of* The Search after Truth, eds. and trans. Paul J. Olscamp and Thomas M. Lennon (Cambridge: Cambridge University Press, 1977), pp. 563–5.

2   G. W. F. Hegel, *Science of Logic*, trans. George di Giovanni (Cambridge: Cambridge University Press, 2010), pp. 29–30.

3   Plato, *Cratylus*, 400 c.

4   Malebranche, *Elucidations of* The Search after Truth, p. 582: 'We can see, then, that since the first man let his mind's capacity be gradually shared or filled by the lively sensation of a presumptuous joy, or perhaps by some pleasure or love, God's presence and the thought of his duty were erased from his mind . . . Having thus been distracted, he was able to fall.'

5   This prohibition is what enables the state of nature to function. One is reminded of the prohibition of incest (it too is punctual), which makes possible the functioning of primitive societies; they too are subject to relations based on *sex* [author's note].

7 What is Practice?

1   Aristotle, *Nicomachean Ethics*, VI, 1140a.

2   Cf. Louis Althusser, 'A Letter from Louis Althusser on Gramsci's Thought', trans. Warren Montag, *Décalages*, 2/1, 2016, available at http://scholar.oxy.edu/decalages/vol2/iss1/1.

9 Scientific Practice and Idealism

1   Karl Popper, *Conjectures and Refutations: The Growth of Scientific Knowledge* (London: Routledge, 2004), pp. 69–71.

2   Kant, *Critique of Pure Reason*, p. 409: 'It can be said that the object of a merely transcendental idea is something of which we have no concept, even though this idea is generated in an entirely necessary way by reason according to its original laws.'

3   See Chapter 2, n. 7.

4   See, for example, Karl Popper, *The Open Society and its Enemies: The High Tide of Prophecy – Hegel, Marx, and the Aftermath*, Volume 2 (London: George Routledge & Sons, 1947), pp. 190–203. See also Popper, *Conjectures and Refutations*, pp. 69–75.

10 Scientific Practice and Materialism

1   Louis Althusser, *For Marx*, trans. Ben Brewster (London: Verso, 2005), p. 183.

2   Karl Marx, *A Contribution to the Critique of Political Economy* (Marston Gate: Forgotten Books, 2014), pp. 294–6.

3   Louis Althusser, 'Three Notes on the Theory of Discourses', in *The Humanist Controversy and Other Writings (1966–67)*, ed. François Matheron, trans. G. M. Goshgarian (London: Verso, 2003), p. 77: 'There is no such thing as a *subject* of science as far as scientific discourse, scientific statements, are concerned . . . any more than there are individuals "who

make history", in the ideological sense of that proposition.' See also Althusser, 'Marx's Relation to Hegel', in *Politics and History: Montesquieu, Rousseau, Marx*, trans. Ben Brewster (London: Verso, 2007), pp. 182–5; Althusser, 'Remarks on the Category: "Process without a Subject or Goal(s)"', in *On Ideology*, trans. Brewster (London: Verso, 2008), pp. 133–9.

4 See Chapter 4, n. 11.

5 Gaston Bachelard, *The Poetics of Reverie: Childhood, Language, and the Cosmos*, trans. Daniel Russell (Boston, MA: Beacon Press, 1971), p. 76.

6 Karl Marx, *Capital*, Volume 1, in *Marx and Engels Collected Works*, Volume 35 (London: Lawrence and Wishart, 2010), p. 565: 'The conditions of production are also those of reproduction. No society can go on producing, in other words, no society can reproduce, unless it constantly reconverts a part of its products into means of production, or elements of fresh products.' Marx, *Capital*, Volume 3, trans. David Fernbach (London: Penguin Books, 1981), p. 929: 'It is in the interest of the dominant section of society to sanctify the existing situation as a law and to fix the limits given by custom and tradition as legal ones ... this happens automatically as soon as the constant reproduction of the basis of the existing situation, the relationship underlying it, assumes a regular and ordered form in the course of time; and this regulation and order is itself an indispensable moment of any mode of production that is to become solidly established and free from mere accident or caprice. It is precisely the form in which it is socially established, and hence the form of its relative emancipation from mere caprice and accident.'

11 Ideological Practice

1 Vladimir Lenin, 'What the "Friends of the People" Are and How They Fight the Social-Democrats', in Lenin, *Collected Works*, Volume 1 (Moscow: Progress Publishers, 1977), p. 180: 'The relation of forms to the material conditions of their existence – why, that is the very problem of the interrelation between the various aspects of social life, of the superstructure of ideological social relations on the basis of material relations, a problem whose well-known solution constitutes the doctrine of materialism.'

2 Althusser may (also) have in mind a passage originally included in the present chapter, part of which he struck in revising his text: 'Let us consider, for example, the practice of material production. It is a labour-process, in which one or more workers (labour-force) use means of production (tools, machines) to transform raw material (ore, wood, etc.) into a finished product. This process unfolds under the domination of abstract relations that define the material relation which has to obtain between these different elements (a particular tool is needed to work on wood, as opposed to iron) if the desired result (a particular product) is to be attained. We may therefore say that these relations of production are technical relations. But if we consider the same process not *abstractly*, as we have just done (that is, independently of any specific society), but concretely, then we have to bring into play not just these technical relations of production, but the social relations that command the elements and their places and functions in production. We know that these relations are, in the last instance, double: relations between groups of people (constituted either by the division of labour or the division into classes) and relations between those groups of people and the means of production. When the means of production (raw material, instruments of production) are held collectively by the whole group and are put to work collectively, we have communal relations of production (primitive societies, communist society). When, in contrast, the means of production are held by a particular group, while all others in the same society are deprived of them, and this in organic fashion, we have a class society, in which the class that possesses the means of production exploits the class deprived of them, appropriating the surplus labour that it compels this class to perform by means of a whole series of constraints, first and foremost the state, instrument of its class domination. Things go so far that, if we fail to take into account the social relations of production or, to put it more exactly, the existing social relation of production – if, neglecting this relation, we treat the "phenomena" observable in production and analyse what enters into production, how the product circulates, and how its value is distributed, we have the impression that we are doing what is called Political Economy and, thus, scientific work. But we are doing nothing of the sort.'

12 The Ideological State Apparatuses

1 In 1970, Althusser assembled extracts from 'La reproduction des relations de production' (see Chapter 1, n. 1) to produce a paper that appeared in the review *La Pensée* in June of that year and in English translation a year later: 'Ideology and Ideological State Apparatuses (Notes Towards an Investigation)'. The present chapter includes a reply to those who criticized this paper for 'functionalism' and pessimism about the possibility of ending the bourgeoisie's ideological domination. It is partly based on a strategy applied in Chapters 7 and 8 of 'On the Reproduction of Capitalism', different drafts of a historical excursus which proposes to show that the French bourgeoisie was able to maintain its dictatorship after the 1789 Revolution only at the price of a protracted class struggle against feudal survivals on the one hand and the working class on the other. In 1977,

Althusser published another, more theoretical reply to his critics in German, the core of which is a somewhat different version of pp. 123–7 below. Released posthumously in the original French in 1995, it is available in English under the title 'Note on the ISAs', trans. G. M. Goshgarian, in *On the Reproduction of Capitalism*, pp. 218–31.

2   In 1976–7, Althusser led a public campaign against the abandonment of the concept of the dictatorship of the proletariat by the French Communist Party, of which he had been a member since 1948. The term 'public service', frequent in his polemical discourses and lectures of the day, figures prominently in an article published in 1976 by a leading Communist intellectual, François Hincker, who had suggested that a 'democratized' state could play the role of a public service provider. This idea resurfaces in a book by Hincker, Jean Fabre and Lucien Sève written to justify the Party's revision of the classic Marxist conception of the state and, by the same stroke, the Party leadership's ambition to join a 'Left government' after a widely anticipated victory in the 1978 legislative elections: see *Les communistes et l'État* (Paris: Éditions Sociales, 1977), p. 180. The notion that the state could be confined to the role of a benevolent purveyor of 'public services' epitomized, in Althusser's view, the 'very dubious, or even openly bourgeois, right-wing positions' that he was combating in the PCF, to cite a phrase from a book-length manuscript on the dictatorship of the proletariat he completed in 1976, but left unpublished: *Les Vaches noires: Interview imaginaire*, ed. G. M. Goshgarian (Paris: Presses universitaires de France, 2016), pp. 106, 147.

3   Crossed out: 'On the other hand, we can raise an extremely interesting question about this concept. It is indeed possible to ask: But since the state is one, why talk about state ideological apparatus*es*, in the plural? Why not talk about *an* ideological state apparatus, just as we talk about *the* repressive state apparatus? What point is there in highlighting this diversity and, especially, why this diversity, when the "list" of ideological state apparatuses has obviously not been closed, when we might well add to it the medical ideological state apparatus, the architectural ideological state apparatus, and no doubt others as well – perhaps even the economic ideological state apparatus, since firms are also a setting for manifest ideological inculcation? It may be that, initially, I proposed the plural as a kind of open research programme, even as I also felt the need to unify this diversity. Does Engels himself not say, in passing, it is true, that "the state is the first ideological power"? That is a reason to insist on the state character of the ideological apparatuses, but it also suggests that the unity the state imposes on them could find expression in a unifying term such as "the ideological state apparatus", subsuming all the diversity we have discerned. I admit, on reflection, that I am unable to make an informed, clear-cut decision with reference to the different modes of production or historical periods. But I also admit, after taking into consideration the

whole history of the class struggle indispensable to a dominant class if it is to anchor its domination in the consent of its own members as well as the members of the exploited class by means of the ideological state apparatuses, that it seems to me preferable to bring out the fact that this diversity is the prior material condition for any unification of the dominant ideology.'

4   Cf. Louis Althusser, 'Philosophy and Marxism: Interviews with Fernanda Navarro, 1984–87', in *Philosophy of the Encounter: Later Writings, 1978–87*, ed. François Matheron, trans. G. M. Goshgarian (London: Verso, 2006), p. 264.

5   Crossed out: 'not plural like the ideological state apparatuses'.

6   Cf. Louis Althusser, 'Ideology and Ideological State Apparatuses (Notes Towards an Investigation', trans. Ben Brewster, in *On the Reproduction of Capitalism: Ideology and Ideological State Apparatuses*, ed. Jacques Bidet, trans. Brewster and G. M. Goshgarian (London: Verso, 2014), p. 181.

7   *Sic*. Althusser probably intended to write 'on those realities'.

13 Political Practice

1   In the manuscript, the chapter title reads 'Philosophical Practice' – no doubt a slip of the pen.

2   Karl Marx, Letter to Joseph Weydemeyer of 5 March 1852, in *Collected Works of Marx and Engels*, Volume 39 (London: Lawrence and Wishart, 2010), p. 60.

3   Althusser summarizes the two late feudal theories of the encounter in a slightly different way in 'On the Reproduction of Capitalism', trans. G. M. Goshgarian, in *On the Reproduction of Capitalism: Ideology and Ideological State Apparatuses*, ed. Jacques Bidet, trans. Goshgarian and Ben Brewster (London: Verso, 2014), pp. 171–2, n. 1.

4   Althusser revisits the theses developed in the following ten paragraphs in 'The Underground Current of the Materialism of the Encounter', in *Philosophy of the Encounter: Later Writings, 1978–87*, ed. François. Matheron and Olivier Corpet, trans. G. M. Goshgarian (London: Verso, 2006), pp. 163–208.

5   Karl Marx, *A Contribution to the Critique of Political Economy* (Marston Gate: Forgotten Books, 2014), pp. 11–12.

6   Althusser develops the thesis presented here in much the same terms in a still unpublished, fragmentary 1973 text, 'Livre sur l'Impérialisme'.

7   Yves Duroux [author's note].

8   The manuscript reads 'feudal', an obvious slip.

9 Althusser first presents the idea that capitalism was 'born and died' several times in 'Livre sur l'Impérialisme'. On the feudal bourgeoisie as 'a fairly well integrated part of the feudal system itself', see Althusser, 'Montesquieu: Politics and History', in *Montesquieu, Rousseau, Marx*, trans. Ben Brewster (London: Verso, 1972), pp. 100 ff.

10 Étienne Balibar, *Cinq études du matérialisme historique* (Paris: Maspero, 1979), p. 99, n. 12: 'I suggest this expression as a deliberate echo of the formula Althusser used with respect to Lenin when he spoke of "a new practice of philosophy" . . . In fact, since, as Althusser has shown, philosophy is nothing more nor less than politics in theory, one and the same problem is in question here, in two different modalities.'

11 Presumably a slip for Münzer.

12 First version: 'is proof of the necessity of this encounter' [*prouve la nécessité de cette 'rencontre'*].

13 The title of Chapter 21 of *Citations du Président Mao-Tsé-Toung* (Beijing: Éditions en langues étrangères, 1966) begins with the words 'Compter sur ses propres forces' [Count on your own strength]. The original is '自力更生，艰苦奋斗' [Self-reliance and arduous struggle], a phrase taken from 'The Situation and our Policy after the Victory in the War of Resistance against Japan', *Selected Works of Mao Tse-tung*, Volume 4 (Beijing: Foreign Language Press, 1961), p. 20.

14 'John Lewis: "It is man who makes history." Marxism-Leninism: "It is the masses which make history."' Louis Althusser, 'Reply to John Lewis', in *On Ideology*, trans. Ben Brewster (London: Verso, 2007), p. 77.

15 Karl Marx, *Critique of the Gotha Program* (Moscow: Progress Publishers, 1970), p. 10.

16 The manuscript reads 'on vaults'.

17 First version: 'the communist party'.

14 Psychoanalytic Practice

1 Nicolas Malebranche, *Réflexions sur la prémotion physique*, in Malebranche, *Oeuvres complètes*, Volume 16, ed. André Robinet (Paris: Vrin, 1958), p. 35: 'these feelings and movements [of desire] that God produces in us without us comprise the raw material of sin'; 'God, as efficient cause, produces all our perceptions and impulses in us without us.'

2 Denis Diderot, 'Rameau's Nephew, in *Rameau's Nephew and First Satire*, trans. Margaret Mauldon (Oxford: Oxford University Press, 2006), p. 78: 'If the little savage were left to himself so that he retained all his imbecility, uniting the little reason possessed by a child in the cradle with the passionate violence in a man thirty years old, he'd wring his father's neck and sleep with his mother.'

3   Cf. Louis Althusser, 'On Feuerbach', in *The Humanist Controversy and Other Writings (1966–67)*, ed. François Matheron, trans. G. M. Goshgarian (London: Verso, 2003), p. 135; Sigmund Freud, *The Complete Letters of Sigmund Freud to Wilhelm Fliess*, 1887–1904, ed. and trans. Jeffrey M. Masson (Cambridge, MA: Harvard University Press, 1985), p. 345: 'Not only dreams are wish fulfilments, so are hysterical attacks. This is true of hysterical symptoms, but probably applies to every product of neurosis, for I recognized it long ago in acute delusional insanity.'

4   For the first topography, see Sigmund Freud, 'The Unconscious' (1915), trans. James Strachey, in *The Standard Edition of the Complete Psychological Works of Sigmund Freud*, ed. Strachey, Volume 14 (London: Hogarth Press, 1957), pp. 159–96. For the second topography, see 'Beyond the Pleasure Principle' (1920), trans. Strachey, in Freud, *The Standard Edition*, Volume 18, pp. 7–65.

5   Crossed out: 'or base (the Freudian topography may be profitably compared to the Marxist topography of base and superstructure)'.

6   First version: 'This attitude seems to be more correct, even if Lacan has not resisted the temptation to philosophically complete a theory that Freud, unwilling to anticipate the discoveries of neighbouring sciences, jealously maintained in a state of prudent scientific incompletion.'

7   First version: 'although every psychoanalysis is interminable'.

8   Jacques Lacan, *Séminaire IX*, *L'Identification*, seminar of 15 November 1961, www.gaogoa.free.fr/Seminaires_HTOL/09-ID15111961.htm. 'In the philosophical lineage that has developed on the basis of Descartes' investigations of what is called the cogito, there has only ever been one subject, which I shall pinpoint . . . in the following form: the subject supposed to know . . . The Other is the dumping ground for representatives representative of this supposition of knowledge; it is that which we call the unconscious insofar as the subject has itself been lost in this supposition of knowledge.'

9   First draft: 'in a relatively disputable way'.

10   Althusser probably has in mind *Cahiers pour l'analyse* (1966–69), a Lacanian review that some of his students helped to found. It is available online: cahiers.kingston.ac.uk.

11   Althusser refers to the 'parallelism' of the Spinozist attributes elsewhere, notably in 'Three Notes on the Theory of Discourses', in *The Humanist Controversy*, p. 65; in 'The Underground Current of the Materialism of the Encounter', in *Philosophy of the Encounter*. pp. 9, 177–8; and, especially, in *Être Marxiste en philosophie*, ed. G. M. Goshgarian (Paris: Presses universitaires de France, 2015), p. 168.

15 Artistic Practice

1 Cf. Louis Althusser, 'On Brecht and Marx', trans. Max Statkiewicz, in Warren Montag, *Louis Althusser* (New York, NY: Palgrave Macmillan, 2003), p. 138.

2 Karl Marx, *A Contribution to the Critique of Political Economy* (Marston Gate: Forgotten Books, 2014), p. 312.

3 Aristotle, *Poetics*, 1449 b.

4 Sigmund Freud, 'Creative Writers and Daydreaming', trans. James Strachey, in *The Standard Edition of the Complete Psychological Works of Sigmund Freud*, ed. Strachey, Volume 9, pp. 141–55.

5 G. W. F. Hegel, *Encyclopedia of the Philosophical Sciences in Basic Outline*, Part 1: *The Science of Logic*, trans. Klaus Brinkmann and Daniel O. Dahlstrom (Cambridge: Cambridge University Press, 2010), §25, pp. 66–7.

16 Philosophical Practice

1 J. L. Austin, *How to Do Things with Words* (Oxford: Oxford University Press, 1976), p. 53 ff.

2 Althusser, who himself conceived of philosophy 'in the mode of scientific practice' in the first half of the 1960s, began to revise his point of view in May 1966. He first presented his new conception of the 'political nature of philosophy' in the concluding chapter of a text still unpublished in French, 'The Historical Task of Marxist Philosophy' (May 1967), which was released in a Hungarian version shorn of this chapter in *Marx – az elmélet forradalma*, ed. Péter Józsa, trans. Ernö Gerö (Budapest: Kossuth, 1968), pp. 272–306, and in an unabridged English version in *The Humanist Controversy and Other Writings (1966–67)*, ed. François Matheron, trans. G. M. Goshgarian (London: Verso, 2003), pp. 155–220.

3 This thesis, summarized in Louis Althusser, 'Lenin and Philosophy', in *Lenin and Philosophy and Other Essays*, trans. Ben Brewster (London: Verso, 2001), p. 34, is developed at greater length in Althusser, 'Philosophy and the Spontaneous Philosophy of the Scientists', trans. Warren Montag, in *Philosophy and the Spontaneous Philosophy of the Scientists and Other Essays*, ed. Gregory Elliott (London: Verso, 1990), p. 77.

4 Niccolò Machiavelli, *The Prince*, ed. and trans. Peter Bondanella (Oxford: Oxford University Press, 2005), pp. 43–6.

5 *Wer den Feind will verstehen / Muss in Feindes Lande gehen.* This is an adaptation by Ivan Turgenev, cited by Lenin in *Materialism and Empirio-Criticism: Critical Comments on a Reactionary Philosophy* (Moscow:

Progress Publishers, 1970), p. 306, of two lines by Goethe: *Wer den Dichter [the poet] will verstehen / Muss in Dichters Lande gehen.*

17 Dominant Ideology and Philosophy

1 Thomas Hobbes, *Leviathan*, ed. Richard Tuck (Cambridge: Cambridge University Press, 2003), p. 89.

2 René Descartes, 'Letter to Marin Mersenne of 15 April 1630', in *Philosophical Letters*, ed. and trans. Anthony Kenny (Oxford: Basil Blackwell, 1970), p. 11. 'The mathematical truths which you call eternal have been laid down by God and depend on him entirely no less than the rest of his creatures . . . it is God who has laid down these laws in nature just as a king lays down laws in his kingdom.'

18 Philosophy as Theoretical Laboratory

1 Cf. Louis Althusser, 'Philosophy and the Spontaneous Philosophy of the Scientists', trans. Warren Montag, in *Philosophy and the Spontaneous Philosophy of the Scientists and Other Essays*, ed. Gregory Elliott (London: Verso, 1990), pp. 103–4.

2 Althusser incorporated, in modified form, certain ideas developed in this and the following paragraphs into the final version of Chapter 2, while leaving the present chapter essentially intact.

3 The manuscript reads 'science'.

4 G. W. F. Hegel, *Outlines of the Philosophy of Right*, ed. Stephen Houlgate, trans. T. M. Knox (Oxford: Oxford University Press, 2008), p. 16.

5 This idea is developed polemically in Louis Althusser, 'On the Reproduction of Capitalism', trans. G. M. Goshgarian, in *On the Reproduction of Capitalism: Ideology and Ideological State Apparatuses*, ed. Jacques Bidet, trans. Goshgarian and Ben Brewster (London: Verso, 2014), p. 157.

6 John Duns Scotus, *De Primo Principio*, in *Works*, Volume 8, ed. and trans. Evan Roche (St. Bonaventure, NY: Franciscan Institute, 1949), p. 33: 'Plurality is never posited without necessity.' *Entia non sunt multiplicanda praeter necessitatem*, the equivalent formula that Althusser cites here, is often attributed to William of Ockham, but seems to occur neither in Ockham nor in Duns Scotus.

7 Undated letter (1679) to an unidentified correspondent (Duc Jean-Frédéric de Brunswick-Calenberg?), in G. W. Leibniz, *Sämtliche Schriften und Briefe*, Series 2, Volume 1, ed. Deutsche Akademie der Wissenschaften

(repr., Berlin: Akademie, 2006), p. 782: 'We will soon forget the beautiful novel about physics that [Descartes] has given us.' See also Leibniz, Letter to Molanus (?), 'On God and the Soul' (1679), in *Philosophical Essays*, trans. Roger Ariew and Daniel Garber (Indianapolis, IN: Hackett, 1989), p. 245.

19 Ideology and Philosophy

1   Friedrich Engels, 'Supplement to the Preface of 1870 for *The Peasant Wars in Germany*', in *Collected Works of Marx and Engels*, Volume 23 (London: Lawrence and Wishart, 1988), p. 632. See also Vladimir Lenin, 'What is to be Done?' in Lenin, *Collected Works*, Volume 5 (Moscow: Progress Publishers, 1991), pp. 370–2.

2   Karl Marx, *Capital*, Volume 1 (London: Penguin, 1976), p. 875. Cf. Louis Althusser, 'Marx in his Limits', in *Philosophy of the Encounter: Later Writings, 1978–87*, ed. François Matheron, trans. G. M. Goshgarian (London: Verso, 2006), p. 59.

3   Louis Althusser, 'Lenin and Philosophy', in *Lenin and Philosophy and Other Essays*, trans. Ben Brewster (London: Verso, 2001), p. 42: 'Marxism is not a (new) philosophy of praxis, but a (new) practice of philosophy.'

4   Louis Althusser, 'Reply to John Lewis', in *On Ideology*, trans. Ben Brewster (London: Verso, 2007), p. 67.

20 Philosophy and the Science of Class Struggle

1   Cf. Louis Althusser, 'Philosophy and the Spontaneous Philosophy of the Scientists', trans. Warren Montag, in *Philosophy and the Spontaneous Philosophy of the Scientists*, ed. Gregory Elliott (London: Verso, 1990), pp. 102–5.

2   Gyorgy Lukács, *History and Class Consciousness: Studies in Marxist Dialectics*, trans. Rodney Livingstone (Cambridge, MA: MIT Press, 1971), esp. Chapter 3, Section 6.

3   Joseph Stalin, 'Dialectical and Historical Materialism', in *History of the Communist Party of the Soviet Union (Bolshevik)* (New York, NY: International Publishers, 1939), pp. 105–32.

4   Althusser closely followed the composition of Lecourt's book and wrote an introduction to it. See Louis Althusser, 'Introduction: Unfinished History', in Dominique Lecourt, *Proletarian Science? The Case of Lysenko* (London: New Left Books, 1977), pp. 7–16.

5   Vladimir Lenin, 'Philosophical Notebooks', in Lenin, *Collected Works*, Volume 38 (Moscow: Progress Publishers, 1972).

6   Marx and Engels, 'The Manifesto of the Communist Party', in *Marx and Engels Collected Works*, Volume 6 (London: Lawrence and Wishart, 1976), p. 505.

7   Cf. Louis Althusser, 'The Transformation of Philosophy', trans. James Kavanaugh, in *Philosophy and the Spontaneous Philosophy of the Scientists*, ed. Gregory Elliott (London: Verso, 1990), p. 246 f.

8   Friedrich Engels, *Ludwig Feuerbach and the End of Classical German Philosophy* (Peking: Foreign Language Press, 1976), p. 11.

9   Ibid., p. 18.

21 A New Practice of Philosophy

1   For example, Louis Althusser, 'Matérialisme historique et matérialisme dialectique', *Cahiers marxistes-léninistes*, 11 (April 1966), pp. 97, 113: 'In founding this new science [the science of history], Marx founded, by the same stroke, another theoretical discipline, dialectical materialism, or Marxist philosophy ... The object of dialectical materialism is ... the history of the production of knowledge as knowledge ... Marx's philosophical revolution ... brought philosophy from the state of an ideology to that of a science.'

2   Crossed out: 'or a dialectical-materialist position in philosophy'.

22 The Dialectic: Laws or Theses?

1   G. W. Leibniz, Letter to P. Swelingius, in *Die philosophischen Schriften von G. W. Leibniz*, Volume 4, ed. Carl I. Gerhardt (repr., Hildesheim, Germany: G. Olms, 1961), p. 329.

2   Friedrich Engels, *Dialectics of Nature*, trans. Clemens Dutt (Moscow: Progress Publishers, 1964), esp. Chapter 2.

INDEX